SOME OF THE MORE IMPORTANT
Prehistoric Sites in Europe

Miles
Kilometers

0 100 200 300 400

0 100 200 300 400

BALTIC SEA

Barum

nose Swamp

Gagarino

Prědmostí

Willendorf   Dolní Věstonice

Vérteszöllös

Hallstatt

Krapina

BLACK SEA

BOSPORUS

onte Circeo

Nea Nikomedeia

Troy

Çatal Hüyük

Asprokhalico

Hacilar

evanzo

Athens

Cyclades

Mycenae

onte Pellegrini

Sparta

SICILY

CYPRUS

Knossos   Mallia

Mokhlos

MALTA

CRETE   Phaistos

PREHISTORIC EUROPE

From Stone Age Man to the Early Greeks

PREHISTORIC

From Stone

W · W · NORTON & COMPANY · INC · NEW YORK

Philip Van Doren Stern

EUROPE

Age Man to the Early Greeks

I would write of that prehistoric life when man was knit close to nature. I would describe the people who were brothers of the red earth and the red rock and the red streams of the hills. . . . I would show you the unknown, the hideous shrieking mystery at the back of this simple nature. Men would see the profundity of the old crude faiths which they affect to despise. I would make a picture of our shaggy, sombre-eyed forefather who heard strange things in the hill silences. I would show him brutal and terror-stricken, but wise, wise, God alone knows how wise!

—JOHN BUCHAN, *The Watcher by the Threshold*

What a marvelous romance, surpassing in its reality all the imaginative dreams of Jules Verne and H. G. Wells!

—HENRI BREUIL, *Beyond the Bounds of History*

To be ignorant of what happened before you were born is to be ever a child. For what is man's lifetime unless the memory of past events is woven with those of earlier times?

—CICERO

Contents

PHASE SIX

PHASE SEVEN

PHASE EIGHT

Introduction

THIS BOOK DEALS WITH man's beginnings in Europe. Our knowledge of those long-ago times comes only from the things we have found, physical objects, all of them. Since prehistory is the record of man before writing was invented, no words remain to tell us what these early people thought or felt.

Attempts have been made to understand them by drawing analogies with the few primitive tribes that still exist. But it must be remembered that our modern primitive people have not stood still since prehistoric times; during those thousands of years they established traditions, devised new customs, and invented implements, weapons, and techniques which may be very different from those used by early man.

Fortunately, some of our prehistoric ancestors were artists who left us paintings, engravings, and sculpture that tell us a great deal. But art came late. The earliest traces of it are not much more than 30,000 years old while Europe has been inhabited for more than 700,000 years. For all the time before art came into being we have only some bits of chipped flint, a few bones, and scattered odds and ends.

The evidence may seem scant but with it prehistorians have been able to reconstruct the way these early men lived. Furthermore, they have made them seem real. We know now how expert they were as hunters of big game, and we have also learned how important animals were to them, not only as food but as creatures endowed with mysterious powers that border on the realm of magic. Sex, too, dominated these ancient peoples' lives, as the symbols in their art and ornament show.

Less than a hundred years ago the men who lived before the dawn of history were thought of as savages, but we know now that they had very human feelings 50,000 or 60,000 years ago.

Much of our knowledge of prehistoric people can be 9

found only in the field reports that come in in large numbers from all over the world. It sometimes takes years before this information is made public and then it is written in the specialized language that experts use when they address one another. And their writings often cover only a single aspect of their subject. Nor do the experts always agree.

THIS BOOK was written by a man who was trained in an allied field—in history rather than in prehistory. Yet the two are not far apart, for the need to weigh sources, select major themes, organize material, and then present it logically is common to both.

The author read the specialists' reports, journals, and books, and visited the sites and museums before writing this account for nonspecialists.

Since our knowledge of prehistory changes rapidly as new discoveries are made and new theories are presented, only very recent references can be depended upon. Anything more than a few years old is likely to be suspect. An examination of the sources used here (see Bibliography) will show that most of them are dated in the 1960's; a few are in the 1950's; those before that are very few indeed, and most of them were cited because they have become classics. So far as possible, primary sources have been used.

In order to make this introductory account of a large and complicated subject as simple as possible, a great deal had to be eliminated. The Iron Age, for instance, is given relatively slight attention because it is merely an extension of a time when other metals, notably copper and bronze, had already come into use. Nor is there much on prehistoric skulls, methods of chipping flint, or the fine points of identifying and classifying pottery. Such things are important to professional prehistorians, but the average reader wants to get on with the story and not have to spend too much time on technical details.

The story is certainly a great one, one that should concern all Europeans and their widely scattered descendants, for it is about the origins of their ancestors. It is, in fact, Chapter One in the biography of Western Man. And if the proper study of mankind is man, here is where that study begins.

A Note on Chronology

DURING THE YEARS since the Second World War scientists have invented so many new ways of determining prehistoric dates that our concept of the time structure of early man is being revised. In fact, it is being changed almost as rapidly as the plans for a supersonic jetliner. But we do not stop flying in today's planes because faster ones will soon be available; we have to live with what we have. And this applies to prehistory as much as it does to air transportation.

A good instance of the way things are changing in prehistory can be seen in the dating of the Pleistocene, that geological epoch during which man evolved from his ape-like ancestors. In 1911 William J. Sollas of Oxford, in his book *Ancient Hunters,* said that "the duration of the Pleistocene cannot have exceeded some three or four hundreds of thousands of years." Then Sir Arthur Keith, in the second edition of *The Antiquity of Man* (1925), made the Pleistocene even shorter—only 200,000 years, which was an inconveniently brief amount of time to encompass the evolution of man. When Frederick E. Zeuner brought out the first edition of his heavily documented *Dating the Past* in 1946 he gave the Pleistocene a duration of 600,000 years.

All these estimates were based on early methods of determining ancient dates. In 1949, as a result of the work done on developing nuclear bombs, a completely new technique for dating was announced. Willard F. Libby, then at the University of Chicago, where the first atom bombs had been developed, made public the details for establishing dates by the rate of decay of radioactive carbon, a substance which is present in all living things. From it came other isotopic dating techniques, and a revolution in prehistoric chronology began.

Laboratory reports showed that estimates for the duration of the Pleistocene had to be increased. In 1950 J. Putnam Marble, speaking as chairman of the Committee on the Measurement of Geologic Time, gave it a duration of a

million years, although he hedged this by saying that the
Committee's figures were like those in railway timetables—
subject to change without notice.

That he was right was proved in December 1963, when
Ericson and Wollin (1964, p. 191) found that the analysis
of deep-sea cores "indicated that the Pleistocene spanned a
figure of about 1,500,000 years."

This estimate did not stand for long, for potassium-
argon dating of material from the Olduvai Gorge in Africa
soon gave a figure of 1.75 million (± 300,000) years. This
was quickly superseded in 1966 when further analysis of
deep-sea sediments indicated that the Pleistocene was even
older—that it began more than 3 million years ago.

In little more than half a century scientists have had to
make extensive revisions in their ideas about man's antiquity. During that time a number of other supposedly
valid theories also turned out to be untenable and had to be
discarded. Those years also witnessed so many important
discoveries in the field that thinking about prehistory had
to undergo a major overhauling. And laboratory work dis-
credited so many important things—such as the genuineness
of Piltdown Man—that large bodies of literature were made
obsolete.

These massive changes, together with a great deal of
simplification in nomenclature, have made the older books
suspect. They may contain much useful material, but they
have to be used warily. Only a reader who knows enough
about the subject to be able to make mental revisions about
dates and descriptive terms can trust them. It is unfortunate
that this is so, but it is. And this book, like all others on the
subject, must someday be outdated by the passage of time.

THE DATES in the text are as correct as our present state of
knowledge permits them to be. Many will undoubtedly
change when new calculations make existing dates obsolete.
Radiocarbon and historic dates are given in exact figures,
but even those are not above suspicion.

The phrase "——years ago" needs to be fastened down,
for the passage of time keeps thrusting yesterday farther
and farther back into the past. In order to establish a fixed
reference point, the Fifth Radioactive Conference, meeting
in 1962, adopted the year A.D. 1950 as the standard for

computing dates B.P. (Before the Present).

The terms B.C. (Before Christ) and A.D. (Anno Domini) are sometimes confusing. Since there was no year 0, A.D. 1 follows directly after 1 B.C. The time between a B.C. date and an A.D. date is therefore one year less than the total number of years given.

Modern scholars do not believe that the year assigned to the beginning of the Christian Era was correctly calculated in ancient times and think it should be placed at 4 B.C. or perhaps even earlier. This, of course, adds to the confusion.

Fortunately, precise figures are less important for long-ago dates than they are for more recent ones. As a figure becomes larger, more toleration for error can be allowed. More important is the question of which event came before another. We need to know more about that.

Yet we are the first generation to have even reasonably exact dates for time long past. Let us therefore be grateful that our chronology is as good as it is. It will get better.

PREHISTORIC EUROPE

From Stone Age Man to the Early Greeks

PHASE ONE

1. Man's Ancestors Come Down
from the Trees

OUR KNOWLEDGE of man's origins is still fragmentary; the fossil record is incomplete and to a great extent will always have to remain so, because most of it has been obliterated by time, weather, and natural decay. Only small bits and pieces have been put together to give us some idea of what went on in the long-distant past. But we are learning, and much of what we know has been discovered in the last few decades.

Only recently, for instance, has it been determined that the age of the earth is about 4.8 billion years, and that life on it began some 3.5 billion years ago. Air and water both came from gases that were gradually emitted from the interior. Long after the primeval oceans were formed, microscopic creatures swam in them for countless eons and did not evolve into structures large enough to leave visible evidence of their existence until about 720 million years ago.

More than a dozen periods and epochs, from the Cambrian to the Pliocene, each many millions of years long, then followed one another in a majestic procession. Given enough time, Nature can accomplish almost anything—and has. Life-forms left the water; some became vegetables and were forever rooted into place; others became animals, mobile and forever restless. A few water-creatures remained on the borderline, half vegetable, half animal. The true animals went through many transformations as amphibians, reptiles, birds, and mammals. Some of the shapes they assumed may seem monstrous to us, but words like frightening, fierce, or strange are more accurately descriptive. There are no monsters in real life. No matter how grotesque or distorted a living thing may seem to be, it appears repulsive only because we look at it with prejudiced eyes. The scientist, who studies it unemotionally and impartially, sees the unfamiliar creature simply as a specimen to be described and classified. True monsters exist only in the mind—not in the corporeal world. No man ever saw a living dinosaur, for those huge, lumbering reptiles became extinct millions of years before mankind's earliest ancestors appeared on earth.

GEOLOGICAL TIME TABLE

Era	Period	Epoch	Time
Cenozoic	Quaternary	Recent (Holocene)	(10,000)
		Pleistocene	3 million
	Tertiary	Pliocene	12 "
		Miocene	25 "
		Oligocene	35 "
		Eocene	55 "
		Paleocene	60 "
Mesozoic		Cretaceous	120 "
		Jurassic	180 "
		Triassic	200 "
Paleozoic		Permian	285 "
		Carboniferous	350 "
		Devonian	400 "
		Silurian	450 "
		Ordovician	500 "
		Cambrian	600 "

Pre-Cambrian

Life-forms like the dinosaurs, which could not adapt to changing environment or which evolved into self-destructive dead-end organisms, soon perished. The more efficiently constituted ones endured, and some highly efficient ones like spiders, scorpions, king crabs, and sharks have continued almost unchanged for millions of years.

The incredibly long early geological epochs were succeeded by a relatively short one, the Pleistocene. (The

word comes from Greek roots meaning "most" and "new.")
During its 3 million years man evolved into his present
form. The Pleistocene ended only about 10,000 years ago,
when the huge ice sheets that covered much of the Northern
Hemisphere melted and shrank. It is possible, of course,
that we are now living in an interglacial period and that
more centuries-long bitter weather will return at some
future date.

The epoch since the end of the Pleistocene is much
too short to be a true epoch. But this brief span of time
has been named the Holocene. It more than covers all
civilization.

The Greek roots "holo-" and "-cene" mean entirely recent, and that is what this somewhat fraudulent "epoch" is.

GEOLOGICAL eras, periods, and epochs are human inventions; they are man's attempts to put huge stretches of time
in their place and make them seem reasonably comprehen-
sible. Nature was indifferent to such fine distinctions. Time
flowed on continuously with one phase changing imper-
ceptibly into another without dividing itself neatly into
segments.

But man has a way of pushing himself into practically
everything. In describing his coming, some books—especially older ones—present all the antecedent action as
though it were just a setting of the stage on which this
lordly creature was to appear. It is true that he is the most
dominant of all living things, but the world was not created
just for him to become its master. In evolutionary terms he
is only an accident of nature.

The accident that made man into what he is today took
place some millions of years ago in Africa and perhaps in
other tropical Old World areas as well. The New World
played no part in this; the first human beings arrived there
only a few tens of thousands of years ago.

The accident was a change in climate. The climate we
take for granted was not always as it is now. E. C. Colbert
(1953, p. 269) said of this: "Wet and dry seasons in the
equatorial regions, hot and cold seasons in the higher
latitudes . . . were established . . . in Pleistocene times. . . .
But this climatic pattern, so generally accepted by us, is far
from typical in the history of the earth; in fact, the present

19

climates of the world make up an atypical pattern, quite at variance with what was held through much of geologic history."

One of the major climatic changes occurred in South and East Africa, where some of man's apelike ancestors had been living a reasonably safe and arboreal life. The trees, which need plenty of moisture, began to die when the land dried up. This did not happen suddenly; in fact, the change was exceedingly slow, so slow that it went on for millions of years, but it continued inexorably until open savannahs dotted with small groves of trees replaced the vast woodlands. What happened to the arboreal creatures who wanted to remain in the trees has been vividly described by Hockett and Ascher (1964, p. 140): "Population pressure within a diminishing grove would force bands into competition over its resources, and the less powerful bands would be displaced. Also, when a migrating band managed to reach another grove, it would often happen that the new grove was already occupied, and once again there would be competition. Thus, in the long run, the trees would be held by the more powerful, while the less powerful would repeatedly have to get along as best they could in the fringes of the forest or in open country. Here is a double selective process. The trees went to the more powerful. . . . Some of these successful ones were ancestral to the great apes of today. Our own ancestors were the failures. We did not abandon the trees because we wanted to, but because we were pushed out."

The authors also point out that the unhappy proto-hominids "were not striving to become human; they were . . . trying to stay alive."

These seemingly luckless creatures, who have been called "the waifs of the savannahs," now had to learn how to live on dangerous stretches of open ground. Nothing in man's long career was as decisive as this forced change of habitat.·

The new ground dweller had had some preparation for his altered way of living. As a tree dweller swinging from the branches, he was already different from four-footed beasts, for his body had long been used to being held in an upright position, and his heart had long been pumping blood upward to his brain. His vision, needed for moving

20

rapidly from tree to tree, had become stereoscopic, so that he saw a colorful three-dimensional world in which he could judge spatial relationships quite accurately.

Once this newcomer was established on the ground, his arms, which were no longer needed for climbing, grew shorter. Most important of all, he learned to stand upright, perhaps to peer over the tall savannah grass. This erect posture freed his forelimbs from walking or crawling. As a result, his hands, with their fingers and opposable thumbs, became more adept at picking things up. And all these bodily changes were making his brain grow larger and more complex. He could not only act better but think better. Whether this is a good thing or not is open to question in philosophical terms. G. H. R. von Koenigswald, the distinguished Dutch anthropologist, has said (1964, p. 74): "It is the large brain capacity which allows man to live as a human being, enjoying taxes, canned salmon, television, and the atomic bomb."

WHEN he came down from the trees, the adventurous surface dweller's diet changed, not from choice but from necessity. The arboreal monkeys and apes could live on fruit that was to be had for the picking, but the ground pioneers found that food was much harder to get. Periods of near starvation forced them to experiment with eating eggs, insects, grubs, snails, frogs, lizards, carrion, and very young or very old—and therefore easily captured—larger animals. Baboons and chimpanzees still carry on this tradition.

Kenneth Oakley (1961b, p. 189) reminds us that in Africa "after a kill by one of the larger carnivores, there is a scavenging food queue; when the lions, for instance, have had their fill, the hyenas and then the vultures enter the scene of slaughter. The protohominids may have first obtained the meat of larger animals by entering this queue at an early stage. It has been reported that African children have been known to drive lions from their kill by beating tins. It is certainly conceivable that the protohominids used tactics of intimidation to facilitate their scavenging and that this preceded the hunting of larger wild game."

But, again, luck favored us. Something—just what is not known—finally induced our ancestors to give up scavenging. Had they continued to make a regular practice of it, we would still be furtive, cringing creatures waiting timorously in line for our turn to get what was left of a torn carcass after the big carnivores were satiated with their kill; we would still be contesting for carrion with vultures, hyenas, and insects.

The new ground dwellers' altered diet began to change their teeth and jaws. Darwin thought that their canines became smaller because they were no longer needed for fighting after hand-wielded weapons had replaced sharp teeth. But fighting, whether defensive or offensive, does not take place every day whereas eating does. It therefore seems much more likely that long canines, which were required for tearing tough tropical vegetable skins and fibers apart, became reduced in size when meat was eaten regularly.

High-protein meat is more easily and quickly digested than plant food, and it is also a more highly concentrated source of sustenance. Gorillas, which stayed with their vegetarian diet, have to consume enormous quantities of food, so they spend most of their waking hours eating. These huge, placid jungle dwellers, which have become so powerful that they have no reason to fear most of the predators around them, lead lives that are all too easy. George B. Schaller, who spent more than a year in Africa studying them, said (1965, p. 253) that "the very existence of the gorilla, free from want and free from problems, is mentally an evolutionary dead-end."

But the evolving protohominids were leading hard lives in harsh surroundings. As hunters they were always on the go and so became slim, swift, and muscular. A slow-moving, round-bellied gorilla has only to reach out to get food, but these waifs of the savannahs had to run it down every day. They learned to hunt in organized bands that required leadership, planning, quick thinking, and vocal communication to produce rapid co-ordinated action.

Their hands became still more skillful at grasping sticks, stones, and the bones of large animals to use as weapons to kill for food. But it was taking time for them to comprehend the idea that they could shape such things into more efficient tools. Slowly, very slowly, they found out that they could break pebbles to produce sharp cutting edges. When they discovered this elementary fact they were content to live

Single-faced chopper tool

22

with it for thousands of years before they went on to make still better cutting devices. They had often encountered fire when lightning, volcanic action, or spontaneous combustion produced it. But the notion of taming the bright red flames for their own use was still far ahead. Prometheus was as yet unborn, nor is it known when or where fire was first domesticated. But when this happened, tools and fire were forever to separate men from beasts and give them the power to dominate the world.

IT MUST BE MADE clear at this point that man is not a direct descendant of the apes. Both have common ancestors, but that is all. Darwin emphasized this in 1871 in his *Descent of Man* when he said: "We must not fall into the error of supposing that the early progenitor of the whole simian stock, including man, was identical with or even closely resembled any existing ape or monkey."

It was formerly believed that the hominid evolutionary line divided protoapes and protomen about 20 million years ago. But new light was recently cast on this when two biochemists at the University of California at Berkeley, Dr. Vincent M. Sarich and Dr. Allan C. Wilson, devised a new method of using albumin molecules in the blood to determine when certain evolutionary developments took place. Their results indicate that men and African apes are descended from a common ancestor that lived no more than 5 million years ago. And then they also calculated that the line leading to the Asiatic orangutan separated from the one leading to the African apes some 8 million years ago, while the gibbon lineage separated about 10 million years ago (*Science*, December 1, 1967).

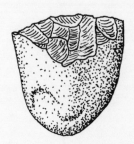

Two other scientists, Dr. Adrian Kortlandt and Dr. J. von Zon of Amsterdam University, after working in Africa, reported that modern chimpanzees living on open grassland are more aggressive than those that have remained in the forest.

The animals that were to remain apes and those that were to evolve into man changed very slowly, so slowly that the two ever-divergent forms almost paralleled each other for several million years. But the protomen eventually developed large and complex brains and skillful fingers, while the apes remained less intelligent and clumsier in their

Pebble tools from the Olduvai Gorge in Africa

23

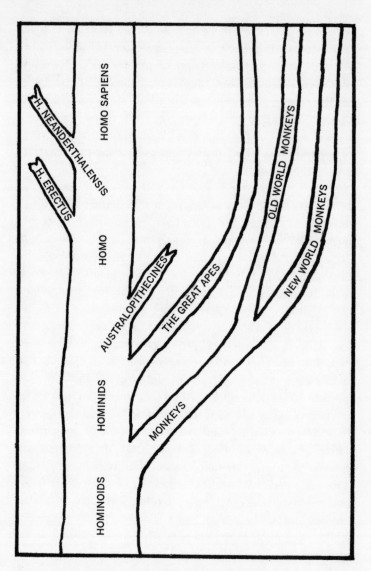

*The evolution of
men and apes*

digital manipulations. Present-day apes are different from those that were contemporary with the earliest humans, for they too have evolved further although not with the amazing speed of men.

There are four modern anthropoid apes—the small gibbons and large orangutans of Southeast Asia and the medium-sized chimpanzees and big gorillas of tropical Africa. (Baboons are monkeys.) According to Cole, who has 24 worked with Leakey in Africa, gorillas and chimpanzees seem to have fairly legitimate claims to be classified as members of the Hominidae, for their blood proteins and chromosomes are very similar to men's. The Hominidae belong to a family that includes all the species of men, even the very early australopithecines. As apes, the gorillas belong to the superfamily Hominoidea, which includes both the Hominidae and the Pongidae. The pongids are apes. Men and apes alike are hominoids; men are hominids; the common ancestors of men and apes are protohominoids; the earliest creatures evolving into men are protohominids. Men, apes, monkeys, tarsiers, lorises, and lemurs are members of the Order Primates, the most highly developed mammalian form of life.

DURING the long period since the time when man's ancestors descended from the trees to live on the ground, one variant evolutionary form succeeded another in a bewildering and still incompletely known series of primitive creatures whose bones have been dug up in Africa, Java, China, Europe, and the Middle East. Their fossil remains have been given individual names by their discoverers even though it was obvious that some of them were representative of already established biological classifications. This confusing nomenclature has to be simplified, and steps are now being taken to do so. Until this is done—and the decisions are generally agreed upon in scientific circles—the layman will have difficulty trying to find his way through a polysyllabic maze of names that mean very little to him.

Fortunately, we do not have to lose our way in that maze in a book on European prehistory, so we will merely summarize the findings in that very early field. There are many extinct higher primates, but the most important one seems to be *Proconsul Africanus,* a Miocene ape. Dr. and Mrs. L. S. B. Leakey, who have contributed so much toward our knowledge of man's origins, found the first Proconsul skull in Kenya in the 1940's. Proconsul was a tree dweller that spent only part of the time on the ground, but he was apparently an ancestor—or one of the ancestors—of the gorilla, the chimpanzee, and perhaps of man, for his face, jaw, and teeth have some hominoid characteristics. He is not very near to us in either biology or time, for he lived somewhere between 22 and 15 million years ago. But he was

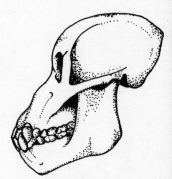

Proconsul skull

25

a beginning, an early prototype of the prototypes of man.

It was not until August 1965 that the next bit of very ancient evidence for man's beginnings was found. Harvard University made the discovery public in January 1967 when it announced that Professor Bryan Patterson (those who remember the Scopes Trial in Tennessee will appreciate the irony of his first name) had picked up a fragment of upper arm bone that was definitely human. Potassium-argon dating of the lava enclosing it showed that it was 2.5 million ± 20,000 years old—the oldest bit of bone yet found that could come from a creature which might be called human—or even near human.

It had been deposited in the Kanapoi dry wash in the great Rift Valley that runs down Africa and gives birth to many volcanoes. Olduvai Gorge, where Leakey has found numerous other specimens of early hominids, is in this same fossil-rich area.

Also in Africa, but much farther south, Raymond A. Dart had come across a skull and brain cast in November 1924 (the Taung skull) which was the first find that made scientists aware of the existence of the australopithecines. These had certain human features. The term "missing link," which was popular in the nineteenth century, would have been applied to them, but it has now fallen into disfavor because scientists believe that there was not only one missing link but a whole series of them starting at the point where the Hominidae and the Pongidae branched apart.

The australopithecines "represent stages in evolution at which an ape is seen almost in the very process of merging into man" (Montagu, 1945 and 1960, p. 116). They walked erect and did not need to use their knuckles for support as the great apes do. They had teeth like men's, ate meat, and could make tools, as is shown by the crudely shaped stone implements found with their remains. That they used weapons to slaughter animals for food is indicated by the discovery of a number of baboon skulls associated with australopithecine remains. Out of 58 of these, 42 (or 72 per cent) had depressed fractures which seem to have been made by some kind of rounded implement, perhaps a large animal bone.

The australopithecines must have been numerous, for many of their bones have been found, mostly in South and

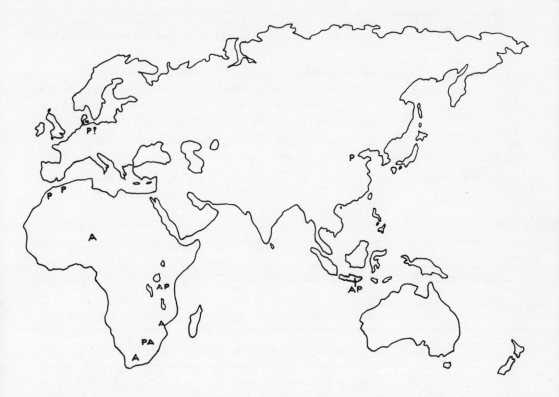

East Africa. They were fairly small in stature, with large jaws, and a cranial capacity of 435 to 700 cc. W. W. Howells has said (1959, p. 118) of their hip and leg bones: "They are not exactly like ours in every detail, but they are not at all like an ape's: they are *not halfway between.*"

Since they were not apes, not men, nor halfway between, they were at least somewhere along the way. They probably could not speak, but presumably could communicate with each other by using nonwordlike sounds like those uttered by present-day apes.

The australopithecines date back to 1.75 million or more years ago and continued to live on for many hundreds of thousands of years.

The name australopithecine has nothing to do with Australia. Their discoverer, Raymond Dart, said (1959, p. 16) of the South African Taung skull: "Because it had come from the Southern Hemisphere and not from the tropics I named it *Australopithecus* from *Australis,* 'south,' and *pithecus,* 'ape.'" The taxonomist George Gaylord Simpson, how-

Australopithecine and pithecanthropine sites [After Montagu and Brace]

27

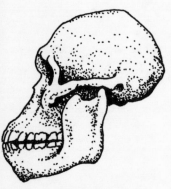

Australopithecus skull

ever, says (1963, p. 6): "*Australopithecus* does not mean 'southern ape.' Its meaning (defined by its referent) is simply one taxon to which the nomen was first attached and to which it was the first nomen attached."

Because australopithecine bones, implements, and food leavings have been so well preserved in arid areas, we know more about them than we do about their immediate successors. There were several varieties of australopithecines; some were larger; some may have been vegetarians; and some of the later ones were more manlike than their predecessors. Their discoverers have given them different names —Telanthropus, Paranthropus, Zinjanthropus, etc.,—but they were all australopithecines just as we are all *Homo sapiens* no matter what our color or size or what kind of facial features or hair we may have.

Darwin, who was so often right about man's origins, said that it "was probable that Africa was inhabited by extinct apes closely allied to the gorilla and the chimpanzee; and as these two species are man's nearest allies, it is somewhat more probable that our early progenitors lived on the African continent than elsewhere." In connection with this, it is interesting to note that the australopithecines lived east and south of the area now occupied by gorillas and chimpanzees. The australopithecines were followed by the pithecanthropines, who dwelt in the Far East and Africa—and perhaps elsewhere—from 1 million to 500,000 years ago. They have recently been given the taxonomic name *Homo erectus*, which makes them the first creatures to be designated as man. They were followed in much later time and evolutionary development by *Homo neanderthalensis* and *Homo sapiens*—or, to be more exact—by *Homo sapiens neanderthalensis* and *Homo sapiens sapiens*.

A species is defined as "a population or group of populations of actually or potentially interbreeding organisms that are reproductively isolated from other such organisms." Interbreeding is the key word. If *H. neanderthalensis* could interbreed with *H. sapiens,* he belonged to the same species. Most experts believe that such mingling of stocks was not only possible but even probable.

Of *Homo erectus,* the noted English taxonomist W. E. LeGros Clark has said (1964, p. 116): "There is . . . a general consensus of opinion that *H. erectus* stands in an

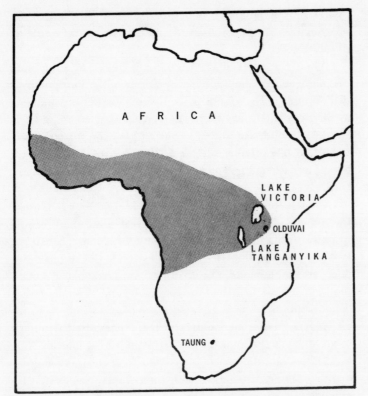

*Primate areas in Africa.
Shaded section shows
where gorillas and
chimpanzees now live*

ancestral relationship to *H. sapiens* (and also *H. neander-thalensis*). This does not mean that the Far Eastern popu-lation of this species was itself the ancestral group—it means, at the most, that the species as a whole was ancestral to the later species; if so, of course, the transition from one to the other may have occurred in some other part of the world."

Scientists' attitudes toward the origins of man are under-going such rapid changes that it is hard to keep up with them. Generally speaking, the name game is being simpli-fied, and, as more and more dates are determined, the earlier hominids are being pushed backward in time.

IT WAS SAID above that the early protohominids may have communicated with each other by mouth-uttered sounds as monkeys and apes do now. Such calls have limited mean-ings, but they can be used for warnings, for territorial threats, for sexual, maternal, and social contacts, and for the glad news that food has been found. Yet these calls are the

29

beginnings of language and are the humble substructure on which Shakespeare, Molière, and Joyce were eventually to build.

When the forerunners of mankind evolved into more complex beings they learned to do what anthropologists call "symbol." To symbol is to assign a certain meaning to a thing and then let others know what that meaning is. It can be a sound, a gesture, a color, a blaze on a tree, a pictogram, a hieroglyph, a letter of the alphabet, a numerical figure, a mathematical sign, or a hole in a computer punchcard.

Animals react to certain man-made symbols. A well-trained cart horse will stop at a red traffic light, a dog will respond to his master's whistle, a rat in a maze can learn that a simple bold pattern indicates food. But animals are poor at spontaneously originating new symbols although they can do so to a certain limited extent. The dog that comes running to his master with a ball in his mouth to invite him to play is symboling. So is the horse that whinnies to go home at the final turning point in a long journey. But these are domesticated animals that have learned a great deal from long association with their human owners. Wild animals are far less likely to be able to originate symbols, and the lower orders of life cannot do so at all.

To symbol well requires intelligence. And symboling over centuries-long periods seems to increase intelligence. Most important of all, symboling in its highest-form makes it possible to disseminate knowledge and pass it on to future generations. It is thus responsible for man's greatest achievements in art, literature, science, and philosophy.

Konrad Lorenz, in his book *On Aggression* (p. 68), says: "Among animals, symbols are not transmitted by tradition from generation to generation, and it is here, if one wishes, that one may draw the borderline between 'the animal' and man. In animals, individually acquired experience is sometimes transmitted by teaching and learning from elder to younger individuals, though such true tradition is only seen in those forms whose high capacity for learning is combined with a higher development of their social life. True tradition has been demonstrated in jackdaws, greylag geese, and rats. But knowledge thus transmitted is limited to very simple things, such as pathfinding, recognition of certain foods and of enemies of the species, and—in rats— knowledge of the danger of poisons. However, no means of communication, no learned rituals are ever handed down by tradition in animals. In other words, animals have no culture."

Culture, in its anthropological sense, was defined as long ago as 1871 by Edward Burnett Tylor as "that complex whole which includes knowledge, belief, art, morals, law, custom, and any other capabilities and habits acquired by man as a member of society." In more recent years, physical objects such as tools, implements, clothing, ornaments, and other man-made paraphernalia have been included in the definition.

And culture, according to the modern anthropologists C. Loring Brace and M. F. Ashley Montagu (1965, pp. 215–16), "is the only discernible specialization which man has ever developed. . . . The evidence for human cultural traditions commences in the early Pleistocene and continues without break right up to the present time with subsequent traditions being clearly derived from earlier ones by cultural evolution." Furthermore, they add, "culture as a major means of adaptation is unique in the world of living organisms."

And culture, even in its more popular sense, which limits it to the finer things of life, is also a product only of mankind. So is language, that subtle instrument which makes it possible to communicate ideas, plans, projects, intentions, emotions, information, and instructions to others. And writing, which is stored language, is still a step further. So are phonograph records, tapes, and computer data.

Man is therefore more than the highest animal. Despite his dreadful faults and failings, he is the most advanced lifeform this earth has yet produced. And it is only he, among all living creatures, who has any interest in learning about his own past.

ALL THE variant forms of near-men are now extinct; every living human being belongs to the genus *Homo*, species *Homo sapiens*. Since European prehistory deals only with highly developed forms of men, this phase of their story is fairly clear. As it progresses it takes on color and eventually brings us face to face with prehistoric men themselves.

31

Portraits of them exist, as do actual footprints, the outlines of their hands, fingerprints, and the marks made by their sticks and spears. We even have some of their bodies, miraculously preserved because they were buried in peat bogs.

But one thing we do not have and never will. Since these people lived before writing began, we can never recover any of the words they spoke. We have many of their personal belongings, but we do not know what they called them. We know the places where they lived, but we do not know the names of their communities. Roots from their languages may be embodied in some of ours, but we cannot be sure. We do not know for certain whether these first men sang or chanted or prayed. Or whether they told stories or devised legends about their memorable deeds or outstanding men. We think they did, but we cannot recapture anything so evanescent as sound. The words and the music and the legends are lost forever.

We have accumulated a great deal of knowledge about our early ancestors, and we are constantly learning more. We know now that the story of the long period between utter savagery and the beginnings of civilization is one of the most fascinating in the drama-filled epic of man. These are his childhood years when he was learning to improve his lot, when he was preparing for the role that was to make him pre-eminent among all the creatures that contest for the right to inhabit the earth. And it is a story of personal interest to each one of us, for these men were our forefathers. We are the end products of their blood and their genes. Our good qualities as well as bad have been inherited from them. In order to understand ourselves better we need to know more about them.

2. . . . And Begin to Make Tools

In 1778 Benjamin Franklin noted that "man is a tool-making animal." Yet some animals use them. The Galapagos Island finch holds a cactus spine in its beak to dig out insects; the British greater spotted woodpecker sticks a pine cone or an oak apple into a split tree trunk so the food-bearing object stays firmly in place while the bird tears it apart; the California sea otter brings up a stone from the bottom to break mussels or crabs that it holds on its chest while swimming on its back; and the East African vulture picks up a stone in its beak and throws it at an ostrich egg to crack it open. Its aim is far from accurate, but eventually it hits the mark.

The most noted of all animal tool users is the clever chimpanzee, which thrusts a twig into a termite nest to bring up a mouthful of edible insects. He also crumples and chews up leaves to make a sponge that can be dipped into a hollow containing rain water in order to get a drink. And he sometimes uses leaves to clean off his body. In captivity, the chimpanzee can manipulate brushes well enough to paint "abstract" pictures. This highly intelligent animal even makes tools, for he can fit a stick into a hollow rod to manufacture an instrument which enables him to get food that has been placed out of his reach.

If such animals were given enough time—evolutionary time, not clock time—they would doubtless be able to improve their tool-using and tool-making abilities. But man is far ahead of them because he has already gone through his early learning stages.

Some millions of years ago, when the creatures that were evolving into men found naturally broken stones with sharp edges, they picked them up out of curiosity and may have cut themselves—and others—while handling them. It took a great many years for the idea to sink in that such edges might have some practical use. Then these keen-edged fragments were sought after and treasured until they became dull and had to be discarded. After a while some inventive

33

genius discovered the amazing fact that certain kinds of stone could be smashed deliberately in order to produce good cutting edges. More millenia passed before it was found out that it was possible to control the method of producing the wanted shapes and edges.

It is difficult for modern man, with his trained mind and the enormous store of knowledge he has accumulated over the ages, to understand how very slowly his remote ancestors progressed. They must have learned things, forgotten them, and relearned them many times before a new concept was retained in their simple minds. And then the novel idea had to be passed on to others, which was an exceedingly slow process in an age when communication was also rudimentary.

But these protohominids learned, and they continued to learn while the animals around them did not.

Zinjanthropus Bosei skull

ON JULY 17, 1959, in the now famous Olduvai Gorge, Mrs. Mary Leakey found the skull of an African australopithecine, which flourished about 1.5 million years ago. This truly low-browed predecessor of man was named *Zinjanthropus Bosei*. It had a cranial capacity of only 530 cc., which is in the same range as that of modern anthropoid apes—350 to 750 cc. But unlike any ape, past or present, it could make stone tools, as was shown by the fact that roughly shaped pebbles with cutting edges were found with the skull. These cutting edges were needed for preparing meat, because the tough, skin-enclosed bodies of most slain animals are almost impervious to anything except the powerful teeth of the big predators or the sharp blades used by men. Such tools were also needed to put points on wooden spears and, much later, to scrape the hair off animal skins before making them into leather.

These broken pebbles are believed to be the first stone tools purposely shaped by man's predecessors. Similar ones of later date have been found in European sites. There can be no doubt of their human origin because they came from deposits with the remains of early men.

They are called pebble tools because part of the smooth, rounded original surface was left intact to serve as a convenient hand grip. Since flint is rare or nonexistent in most of the areas where these early tools are found, they usually

34

had to be made of quartzite or other hard stones that are less easily shaped than flint. Part of their crudeness comes from the intractable material, part from the fact that their makers had not yet developed much skill. Some of them are so roughly made that only the fact that they were found in sites which are known to have been occupied by early men entitles them to be considered genuine.

This brings up the question of eoliths, which were once thought to be man's first stone tools. These are bits of flint and other hard rock which look as if they might have been shaped by human hands. Some of them may have been, but there is no way to prove that they were when they are found as isolated specimens.

Eoliths were popular in the early days of prehistoric study, so much so that a large collection of oddly shaped flints found in Kent by an amateur named Benjamin Harrison was widely publicized in the 1890's. Then came the reaction. It was shown convincingly that stones broken and chipped by glaciers, water, and other natural forces could resemble eoliths so closely that it was impossible to tell them apart. Nowadays, prehistorians are skeptical about them unless they are found in association with definite proofs of human occupation.

PEBBLE TOOLS came first; then the predecessors of modern man developed a more effective tool, the hand-axe. They made these out of easily worked flint when they could get it; when they could not, they used any fine-grained rock that could be chipped into shape.

Flint, however, is the primary raw material used by early European men. It is common in England and France and is obtainable in many other places on the continent. It is, in fact, so widely distributed throughout the Northern Hemisphere that practically everyone who reads this is likely to have had some direct experience with it. He has probably picked up fragments, seen the large, smooth, oddly shaped nodules from which the fragments came, or examined flint artifacts. He may even have broken pieces of it to see how it fractures. It is fascinating material, very smooth to the touch on flat areas, but razor-sharp on fresh edges. It is harder than steel and apparently indestructible. But invulnerable as it seems to be, flint can be affected by

35

Hand-axe from Mercin Pommier, near Soissons [Author's collection]

weather or soil chemicals which form a patina on its sur-face. This patina is normally white, but iron and other min-erals can color it. Long exposure will make the patina quite thick. You may have seen broken pieces of flint with an outer light-colored layer; this is the accumulated patina. Since it is soft, flints coated with it make poor implements. The best flint for such use is that which has been freshly dug from deep underground sources. Prehistoric men even-tually found this out and opened up flint mines which can still be seen in several European countries.

Nearly everyone recognizes flint when he sees it, but few people know what this common stone really is, for it has a strange origin. It occurs in grotesque-looking nodules in deposits which were formed nearly 100 million years ago when much of western Europe was under water. Countless billions of tiny sea creatures left their calcium-rich remains on the bottom to become limestone or chalk. Also living in those seas were sponges with glassy skeletons made of silica. Enormous earth pressure solidified the sponge skeletons into compact nodules which became flint. When these nodules are broken open, they sometimes reveal impressions of sea shells, and flint casts of sea urchins have also been found in them. There is no doubt of flint's marine origin.

Since the sponges that were converted into flint orig-inally grew on flat sea bottoms, the flint nodules derived from them usually occur in level layers—or in layers that were level before earth movements shifted them.

36

The flint itself comes in many colors. Black is common, especially in England; so is yellowish-tan in many places, while blue, gray, brown, red, or white are somewhat rarer. The honey-colored, very smooth flint found near Pressigny-le-Grand in France was so highly thought of in prehistoric times that it served as an article of trade. It was prized because a skilled worker could strike perfect blades a foot or more long from it.

Chert is so similar to flint that only an expert can tell the difference. It was deposited in layers instead of nodules and may therefore fracture along the seams. It is as hard as flint but is not as easily worked.

Volcanic obsidian, a black glasslike substance with very hard edges, was also used for making chipped implements. So were various kinds of semiprecious stones, for ancient men naturally had no idea of the value we put upon them.

MUCH modern research has gone into finding out just how flint factures. Actually, the art of shaping it has never been lost, for a few highly proficient knappers still make gun flints in Brandon, a village near Cambridge, England. That there is a good supply of high-quality flint in this area has long been known because the Neolithic flint mines called Grime's Graves are only a few miles away.

If you plan to experiment with chipping flint, wear shat-

*Flint flakes used
as cutting blades
[Author's collection]*

37

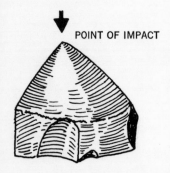

POINT OF IMPACT

Flint percussion cone

terproof goggles to protect your eyes from flying splinters, and cover the knee or the hand holding the flint with a piece of leather. Anyone who has ever tried to chip flint knows that the beginner makes a sorry mess of it. It breaks easily enough, but to compel it to break the way you want it to requires some knowledge of the way it fractures. Kenneth Oakley (1961a, p. 9) has described this: "A sharp blow directed vertically at a point on the surface . . . knocks out a solid cone (resembling a limpet-shell in shape), with the apex or origin at the point of impact. Fracture of this type is called conchoidal. . . . When a blow is directed obliquely near the edge of a slab of material which breaks conchoid-ally, a chip or *flake* is detached. The fractured face of the flake looks like a mussel-shell; it has a half-formed *cone of percussion* at the point of impact, passing into a salient or swelling, called the *positive bulb of percussion,* followed by low concentric ripples. There is a corresponding rippled hollow, or *flake-scar,* with *negative bulb of percussion* on the parent lump, or core."

Oakley (1961b, p. 187) stresses the importance of the brain in tool-making. Unlike even the cleverest animals, he says, "man can see a tool in a formless lump of stone. This ability of conceptual thought may have been present in a few individuals in a group, becoming extended by selection when conditions demanded."

The part played by more intelligent individuals in aiding mankind's evolution has never been sufficiently emphasized. Or perhaps it has just been taken too much for granted. But in almost every instance it was some more than ordinarily bright individual who saw how a new tool, a different and better method, or a novel way of performing a tradition-bound act would improve living conditions for himself and his fellow creatures. These nameless and forgotten innovators, inventors, creators, makers, thinkers, and doers are responsible for raising man above his beastlike origins. A long-deserved monument to them would give credit to the pebble-tool and hand-axe people, the human and not god-like Prometheans, the ingenious unknowns who first thought of using animal skins for clothes and footwear, of domesticating animals, planting seeds, building houses, making wheels, and fabricating pottery. They and not the warriors and the chieftains were the greatest benefactors of mankind.

Oakley also says that "it seems a mistake to think that tool-making depended upon any evolution of the hand; probably a generalized Pongid hand could make tools if enough brain capacity were present. . . . Manual skill depends upon initiation and co-ordination in the cerebral system. Men have developed manual skill even when their hands and limbs were maimed. Refined stereoscopic-color vision and erect posture with a vertical position of the skull are probably important. These allow close visual concentration over a wide field. The earliest hominids would have been anatomically equipped to use tools. . . . Tools are additions to the body that supplement the hands and the teeth."

Flint nucleus from which long blades have been struck off [Lubbock]

THE EVOLUTION of stone implements from pebble tools to hand-axes was accompanied by the evolution of the creatures who made them. The African pebble-tool users were more ape than man, but the African hand-axe makers were more man than ape.

More thought, planning, and manual dexterity were required to make hand-axes than to produce rough pebble tools, for the hand-axes had to have more chips carefully removed to obtain the desired almond or pear shape. As the name indicates, they were intended to be held in the hand.

Hand-axes have two chipped faces (the French call them *bifaces*). The end to be held by the hand is bulbous and rounded; the other is pointed. Sizes vary greatly and range from less than six inches to more than eighteen.

They were used to dig for edible roots, for insects, and for burrowing animals. They also were good for dressing meat, scraping hides, and smashing bones to get at the marrow. They could, with some effort, cut wood and even sharpen spears. But anyone who has tried to use a hand-axe will have noticed that it is clumsy and inefficient. Early men clung to them for so long because they did not know how to make anything better. Somewhere along the line they learned to haft them to long sticks which could then be used as spears. The very large ones may have served as sharp, heavy points on suspended logs that would drop on a passing animal when triggered.

Actually, we do not really know how hand-axes were used because we have no direct information. All the probable uses described above came from modern experiments

39

*Very long Neolithic
flint blades from
Denmark [Lubbock]*

with originals and replicas. What we do know is that they continued to be man's most useful stone implement for hundreds of thousands of years and that their manufacture eventually spread from Africa to southern Asia and western Europe. They were not improved or replaced until man's evolving brain and increasingly clever fingers enabled him to make a whole kit of more specialized tools from flint, bone, and antler.

This, however, does not mean that he was satisfied with the hand-axe alone, for the by-products, the flakes that were chipped off during the shaping, were found to be almost as useful as the basic tool itself. Some of these flakes had very sharp edges that were excellent for cutting meat. Like any knife, they also had countless other uses. Hand-axes and flint flakes were to be man's chief mechanical aids for a long while to come. Museums have many thousands of them, so many that most of them are stored away and are not shown to the public. There is no reason why they should be, for they are endlessly repetitive, and vast numbers of similar stone objects mean little to anyone except the specialists who use them to trace the locales and tool-making techniques of early men.

Since prehistoric men left these imperishable stone implements behind them wherever they went, we can follow their trail across the Old World by searching for the hand-axes they lost or abandoned. The hand-axes are easily recognized, but the flakes are not. Since they look like ordinary bits of stone, only experts can identify them, and even they cannot always be sure unless they find them associated with positive evidences of human occupation.

The number of hand-axes made over long periods of time must have been enormous. Some indication of how plentiful they must have been in Europe alone can be obtained by making a simple arithmetical calculation. Multiply the 700,000 years during which such implements were made in Europe by any reasonable population figure you choose to guess at and then multiply the result by as many hand-axes as you think an adult male might produce in his lifetime and you will arrive at a figure that runs into many millions.

The actual total of hand-axes produced was probably even larger than any figure you may come up with. One

40

thing is sure: vast quantities of them will never be recovered, for they are deep under water or buried under tons of rock in remote areas that no one will bother to excavate. Indestructible as they may seem to be, countless others have been destroyed, smashed by glacial action or worn down by being tumbled around in rivers and seas until they have become unrecognizable small stones, pebbles, or even sand.

HAND-AXES played an important part not only in prehistory but in making us aware of it. Until fairly recent times, people believed that the Bible told all there was to know about the creation of the world and the origin of humanity. In 1658 James Ussher, Archbishop of Armagh, Ireland, stated very positively that God had brought the world into existence in the year 4004 B.C. Then a Dr. John Lightfoot, a Biblical scholar and Hebrew-expert from Cambridge University, refined this still further by declaring that the exact moment was 9:00 A.M., Sunday, October 23. The Garden of Eden and Adam and Eve's expulsion from it doubtless followed some time later. Ussher helpfully dated the Flood at 2501 B.C.

SINCE stone axes were so plentiful, they have long been known. At one time it was popularly believed that they were of meteoric origin and had fallen from the sky as thunderbolts. They were therefore called thunderstones, or, in more erudite language, ceraunites. It was also thought that they had supernatural power and could purify water and cure disease. But only countryfolk had such notions; educated men refused to believe that the stones had any meaning at all.

In 1690 the skeleton of an "elephant" (actually a mammoth) was dug up near Gray's Inn in London. With the bones was a hand-axe. The "elephant" was dismissed as being one of those brought to England by the Romans in the time of Claudius, but the hand-axe was thought to be a British weapon made before the native inhabitants learned about the use of metals from the Roman invaders. This, of course, was true.

Then, on June 22, 1797, a paper entitled "Account of Flint Implements Discovered at Hoxne" was read by John Frere to the Society of Antiquaries of London. It described

41

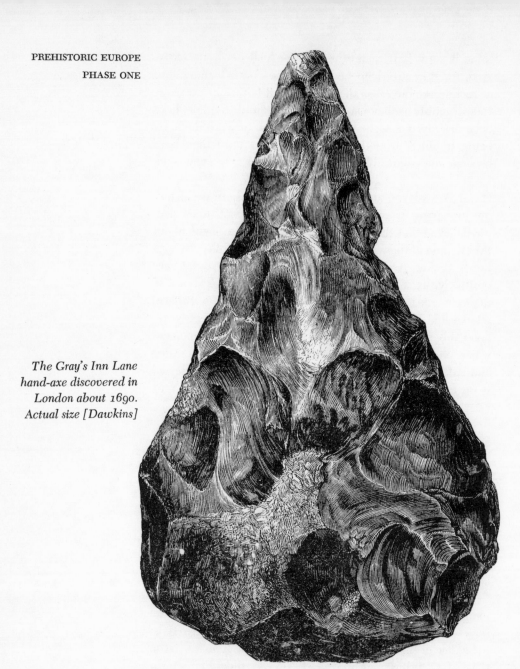

*The Gray's Inn Lane
hand-axe discovered in
London about 1690.
Actual size [Dawkins]*

the many hand-axes that had been dug up in the clay of a
brickyard along with an enormous thighbone and a huge
animal jaw equipped with teeth. Their finder said that the
42 hand-axes were so numerous that basketfuls of them had

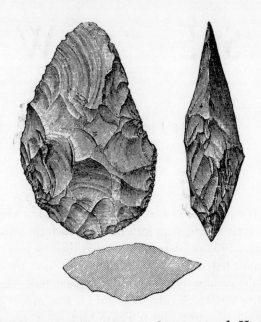

been thrown into the ruts of an adjoining road. He thought
that they were "weapons of war, fabricated and used by a
people who had not the use of metals" and that the location, deep in the earth, where the implements were discovered, "may tempt us to refer them to a very remote period
indeed."

*One of the flint hand-
axes dug up from 12 feet
below the surface at
Hoxne, Suffolk, in 1797
[Dawkins]*

been thrown into the ruts of an adjoining road. He thought
that they were "weapons of war, fabricated and used by a
people who had not the use of metals" and that the location, deep in the earth, where the implements were discovered, "may tempt us to refer them to a very remote period
indeed."

He spoke the truth, but no one paid much attention to
what he said even though his paper, illustrated with copper
engravings of the hand-axes, was published in the Society's
important journal, *Archeologia,* in 1800. But a new century
was dawning, the century of Chambers, Darwin, Huxley,
Haeckel, and other pioneers who were to change man's
thinking about his own origins. Before that century ended,
Archbishop Ussher's confidently placed date of 4004 B.C.
would seem absurd.

PHASE TWO

3. The First Europeans

MOST, BUT BY NO MEANS ALL, paleoanthropologists now think that the evolution of man into his modern form took place more than a million years ago and that there is no need for the complicated series of different names that have been given to the various discoveries of fossil hominids. The present tendency is to classify them into a few major groups, the australopithecines, the pithecanthropines (*Homo erectus*), the Neandertals, and modern man (*Homo sapiens*)— with an increasing tendency to consider *Homo neanderthalensis* as an early but somewhat different and now extinct form of *Homo sapiens*.

John W. Crenshaw, Jr., who is an ecologist with a special interest in evolutionary genetics, stated the case for this (1964, p. 12) when he said: "I am inclined to agree . . . that *all* hominids now known belong morphologically to a single species, or successional species at most, and to suggest that below the braincase, macro-evolution in the genus *Homo* came to an early end." And Crenshaw is not the first or the only scientist to say this.

The second major stage of mankind's evolution, *Homo erectus*, lasted from approximately 1 million to 500,000 years ago. The first fossil specimen for this period was discovered in 1891 in Java by Eugene Du Bois, who named his find *Pithecanthropus erectus* (now classified as *Homo erectus*).

Homo erectus was amazingly like modern man so far as his postcranial skeleton is concerned. He was about our height, and his thighbones are almost indistinguishable from ours. He walked erect; his brain capacity was just under 1,000 cc., and the fact that the left side of the lobe was somewhat larger than the right indicates that he was probably right-handed. (So were the Neandertals, for that mat-

44

ter. Right-handedness is an ancient trait. About 90 per cent of the world's present population favor the right hand. Oddly enough, however, some prehistorians believe that the cave painters' work shows that they were predominantly left-handed.)

But the head and face of *Homo erectus* were very different from ours. The bone structure was thick, the jaw prognathous, the rami broad, the chin almost nonexistent, the nasal openings wide, and the supra-orbital ridges over the eyes were very heavy. Yet the teeth were basically hominid in shape. There is no doubt that this early creature deserves to be called a man. It is believed that he may have been able to speak words and phrases.

In some ways, his skulls resemble those of his successors, the Neandertals, especially the so-called "Classic" ones. They are, however, even heavier and more primitive looking.

A modern European skull with technical names of some of its parts

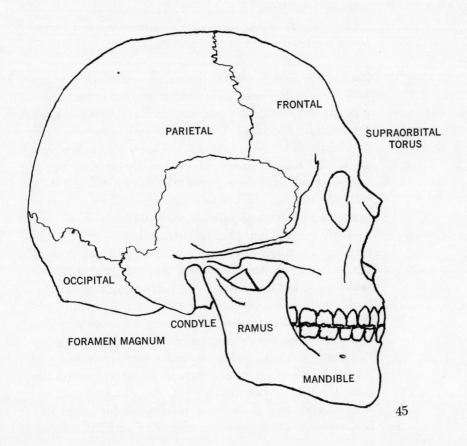

45

The fact that representatives of *Homo erectus* are known to have lived in Java and China many hundreds of thousands of years ago has led some scientists to believe that mankind may have had more than one place of origin—Asia as well as Africa. The matter has not been settled, nor is it likely to be settled soon. At the moment, the southern half of Africa is the favored place. But Carleton S. Coon, writing about this in *The Origin of Races* in 1962 (p. 230), said: "The currently popular theory that tool-making began in Africa in the Late Lower Pleistocene and spread to Europe and Asia only at the beginning of the Middle Pleistocene has not yet been disproved, but it faces many challenges as more and more archeological work is carried out in India, southeast Asia, and Indonesia."

Whether man orginated in Africa or Asia—or both—it is fairly certain that he did not have his beginnings in Europe's cool climate. His naked, unprotected body required tropical warmth even though it had more hair then.

Somewhere and at some unknown time, the first human being must have entered Europe from outside.

AN EXPLANATION is needed here about early man's migrations because the word, in current usage, has come to have a purposeful intent. The migrant hordes of Genghis Khan, the nomadic Bedouin tribes, and the emigrants who came to America did have a purpose; they knew where they were going, and they went toward their destinations as fast as horses, camels, and ships would take them there. But these were all relatively modern migrants who had some kind of transportation and some knowledge of their goals.

Early men did not. They had to travel on foot. Since they possessed no stored-up food supplies, they had to find something to eat every day. They could take only the goods they could carry, but they owned only a few simple things that could easily be replaced. The women and children could not go fast or far, so they moved only a few miles a day while the male hunters scouted for game. In many cases the group was not heading toward a destination but was fleeing from a place where it could no longer remain because the climate had grown worse, because food had become scarce, or because some more powerful group had pre-empted it. The waifs of the savannahs were still wander-

46

ing and would continue to do so for a long while to come.

It was not the far-off hills that beckoned, but the next bit of land, the nearest place with a promise of more food and perhaps a better life. The migrants went because they had to, and ordinarily they went slowly, but it is amazing how much ground can be covered when you keep moving for generations, for centuries, for thousands of years. Time drops away and is no longer a factor. You are where you are today, even though you do not know quite where that is. Then tomorrow—or next year, or years later—you will be somewhere else. Occasionally you come to a good place and stay there for a while. Then, when circumstance demands that you leave, you move on again.

Eventually you—or your descendants—are far away in a strange land where everything is different from the area where you started. Yet it does not seem strange to you, because you entered it very slowly and got used to it before you had gone very far into it.

Actually, primitive men can move into new territory much faster than one might think. Some brilliant theoretical work done by John B. Birdsell (1957, p. 67) shows that Australia could have been settled during the extraordinarily short period of only 2,200 years after the initial entry of a few migrants about 32,000 years ago. During that brief time, according to his figures, the population increased from a handful of the first settlers to an estimated saturation point of 300,000 or more aborigines. This population explosion on what is largely arid land could have been caused by approximately 35 tiny colonizing waves plus natural biological increase. And the settlers could have crossed the 3,200 miles to the farther side of the continent in a little more than two millenia.

By extrapolation, Birdsell arrived at a figure of only 23,000 years for the passage of the australopithecines from South Africa into the grasslands of southeastern Asia. He concludes that "Pleistocene man, when spreading into unoccupied territory, could have saturated it to carrying capacity, without resort to migration, in amazingly short elapsed time."

These figures are not quite as startling as they may at first seem. By using only simple arithmetic, it is evident that if a small group of people were to move away from their

47

origin at an average rate of only one mile a year, their descendants could cover 10,000 miles in 10,000 years, and so on.

It must be remembered, however, that such figures are theoretical. In reality, early migrants almost never averaged much speed. They lingered on in places they liked, sometimes they even turned back, and their rate of progress was also slowed by disease, starvation, and natural disasters. Yet over a long period they did press on until *Homo sapiens* eventually settled the entire earth.

EUROPE, in those early days, was very different from what it is now. At various times much of it was covered by vast sheets of ice. The rocks, stones, gravel, sand, clay, and wind-blown loess (rock dust) deposited when the glaciers melted tell us the story. After many years of research and correlation of observations made in every country that had ever been affected by the ice, scientists were finally able to show that there had been at least four major glaciations during the Pleistocene with many interglacial periods when the ice retreated and the land became warm enough for men to live on it in reasonable comfort. Since a great deal of time was involved, both the glacials and the interglacials were very long. Interglacials are the periods between major glaciations; warm periods within a major glaciation are called interstadials.

There had been other cold periods before these, one of them, the Donau, only a short time before. (Time, as used here, is geological time in which millenia are ticked off like seconds on a clock.) But they had all occurred long before man appeared on the earth and therefore do not concern us here. We know—or believe we know—the following facts about the later ice ages:

1. The world had been warm for more than 200 million years before the Pleistocene glacial periods set in although there had been several previous cold periods.

2. There is no agreement among scientists as to what caused the huge accumulations of ice, but two possible explanations are that (a) when mountains were formed they in turn caused the formation of glaciers, and then the white surface of the ice reflected 80 per cent of the sun's heat back into space; (b) smaller amounts of solar radiation reached

Pleistocene glaciations. Only main features are shown; time periods are not drawn to scale

IV WÜRM

Third Interglacial

III RISS

Second Interglacial

II MINDEL

First Interglacial

I GÜNZ

TODAY

100,000 YEARS AGO

200,000

300,000

400,000

500,000

600,000

the earth either because it was blocked en route or because the sun was sending out less. It may very well be that there were many causes and combinations of causes.

3. At its maximum, the great ice sheet covering northern Europe and most of the British Isles was two miles thick. It extended over all of Scandinavia, the Baltic Sea, and far into Germany (below Berlin) and Russia (beyond Moscow). Separate, less extensive glaciers covered the Alps, the Pyrenees, the Cevennes, and other high mountain areas.

4. Since the ice sheets shrank and then grew large again many times, men and beasts were repeatedly driven back to warmer southern climates. But they always returned, following the retreating masses of ice as they melted.

5. The glaciers changed the face of northern Europe, wearing down mountains, carving out valleys, forming lakes, and leaving behind enormous deposits of material gouged out of the land.

6. During the long time when so much water was tied up as ice in the glaciers, the oceans of the world sank to a level which, at its maximum, was about 500 feet below

Maximum glaciation of Europe

49

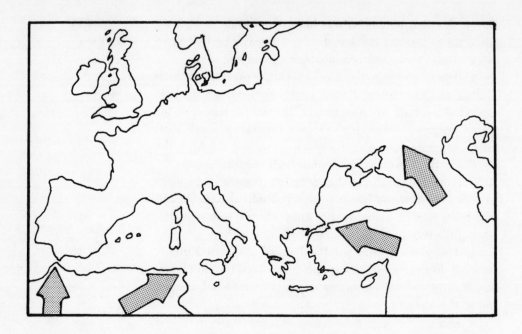

Possible entry points
of man into Europe

where it is now, and the vast weight of the ice caused the land beneath it to sink. This resulted in shorelines that extended much farther out than they do today. The remains and artifacts of the early men who dwelt on these now flooded areas are submerged under many feet of water, and some authorities believe that there is more prehistoric material under the ocean than there is on dry land. This seems likely because coastal areas were probably well settled on account of the seafood available there.

STILL UNANSWERED is the question of where and when the first settlers entered Europe. F. Clark Howell (1960, p. 225) believes that there was a primary dispersal of hominids from Africa to Asia and "that continental Europe was not penetrated" by this first migration because "there are no traces of hominids, either skeletal remains or stone tools, in the European Villafranchian. Such evidence does not appear until well along in the earlier Middle Pleistocene. The circumstances whereby Europe was not populated earlier by man are still difficult to ascertain. It is likely that the high sea levels of the . . . Lower Pleistocene may have been a major factor which inhibited dispersal. The Mediterranean was greatly enlarged, and the otherwise narrow water-gaps

50

(or potential land bridges during the later regressive stages of glaciation) in the western (Gibraltar) and northeastern Bosporus, Dardanelles) reaches of the basin were submerged."

Chester S. Chard, writing three years later (1963, p. 124), concluded that the Straits of Gibraltar were the best possibility for being "the gateway to Europe for the hand-axe people of the Lower Paleolithic. And it follows that we may expect eventually to find the oldest traces of European man on Spanish soil."

Fairly early evidence that men had been in Spain was found in 1961–63 by Howell. Excavations he directed at Torralba and Ambrona yielded artifacts made by elephant hunters who lived there about 300,000 years ago. Unfortunately, there were no human remains. But there were many hand-axes and some bits of charred wood which showed that these ancient men had used fire to drive their prey into a swamp where it would be trapped in the soft mud.

Fire was also used at a much earlier site, the Escale cave (Saint-Estève-Janson) in the Durrance valley in southern France, where "at least five hearths with reddened areas up to a meter in diameter and fire-cracked stones, and traces of ash and charcoals, have been encountered." So says Howell (1966, p. 109), who then adds: "The site shows every promise of being one of the very most important ever discovered in the Lower Pleistocene of Europe."

It is important because it may be the oldest known site in Europe with definite proof of human occupation. Men lived there perhaps as long as 750,000 years ago. It was discovered by Mme. Marie-Françoise Bonifay and Eugène Bonifay in 1960. Their report on it, presented in Paris in 1963 (p. 1136) to the Académie des Sciences, says that the cave contained many extinct animal bones, some of them dating back to a very early period. So far, the artifacts are few and rather disappointing, since they consist only of limestone flakes. But further work may turn up more remarkable finds there.

There are other very early sites in France. The Vallonnet cave near Roquebrune, was found in 1958. And during that year a deep municipal excavation at Montières (near Amiens) uncovered worked flints accompanied by the bones of a long-extinct ancestor of the horse, *Equus stenonis,* which roamed Europe during the earliest Pleistocene (F. Clark Howell in *American Anthropologist,* April 1966, p. 91).

There are still more very early sites, some near Amiens in the valley of the Somme, some in England along the lower Thames. It must be remembered that the English Channel did not yet exist, and the British Isles were connected to Europe.

So far none of these very early European sites has yielded even a scrap of human bone. Stone tools and evidence of fire exist, but nothing remains of the men who opened up the continent.

This is not as strange as it may seem. These first Europeans did not bury their dead, so their bodies were torn apart by wild animals and consumed by insects. Bones scattered in the open do not last long; they have to be protected in alkaline soil to endure. And there were very few people then in Europe to leave remains. It is therefore not surprising that no human fossils have been found for the period before 500,000 years ago.

THE OLDEST ONE yet discovered is somewhat of a mystery. This is the famous Heidelberg Man, who has long been known, for he was brought to light on October 21, 1907. Unfortunately, all that was recovered was a lower jaw, complete with teeth, that was dug out of the 78-foot level of a commercial sand pit in the Neckar River, a few miles southeast of Heidelberg, Germany. Since the find came from the Mauer sands, it is called the Mauer mandible.

It is a mystery because it does not fit into the expected order of European fossil men. Associated with it were bones of elephants, rhinoceroses, and other animals that have long been extinct in Europe. These made it possible to date the mandible—roughly—by association. The date generally agreed upon is approximately 500,000 years ago.

This means that Heidelberg Man could have been a representative of the species *Homo erectus.* Perhaps he was, but his jawbone is unusually large, and it has several curious discrepancies, the chief of which is the fact that its teeth are fairly small and well advanced (manlike), while its receding chin and very wide rami are more apelike. There has been much dispute about it ever since it was found.

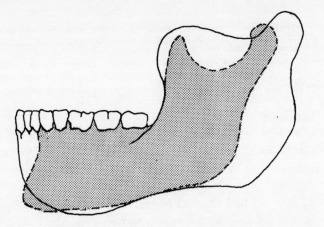

As late as 1965 (p. 238) C. L. Brace and Ashley Montagu still felt "fairly confident in assigning the Heidelberg jaw to the Pithecanthropine (*Homo erectus*) stage." They thought so because "the teeth are the right size, the dating is the same, and the evidence for culture in Western Europe at that time are just what one would expect."

Others do not agree with them. Writing in 1959 (p. 178), William W. Howells said that Heidelberg "cannot be classed with those early and primitive Euhominids of the Far East, Java and Pekin Man." (Java and Peking Man are examples of *Homo erectus*). In the May 1960 issue of *Current Anthropology* (p. 212 *f.*) F. Clark Howell re-examined the Mauer mandible and agreed that its teeth and bone structure have "fundamental differences" from those of Java and Peking Man and then suggested that it may belong to the same ancestral lineage as Montmaurin Man and the first Neandertals. In 1963 Ernst Mayr put it with Java and Peking Man. And then, in 1964, Bernard G. Campbell stated that nothing about it warrants its being classified as *Homo erectus* or placing it in a "subspecific category of its own."

Thus this earliest European man is still very much of an enigma. Carleton S. Coon, writing in 1962 (p. 492), said: "Because there is no Mauer cranium we do not know to which species, *Homo erectus* or *Homo sapiens*, Heidelberg Man belonged. Both the teeth and the narrow intercondylar width fit a higher grade than the other features of the bone itself, and both the jaw and its teeth fail to fit into the pattern of any of the other four lines of human evolution seen elsewhere in the world. Mauer therefore stands at the base of a line of its own."

The Heidelberg mandible compared with a modern European jaw (shaded area)

53

And there it must remain until further discoveries of fossil men cast more light on this baffling fragmentary specimen of the first known European, a mysterious creature who still defies classification.

THE ONLY OTHER BIT of really old human bone so far found in Europe was dug up on August 21, 1965, when Lazlo Vértes found part of a skull (the occiput) in a travertine quarry near Vérteszöllös, 30 miles west of Budapest, Hungary. Three human teeth had already been taken from the site. So had charred bones which had been split open for the marrow, so the men who had lived there obviously knew how to use fire. The numerous stone implements found with the occiput are noteworthy because they are so crude. There are no hand-axes, only simple choppers roughly made from big pebbles like those used in Olduvai Gorge by australopithecines 1.5 million years ago.

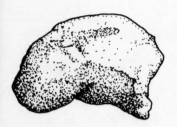

The Vérteszöllös occiput

Animal bones accompanying the Vérteszöllös Man's skull show that he was somewhat younger than Heidelberg Man, perhaps as much as 100,000 years.

The Mauer mandible tells us a good deal because it has all its teeth; the Vérteszöllös occiput is less revealing because that part of the skull has few diagnostic features. But the site from which it came is of the utmost importance because it is the earliest place in Europe that has yielded both artifacts and human remains. And it was found intact, sealed under layers of travertine and loess. Loess is the fine powder from rocks that were ground up under the glaciers. Vast quantities of it were blown about by the winds and deposited in huge areas of Europe after the ice melted.

In the November 1966 issue of *Scientific American*, William W. Howells said that the Vérteszöllös occiput "evidently dates to the middle or later part of the Mindel glaciation and thus falls clearly within the *Homo erectus* time zone as defined here. The bone is moderately thick and shows a well-defined ridge for the attachment of neck muscles such as is seen in all the *erectus* skulls. It is unlike *erectus* occipital bones, however, in that it is both large and definitely less angled: these features indicate a more advanced skull."

Howells reported that Andor Thoma, of the Kossuth University in Hungary, who has carefully examined the

Vérteszöllös occiput, estimates that it had a cranial capacity of 1,400 cc., which is larger than that of *Homo erectus* specimens, and that this early Hungarian therefore "had reached the *sapiens* grade in skull form and brain size." Because of this, Thoma named him a subspecies of *Homo sapiens*.

EVEN IF Europe's two earliest known settlers cannot clearly be classified as belonging to either the species *Homo erectus* or *Homo sapiens*, this does not necessarily mean that *Homo erectus* never got to Europe. He may have arrived there and have evolved into a type that was nearer to modern man by the time Heidelberg and then Vérteszöllös Man appeared in central Europe. Stone implements and traces of fire show that men who left no human remains had been present in western Europe long before them. Since we have nothing to identify these earlier men with we cannot know just who or what they were. But their artifacts are somewhat like those made by *Homo erectus* in other parts of the Old World.

It must be noted, however, that, as Carleton S. Coon (1962, p. 482) has pointed out, "Europe is the only section of the [Old] World in which no skull for *Homo erectus* has been found. The oldest ones whole enough for diagnosis are already *sapiens,* but they are not as old as the earliest *erectus* skulls from Java, China, and Africa. Yet they are older than any *sapiens* skulls found elsewhere."

It will thus be seen that evidence for man's beginnings in Europe is scant, fragmentary, and open to various interpretations. Nor is it likely that it will be clarified until more —and more complete—human remains for this early period are found. The search for them goes on unceasingly, and a new breakthrough may be made any day.

THERE IS a long gap in the succession of European fossil men after Heidelberg and Vérteszöllös. England gave us our next most ancient skull (probably a young woman's) when an occiput and parietals (side sections) were found separately over a period from June 29, 1935, to July 30, 1955, in a gravel pit near Swanscombe on the south shore of the Thames River a few miles below London. Animal bones and stone implements (including many hand-axes

55

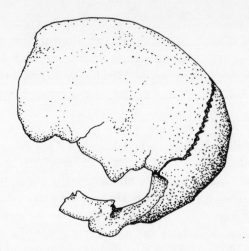

The Swanscombe skull

and flake tools) associated with the skull fragments made it possible to date the find as more than 250,000 years old.

Another very early skull was discovered in one piece near Steinheim, Germany, not far from Heidelberg, on July 24, 1933. Animal bones located near it established the date as somewhat later than that of the Swanscombe fragments, about 200,000 years ago. It, too, probably belonged to a woman and is by far the most complete of all the really old European skulls. Only the lower jaw, most of the upper teeth, and some of the more delicate facial bones are missing. The young lady was probably murdered by a crushing blow to the left eye. The fact that the area around the foramen magnum has been broken away indicates that she may have been the victim of cannibals, who customarily remove the brain through the underside of the skull.

These four skulls—or pieces of skulls—are the only human remains that have so far been found of Europe's earliest inhabitants. Other bones will undoubtedly turn up, but there cannot be many of them. They are scarce because Europe was sparsely settled then, because bones have to be unusually well protected to last 200,000 years or more, and because an expert must be on hand to identify fragmented human remains when they are uncovered. Many a precious bit of testimony has been ruthlessly destroyed by laborers' picks and shovels. Bulldozers will smash and rebury more.

Where do Swanscombe and Steinheim fit into the evolutionary scheme of European men? There is no clear-cut answer, for it is still a moot question as to whether they

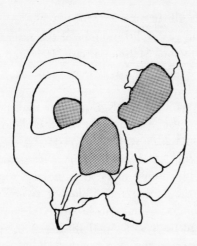

The Steinheim skull

should be classified as late representatives of *Homo erectus*, as precursors of the Neandertals, or as very early members of *Homo sapiens*. Carleton S. Coon believes that they were *sapiens*. In *The Origin of Races* (1962, p. 497) he says that "in 1955 W. E. LeGros Clark accepted these skulls, at least provisionally, as primitive members of *Homo sapiens*. In 1960 Clark Howell discussed the problem at length without committing himself. He emphasized the archaic traits that foreshadowed the Neandertals in both these skulls. Also in 1960, W. W. Howells postulated the first appearance of *Homo sapiens* at "almost certainly . . . some 150,000 years ago." S. L. Washburn, in the same number of *Scientific American* [September], wrote: "The species *Homo sapiens* appeared perhaps as recently as 50,000 years ago. As no one in the Anglo-American world knows more about Steinheim and Swanscombe than these four experts, who are well aware of the date of the skulls, the disagreement is obviously a matter of how one defines *Homo sapiens*."

Still other experts disagree with these. In 1958 J. S. Weiner, writing in the *South African Journal of Medical Science*, (23, 111–120), thought that Steinheim might represent a stage on a separate line leading to *Homo sapiens*. And in 1962 G. H. R. von Koenigswald said (pp. 108–9) that "by underplaying its Neandertal characteristics we can easily change it into *Homo sapiens;* by exaggerating these characteristics we can turn it into 'extreme' Neandertal man. However, the *sapiens* characteristics seem to be the more pronounced of the two."

Nor is this all. In 1960 (p. 202) Ashley Montagu wrote that "there can . . . be little doubt of the essential Neanderthaloid character of Steinheim man. It is not unlikely that he was a descendant of Heidelberg man."

THERE ARE other fairly early European skulls, but they are not as old as the Swanscombe or Steinheim finds. The Montmaurin mandible was discovered in a cave in the lower Pyrenees on July 18, 1949. With it were some crude pre-Mousterian implements made of quartzite and flint. It is smaller than the Mauer mandible but is equally chinless. Its rami, although not quite as broad as Mauer's, are rather wide. They are both wider and thicker than similar Neandertal jawpieces. Ashley Montagu (*ibid*, p. 194) says that it "presents features which give it a position intermediate between Heidelberg and Neanderthal man." He adds that "there can be little doubt that this mandible is of Riss-Würm interglacial age and represents the remains of the oldest fossil man thus far found in France."

Not quite so old are the fragments of two skulls found on August 16, 1947, at Fontéchevade, east of Angoulême in western France. One is the top of a skull; the other a small frontal piece. The larger one shows marks of violence and also of charring.

William W. Howells (1959, p. 220 *f.*) considers the Fontéchevade finds to be of great importance because of their large cranial capacity (more than 1,450 cc.) and the fact that the "vault is indistinguishable from modern man although thicker. . . , but the brow ridge . . . is slight." "This is sensational evidence," he says. "If there is one constant feature of the Neanderthals, early and late, it is the heavy curving brow, and the Fontéchevade skulls certainly lack it. They are therefore damaging to the hypothesis that *Homo sapiens* as we know him did not exist . . . before the heyday of the Neanderthals."

There are still other early European fossil men—Ehringsdorf in Germany, Quinzano in northern Italy, Monsempron in southwestern France, and Krapina in Yugoslavia—but they are later than the ones described above. Some of them are so late that they fall well within the Neandertal time zone.

4. What We Know About the
Early European Settlers

WHETHER HOMO ERECTUS ever got to Europe or not, some kind of "men" certainly reached that continent long before Heidelberg Man did. Since there is no generally agreed-upon name for them, let us call them the early settlers. We know that they were advanced enough to use fire. If they came from Africa they must have learned about it somewhere along the way because no really ancient hearths have been discovered on that warm continent.

The need for artificial heat to protect them from Europe's colder weather may have induced them to find out how to control the comforting but always dangerous flames. At first they probably got their fires from volcanoes or from conflagrations started by natural causes. They then had to guard the precious embers carefully and make sure that they did not grow cold. If the fire did die out, they could probably go to a neighbor—perhaps even an ordinarily hostile one—to ignite some sticks and carry the essential flames home.

The ability to make a fire at will, which marks a great step forward in mankind's cultural development, came much later. It is easy to keep a fire going, but to start one requires knowledge, forethought, and a certain amount of skill, as those who have ever tried to use any of the primitive fire-starting methods can testify.

Kenneth Oakley, who has studied man's use of fire for many years, says (1961b, p. 181 f.) that "discoveries of how to make fire probably occurred through the use and manufacture of tools. The sparks produced by striking stones together must have been very evident to early men working in a dim light. The sparks made by striking flint on flint have only slight incendiary properties. . . . The *percussion method* of making fire was probably discovered through the chance use of a nodule of iron pyrites as a hammerstone for striking flint. Whereas 'flint sparks' have only the heat generated by the percussive friction, and lose it rapidly, pyritic sparks (like iron sparks) develop additional heat through combustion in the air."

As to more advanced techniques, Oakley goes on to say: "It seems rather improbable that the frictional methods of making fire were invented before technology had reached the stage at which bone, antler, ivory, and wood were sawed and shaped by grinding and when holes were bored in such materials by the rapid rotation of a drill. Thus the devices known as the fire saw, the fire plough, and the fire twirl may not have been invented before the end of Paleolithic times. (Indeed, it is unlikely that the true fire drill, which is operated by a bow, was introduced before Neolithic times.)"

Naturally started friction fires, caused by the dead branches of trees being rubbed together by the wind, must have been noticed numerous times by many generations before anyone made practical use of the basic idea. And flint must have been struck many thousands, or even millions, of times before someone saw the sparks from it ignite flammable material that just happened to be nearby.

There is no doubt that much of man's progress came from noticing such fortuitous events. But the observer had to be intelligent enough to make good use of what he saw. And then, once the discovery was made, the new method had to be taught to others and handed down from generation to generation.

We know that European men used fire at Saint-Estève-Janson in France, at Vérteszöllös in Hungary, and at Torralba and Ambrona in Spain. Fire-using was probably discovered independently in China, for traces of it dating back to 400,000 or more years ago have been found in the well-known Choukoutien caves near Pekin.

In most cases, prehistoric men used wood for fuel; where it was scarce or not available at all, they burned animal bones. In Czechoslovakia the marrow from split-open mammoth bones was used to feed the flames. Even fresh bones themselves will burn; Darwin saw the natives use them for fuel when he visited South America on the *Beagle* in the 1830's. Early European men also burned coal in places where they could find it lying near the surface.

When forest or brush fires ravaged the land, animals overtaken by the flames were a free food offering. Some carcasses may have been only slightly charred; others were well roasted. Such delicacies taught the ever-hungry nomads how much better cooked meat is than raw. (Charles Lamb wrote a memorable essay about this.) Our remote ancestors did not know it, but cooking improves the taste of some meats and makes them easier to digest. This new method of preparing more easily chewed food had an effect on the teeth and jaw muscles. Over a long period of time it reduced the chewing apparatus in size, changed facial appearance, and even helped to bring about a new social structure.

Nomads who know how to make fire can travel easily, but those who have to transport glowing embers—and make sure they don't go out—are likely to prefer to stay in one place as long as they can. If they have found a well-protected, dry, and comfortable cave or rock shelter with enough game in the area, they may remain there for many generations.

The use of fire made it possible for men to dwell in caves. Without flames to protect them from wild beasts, a cavern would be a trap. And, as Oakley has suggested (1961b, p. 182), it was a trap in which men were especially vulnerable, because such noisy sleeping habits as snoring "would have continually attracted night-prowling carnivores."

Thus, with the use of fire, the idea of home was born; with the home went the hearth, which was man's first step toward civilization. And a settled abode would lead eventually to seeds accidentally planted around the doorstep; to keeping a few live animals—perhaps as pets at first; to the need for cooking utensils, made, let's say, from the clay that children were molding into toy figures which were hardened when they were left near the fire.

The leaping flames gave not only heat but light. The shelter thus became a warm, illuminated place where its people no longer had to go to sleep soon after sunset. Night, therefore, was less fearful, less to be dreaded than it had been in ages past. The eyes of predators still gleamed threateningly beyond the protecting circle of firelight, but the beasts haunting the darkness were being held at bay.

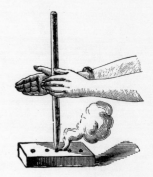

Methods used by modern primitive people for making fire. Top: stick rubbed in a groove; middle: hand-rotated drill; bottom: bow drill [Joly]

61

And on warm, humid nights, smoke from the fire served a useful purpose by repelling stinging insects.

The campfire became a place for meetings, for long talks, for making plans. The man who was the leader in the hunt was not necessarily the leader at these nighttime sessions. In the magic light of the fire not brawn but brain counted. Ideas that were to lead to better ways of living were expressed there. There too, storytelling, legend, and poetry had their origin. Men heard only simple commands from their captains in the field, but the speakers at the fire wanted to voice more complex thoughts that required more elaborate words and phrases. Language took on new and more expressive form. The daily hunt filled men's bellies, but the firelight discussions filled their minds.

Night after night, year after year, century after century, the fire-enchanted circle was drawing farther and farther away from the wild beasts that still dwelt in the darkness outside. Light and knowledge were becoming synonymous. Man was growing up, and most of his mental progress came from what he learned from the give-and-take dialogue that serves as a whetstone for intelligence, for imagination, for conceptual thought, and for the ability to put ideas into words.

DURING THE many hundreds of thousands of years that the early settlers lived in Europe, that broad continent underwent many changes. Huge icecaps came and went, scouring out the land and reshaping it. Sea levels fell hundreds of feet because water was kept away from the ocean for thousands of years while it remained frozen in the enormous glaciers. Cold weather succeeded warm, then the warmth returned, and this was repeated in varying degrees time after time. The climate was usually fairly cool; sometimes it was very cold for centuries on end.

Animal and vegetable life changed with altered temperatures. Semitropical forms were replaced by northern varieties; then it became too hot for the more Arctic kinds. The coming and going of the glaciers, together with the effect that their presence or absence had upon the land, makes a confusing pattern that is hard for the layman to follow. The chart on page 48 shows the major glaciations and places them in time.

One reason for the absence of human remains for the period before 500,000 years ago is that vast ice sheets were covering much of northern Europe, and even where the heavy layers of ice did not encrust the land their presence must have made the climate cold, foggy, and generally unpleasant for hundreds of miles around. As the first men to arrive in Europe pressed farther north, the climate became steadily worse. And there were so few of them that they were scattered across vast empty spaces. Some probably returned to warmer areas, but others remained to die in that hostile land. Their unburied bones were mingled with the glacier-churned soil and were eventually destroyed. Only their hearths and a few of their crude stone tools bear witness to the fact that they were ever there at all.

Heidelberg Man apparently arrived during the First Interglacial that followed the Gunz Glaciation. This was a long spell of warm, dry weather that lasted until the Mindel Glaciation replaced it after Heidelberg and Vérteszöllös men had lived their remote and little-known lives. Then the Second Interglacial, shorter than the First, made it warm enough for the Swanscombe and Steinheim people to remain in Europe. After them came the Riss Glaciation, then another mild Interglacial, the Third, which was followed by the Würm, the cold period the Neandertals knew. The great icecaps melted about 10,000 years ago, and Europe became the temperate area it is today.

There were many short interglacials during the major glaciations, so that the glaciations are usually broken into divisions—Würm I, or Early Würm; Würm II, or Middle Würm, Early Phase; Würm III, or Middle Würm, Main Phase, etc.

We know so little about the early settlers that we cannot tell for sure whether they remained in Europe uninterruptedly, whether they were forced out for a while and then returned many generations later, or whether they were all killed off by bitter winters and were then replaced by later migrants.

There is also an excellent possibility that early Europe was populated at times not only by hand-axe makers but also by a different and more primitive people, the chopper–chopping-tool makers who used chipped pebbles and accidentally produced flakes rather than carefully shaped flint.

63

Jacquetta Hawkes (1963, p. 64) explains this: "The picture is complicated by the fact that the bearers of the two cultural traditions were not usually present simultaneously, but alternated in response to the climatic pulse of Pleistocene times. Though there may well be many discoveries to disprove the universality of this rule, there is now very considerable evidence to show that during the Lower Paleolithic period the hand-axe peoples extended northward through Europe during the warm interglacial conditions, while their rivals, perhaps dominated by the Paleoanthropic stocks, probably hardier and more enduring, took possession of as much of the continent as was habitable during the glacial ages."

An Abbevillian hand-axe
from Chelles-sur-Marne

Our lack of knowledge about this very early period makes its people vague and shadowy, for we have nothing but their stone tools to go by. Even the classification of their implements is still rather tentative. As it stands now, the first European hand-axe culture is called Abbevillian (formerly known as "Chellean"). Jacquetta Hawkes (1963, p. 73) says that "when the final phase of the Second Glaciation rendered northern Europe uninhabitable and most of the rest of the continent bitterly cold, the Abbevillian peoples withdrew southward toward their African cradleland. The peoples who took their place were the makers of a culture known as the Clactonian, which belongs to the group known as flake cultures to distinguish them from the Asiatic chopper-tool and the African hand-axe traditions. Their tools were mostly trimmed from boldly struck flakes, many of them evidently designed as skinning-knives and hide-scrapers, an equipment better adapted to life in a cold climate than that associated with the hand-axe. . . . While later on contacts between the flake-tool and hand-axe makers in Eurasia undoubtedly led to the mingling and transference of cultural traits, there is good reason to believe that at this stage the two people were distinct and that we are free to visualize the departure of the Abbevillians and the arrival of the Clactonians as actual, even if very gradual migrations."

Clactonian "B"
from Swanscombe

As time passed, Abbevillian culture developed into Acheulian, and stone implements were improved. The Mindel-Riss or Second Interglacial made Europe warmer for 150,000 years, during which its population increased and

64

its people mingled together, interbred, and in some places produced both Clactonian flake tools and hand-axes.

With the oncoming of the Riss Glaciation and colder climate, the so-called Levalloisian core-tool culture appeared. Whether its people were descendants of those already living in Europe or were newcomers from outside is not known. Their flake tools are even more specialized for cutting meat and scraping hides than their predessors' had been.

Somewhat later are the Tayacians, a little-known people who lived farther south and east and who developed a culture of their own which may have been derived from the Clactonian. After the Tayacians, the very early peoples give way to the Neandertals, who were close to—and perhaps genetically identical with—*Homo sapiens,* modern man.

*Acheulian hand-axe
from Saint-Acheul*

THE TERMS used above were taken from place names. Clactonian comes from an English village in Essex; all the others are French. Chellean was coined from Chelles, a village in the environs of Paris where artifacts of that type were first discovered. Abbevillian and Acheulian are derived from two towns (Abbeville and Saint-Acheul) in the Somme River valley near Amiens. Levalloisian comes from the site of that name near Paris; Tayacian from Tayac in the Dordogne.

The Somme River valley played an important part in helping us to discover the truth about the antiquity of man, for it was there in 1837 that Jacques Boucher de Crêvecoeur de Perthes, a customs inspector and amateur archeologist from Abbeville, began to examine the gravel beds from which bones of extinct animals and hand-axes had already been taken. He got a rich haul and displayed some of his finds in Abbeville and then in Paris. As was usual in those days, he was scoffed at, but he went on with his work and in 1839 brought out the first of many volumes he was to produce on this then little-known subject. He continued, alone and without recognition, until 1859, the year of Darwin's *Origin of Species.* Then some English scientists and antiquarians went to France to examine what he had found. One of the group was young Arthur Evans, who was later to become world famous for his excavations in Crete.

The visiting Englishmen's report to the Royal Society

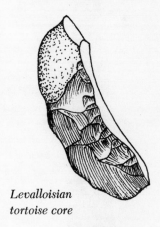

*Levalloisian
tortoise core*

Tayacian from La Micoque

and the Society of Antiquaries brought serious scientific attention to Boucher de Perthes' finds. His own countrymen, however, were still reluctant to admit that the flint implements he had dug up were really old.

It may seem strange to us that so much resistance was offered to the idea that man's origins extend far back in time, but mid-nineteenth-century mentality is almost as far away from us in thinking, if not in time, as it was from the early men it refused to believe had ever existed.

MOST OF THE very old flint implements unearthed in Europe were found in sediments brought down by rivers. Undisturbed occupational sites like the one at Vérteszöllös or the hearths in the Saint-Estève-Janson cave are rare. They are rare because water from the enormous glaciers that covered the continent swept nearly everything away. Flints were tumbled downstream and deposited far from the places where they had originally been shaped.

They were usually left on river terraces, which the ever-flowing streams laid down and then abandoned as they cut their way deeper into the land until they were sometimes many feet below their prehistoric levels. This scouring-out process was especially strong during periods when much of the world's water was locked up in glaciers and the summer runoff coursed swiftly downhill to the lowered sea level. During an interglacial, the ice melted and the oceans rose, sometimes backing up into the rivers, which then silted up their lower stretches. Despite this complicating factor, a series of terraces, perhaps five or six, were formed along ancient rivers like the Somme and the Thames.

In almost every case, the highest terrace is the oldest one. This means that artifacts buried there will not be so far below the present surrounding surface land as more recent ones found deeper down and nearer to the existing river bed.

Because the artifacts were wrenched violently away from their original sites and were then tossed around in fast-flowing streams for countless centuries, they are often badly worn. But so little is left of anything once owned by Europe's first settlers that every fragment is collected, classified, and put away in museums. They tell us nearly all we know about man's beginnings on the continent.

Pointed end of yew spear from Clacton-on-Sea, Essex

66

Oddly enough, however, a few bits of very ancient man-shaped wood remain. Fragments that may be as much as 300,000 years old have been found in the Torralba and Ambrona sites in northern Spain. The pointed end of a yew spear was discovered at Clacton-on-Sea in southeast England. It is now in London's Natural History Museum, where the label describing it says that it was made more than 100,000 years ago. Another yew spear, more than seven feet long and complete with fire-hardened tip, was found in Germany between Bremen and Hanover in the rib cage of an extinct elephant, but this one is somewhat more recent. All were taken from water-soaked ground which protected the wood from the decay ordinarily caused by exposure to air and light.

These pieces of wood somehow seem closer to us than the more impersonal and literally harder stone implements do. Perhaps that is because they are made of organic material, something that once had life and grew.

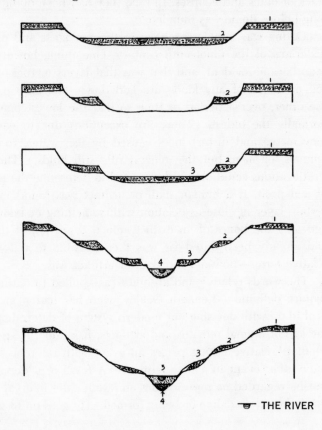

As a river digs deeper into the earth over a long period of time, it leaves a series of terraces behind

☞ THE RIVER   67

5. Dating the Finds

WHEN prehistoric stone implements were examined by learned men in the seventeenth and eighteenth centuries, they had no way of telling how old the odd-looking things were. In England they called them pre-Roman, which meant that it was thought that they had been made before 55 B.C., the memorable year when Caesar invaded an island on which the blue-painted Britons presumably had not yet bothered to keep a record of time. But a twentieth-century astronomer's study of Stonehenge shows us that the British "savages" had been far ahead of the Romans in keeping track of dates and eclipses. In fact, they had been doing so long before Rome was founded.

Dating was a major problem to the geologists and pre-historians of the nineteenth century. One thing, however, soon became evident, and that was that layers of rock—or soil or debris of any kind—are laid down, one on top of the other, over a period of time so that the lowest one is normally the oldest. (There are exceptions due to earth movements and disturbances caused by ice, water, roots, animals, or men, but the general rule still holds.) These stratifications could obviously be used to determine the age of a deposit. If a human skull or artifact was found in a certain layer in close association with something of known age—say the bones of an extinct animal or an object that had already been dated—it was then possible to tell—in relative terms—how old the skull or artifact was.

The words relative and absolute (as applied to dating) require definition. Kenneth Oakley, who has had a great deal to do with devising our modern system of determining the age of animal remains and artifacts, has said (1964, p. 1) that "relative dating places an event with reference to some other event in a time-sequence. A fossil or a deposit can be regarded as representing an 'event': the interval of time when it was alive or being formed." He goes on to say

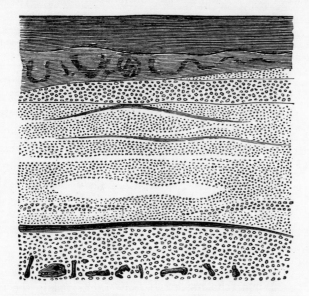

*Stratified gravel levels
at Acton Green;
prehistoric bones are in
the lowest one [Dawkins]*

that since "none of the events occurred everywhere simultaneously, the dating of a specimen . . . does not necessarily imply exact contemporaneity with specimens similarly dated in other parts of the world."

His second statement is needed because some areas were far ahead of others in their development. Hand-axes, for instance, had been in use in Africa for many thousands of years before they appeared in Europe. But advances did not take place in any regular order. Africa may have pioneered in hand-axes, but Europeans and Asians apparently used fire long before Africans did.

Relative dating requires that the rock or soil in which the object to be dated was found be truly contemporary with it. Several cases of intrusive burials deceived prehistorians until more exact methods of determining age proved that the date given the specimen was wrong by thousands of years.

When it comes to dating, many archeologists merely say that the object they are describing is "within the Second Glaciation" (Mindel, 400,000 or more years ago; see chart on page 48) or that the skull "suggests an Upper Pleistocene date, probably during the Fourth Glaciation" (Würm or Last Glaciation). Such references do no more than give a rough indication of the age of the find. This does not matter so much in the case of things that are hundreds of

69

thousands of years old, for a few thousand years leeway is not important then; but it does with more recent things. Fortunately, such material can be dated much more precisely. The skull just mentioned, for instance, can be said to be 20,000 to 30,000 years old. And now it is possible to date some prehistoric objects even more closely than that. It depends on what they are and in what circumstances they were found. Such exact dating is called absolute or chronometric. Oakley (1964, p. 1) defines this by saying that it "relates an event to a regular astronomical event-sequence, particularly the passage of years or solar time." Frederick E. Zeuner, who probably did more work on prehistoric chronology than anyone else, once said (1958, p. 28 n) that "no doubt the day will come when all geological divisions are defined by absolute time."

When scholars first became interested in the study of prehistory, they thought it would never be possible to assign exact dates to objects that were older than written records. Swedish scientists led the way in establishing the first methods for chronometric dating. As early as 1870 Gustav Oscar Montelius began an elaborate survey of prehistoric implements in which he classified them according to their similarity. Once he had arranged them in their probable chronological order, he had established a system of typological dating. In 1889 he published a chronology of the Bronze Age in Europe and soon afterward was able to tie in his findings with definitely known dates in the Near East, Egypt, and Greece, where written records had been in existence for many thousands of years.

The next step toward a better chronology was made by another Swedish scientist, Baron Gerard de Geer, who worked from 1905 to 1910 to show how deposits of silt laid down in annual layers by the melting glaciers of the last Ice Age could be used to determine dates. He was eventually able to establish a series of these varves (as they are called in Sweden) that went back 12,000 years. He also obtained an exact date for the times when the great icecap that had once covered Scandinavia broke up (6839 and 7912 B.C.). Then the Baltic Ice Lake, a vast body of fresh water penned up behind a glacial dam, was able to flow to the Atlantic, thus eventually permitting salty ocean water to enter the Baltic Sea.

Varve dating was soon extended to other parts of Europe, to North America, and to other areas where melting glaciers had left clearly marked layers of sediment.

The basic idea of determining dates by counting the annual growth rings on a cross-cut section of a big tree is more than 150 years old, but it was not put into effect until 1901, when the science of dendrochronology had its beginnings in the United States, where very large and very old trees can be found. Today a forest giant does not have to be cut down to count its growth rings; a long boring tool can extract a slender core without harming the tree. The growth rings in ancient roof beams and fair-sized fragments of timber are even more useful for determining dates. And when they have been partly burned, charcoal shows the rings even more clearly than wood does. Since little wood remains from very early prehistoric times, dendrochronology has only a limited use for establishing dates, because it cannot cover those that are really old.

OAK

BIRCH

Pollen analysis (palynology) reaches farther back in time, for plant pollen can last for thousands of years in lime-free moist soil or peat. But it establishes relative, not absolute, dates. The idea of using ancient pollens for dating is another Swedish innovation. Two Stockholm scientists, Gustav Lagerheim and Lennart von Post, invented pollen dating early in the 1900's. Lagerheim studied peat under the microscope and saw that it was filled with the pollen of many kinds of long-dead plants. Since the pollen of each plant differs from that of every other, it is possible to identify the specific one. Von Post carried this basic idea a step further. He drew up statistical analyses of tree pollens and showed that they had originated at different times which could be arranged in chronological sequences. In this way it became possible to tell not only which trees were growing in a given area at a given time but also how scarce or plentiful they were.

HAZEL

Prehistoric pollen, greatly magnified

The pollens of ancient flora can be related to geological periods or even to the human remains or artifacts found with them and so establish a reasonably close date. Since varve layers often contain pollen, a cross-check between the two techniques can be made.

Glacial deposits, fresh-water and marine shells, insects, animal bones (particularly those of extinct elephants), and

71

the heights of river terraces and former sea beaches can also be used to establish relative dates.

Absolute dates for fairly recent periods can be determined (in some places) by varve and tree-ring methods. But for older dates—and any dates where the special conditions needed for varve and tree-ring counting do not exist— a technique covering longer periods of time was required.

Professor Willard F. Libby, who had worked on the Manhattan Project at the University of Chicago, conceived the basic idea of using radioactive Carbon 14 to determine the dates of prehistoric events with greater accuracy than had ever been achieved before. The technique has limitations, but it is a superb new tool for archeological research, and from it came the use of other isotopes that can tell us the age of rocks and fossils which are millions of years old. The Geiger counter has become our measuring instrument for the long-ago past.

Radiocarbon dating is a complicated technical process with several possible variants but basically it is this: cosmic rays have been bombarding the earth's atmosphere ever since it was formed, and their rate of striking the outer air can be taken as constant over a long period of time. When these rays strike an atom of nitrogen they produce an atom of Carbon 14 and a proton. (C14 is a radioactive isotope of ordinary Carbon 12.) When C14 is formed it combines with oxygen to produce radioactive carbon dioxide, $C^{14}O_2$. This, along with much larger quantities of ordinary nonradioactive carbon dioxide, $C^{12}O_2$, is taken in by plants and is used by them to help build their vegetable structure. Herbivores eat the plants, carnivores eat the herbivores, and omnivorous man eats the plants, the herbivores, and— sometimes—the carnivores. The C14 from the original plants is therefore finally distributed among all living things. In a small way we are all ticking away like radioactive clocks.

When an organism dies it stops taking in C14, and that which is present begins to decay at a constant rate. After $5,568 \pm 30$ years C14 reaches its half-life, which means that at this point there is only half as much of this radioactive isotope left as there was in the organism when it died.

A sample of the specimen to be tested is then taken with great care in order not to contaminate it with more recent material, particularly cigarette ashes, soil containing organic matter, or any other carboniferous substances. This sample, properly packed, is then sent to one of the special laboratories that are equipped with the necessary apparatus needed to measure the exceedingly small amount of C_{14} that remains in the specimen.

A carefully weighed-out portion of the specimen is then ignited in the presence of absolutely pure oxygen to produce carbon dioxide with minute quantities of C_{14} from the original sample in it. This gas is sealed up and inserted (under pressure to concentrate it) into a Geiger counter, which determines the radioactivity of the sample, i.e., it counts the number of C_{14} atoms present. This count is compared with a count made at the same time of the radio-activity of a standard modern sample containing C_{14} and C_{12} as they exist in the air today.

Since the cosmic rays which are now hitting the earth, as well as any other unwanted radioactive emissions that might be around, would distort the findings, the Geiger counter doing the actual counting has to be shielded. It is therefore encased in solid steel walls which must be at least eight inches thick. Inside these is a screen of paraffin wax with boric acid in it to keep out any neutrons that might be generated in the steel walls. Nor is this enough; a ring of Geiger counters inside the massive shield automatically cancels out any stray impulses that might otherwise affect the central counter.

The formula used to calculate the age of the specimen is

$$t = \frac{1}{\lambda} \log_e \frac{I_o}{I}$$

in which t is the time passed since the death of the organism; λ is the radiocarbon's decay constant; I is the activity of the sample; and I_o is the activity of the modern organic material being compared with it.

Looked at in terms of years, the radiocarbon schedule works out like this:

1. At the time of the death of the organism all its original C_{14} atoms were present.
2. After 5,568 years (ignoring the ± 30 years), one half of the original C_{14} atoms still remains.
3. After 11,140 years, one quarter remains.

73

4. After 22,280 years, one sixteenth remains.

Beyond this time, the number of remaining C14 atoms gets smaller and smaller and therefore becomes more difficult to measure. After 50,000 years the amount left becomes so infinitesimal that it cannot be determined by this method. A recently discovered idea, isotopic enrichment, then has to be resorted to. With this, the time range can be extended to about 70,000 years, which seems to be the limit for using C14 measurement.

Radiocarbon dating sounds like the perfect clock for telling exactly how old ancient objects are. But it works only on organic substances like wood, charcoal, nuts, grain, charred bone or antlers, animal or human remains, peat, plant-rich mud or silt, and other things that contain carbon. It does not work on stone, pottery, glass, metals, or anything inorganic. It can, however, date such materials when they are found in close and undisturbed association with carboniferous objects or surrounding soil.

As in any laboratory procedure, radioactive carbon dating is subject to natural faults and human error. The sample may have been contaminated at the source, perhaps ages ago; mistakes can be made in the way it is taken, packed, labeled, opened, or prepared; and there is always, of course, a chance that something can go wrong with the mathematical calculation. These possibilities, however, are not peculiar to handling Carbon 14; they are inherent in any kind of laboratory work. But something else is sadly peculiar to it, and that is that the numerous nuclear explosions set off since 1945 have caused such an increase in radioactive carbon in the atmosphere that by 1964 the amount which had been there 20 years before was doubled. And this is expected to increase until 1975, when it should begin to decline.

Meanwhile, rain soaking through the leaf and root systems of plants that absorb C14 is contaminating the soil and making carbon dating difficult for some time to come. This, however, does not affect deeply buried objects.

OTHER isotopic methods for measuring the age of material that is hundreds of thousands or even millions of years old have been developed. The most useful of them is the potassium-argon technique, which depends upon the transformation of Potassium 40 into Argon 40. The half-life

74

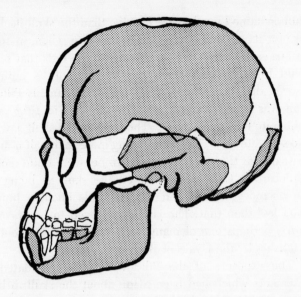

period for this is enormously long, so long that it has to be expressed as 1.30 x 10⁹ years. This method has been particularly helpful in determining the great age of prehistoric material found in Africa's Olduvai Gorge.

The skull of Piltdown Man with its orangutan mandible (shaded area shows extant bones)

The fluorine-dating test is not isotopic nor does it measure elapsed time. It had long been known that fluorine, which is naturally present in water in some areas, gradually accumulates in buried bones and teeth. Comparing the amount of fluorine in human skeletal remains with that in the bones or teeth of other animals found close by would therefore show whether or not they were truly contemporary.

Ancient climatic changes can be determined by analyzing the contents of cores of sediment taken from the ocean floor. Present in them are shells, fish bones, teeth, volcanic ash, and mineral fragments that were carried down from the land.

Other scientific methods for dating make use of terrestial magnetism, the thickness of hydration layers on obsidian artifacts, and thermoluminescence for determining the age of pottery.

IN SEPTEMBER 1949, when Kenneth Oakley told members of the British Association for the Advancement of Science that the animal bones supposedly associated with the Piltdown

75

skull contained much more fluorine than the skull itself, the case for its authenticity began to crumble. Then, in 1953, a serious examination of it, involving all the tests that science could bring to bear upon the problem of its antiquity, showed that "Eoanthropus," as England's famous Piltdown Man was called when it was "discovered" in 1912, was a deliberate fake and a fraud. The fragmented skull, jaw, and two separate teeth, instead of being more than half a million years old, as they were supposed to be, were quite modern. Radiocarbon tests in 1959 dated the skull as being only 620 ± 100 years old and the mandible about a hundred years less than that. The jawbone proved to be an orang-utan's, perhaps one of many such skulls kept for centuries as fetishes by the Dyaks of Borneo.

The exposure of the Piltdown fraud invalidated the statements which had been made about the skull in books about prehistory published between 1912 and the early 1950's. It had been so widely accepted as genuine that the 1925 edition of Sir Arthur Keith's massive two-volume work, *The Antiquity of Man,* featured it with a picture stamped in gold on the covers.

Piltdown is not the only prehistoric forgery that deceived scientists for a while, but it is by far the best known. It did a great deal of damage because it made people believe that such an out-of-place, out-of-time creature as Piltdown Man could live in England 500,000 or 600,000 years ago. The perpetrators of this hoax have never been positively identified, although the evidence seems clear enough. One thing is certain: they knew just what to do to make the bones appear to be old, and they were clever enough to be sure that the parts that might be challenged were missing.

Credit must be given to several scientists who refused to believe that Piltdown Man was genuine. At the time of its finding, David Waterston, Professor of Anatomy at King's College, Cambridge, and Gerrit Miller, Curator of Mammals at the United States National Museum, were exceedingly skeptical about it. And in 1937 the late Franz Weidenreich, who was very well known for his work as a comparative anthropologist, said suspiciously: "The teeth of the Piltdown remains are of three different origins. The two molars embedded within the mandible are typical anthropoid teeth revealing peculiarities such as are found

76

even in the orangutan of today. These teeth, therefore,
correspond entirely . . . to the mandible in which they are
embedded. The isolated left molar is a molar of modern
man. The additional isolated tooth which was found and
called 'canine' neither belongs to the mandible, as is claimed,
nor is it the lower canine of an anthropoid. Its real nature
remains to be determined." Returning to the subject in
1943, he concluded: "The sooner the chimaera 'Eoanthropus'
is erased from the list of human fossils, the better for
science."

Then, in 1944 (p. 257), Theodosius Dobzhansky, of Columbia University, went on record in a scientific journal
when he wrote that "the remains of the alleged 'Piltdown
Man' . . . are a mixture of ape and human bone fragments."

PREHISTORIC chronology is still incomplete, but work on it
proceeds steadily. Isotopic dating is expensive because the
laboratory and skilled labor costs needed for it are high, but
more and more dates are being determined and published
every year. The time structure of long-ago events is thus
being built with meticulous care. Some of the dates that
were thought to be exact when they were originally calculated already need revision, and this will have to be done.

But we have come a long way from the first crude
guesses about the antiquity of man. Most of the more accurate dating methods keep pushing back even the more
recent estimates. Before long we may have a reasonably
exact chronology of mankind's development from earliest
times.

6. The End of the Beginning

You CAN TRAVEL from one end of Europe to the other and not come across a trace of the people who lived there from 750,000 to 100,000 years ago unless you are lucky enough to discover some of their pebble tools or hand-axes. Only in museums are you likely to see evidence that they really did exist, and there you will find only a few bones and stone implements from the earliest periods. Undoubtedly these first Europeans also made things out of wood, hide, horn, and other perishable organic materials, but except for a few bits of wood all such artifacts have disappeared. Much of what we know—or think we know—about life in those remote days comes from observing the behavior of modern savages and present-day anthropoid apes. What we find out from them may or not be true about our early ancestors.

Firm information is scant. Pebble tools tell us that they had learned to smash stones to produce sharp edges. The remains of their feasts—bones and shells—give us some knowledge of the kind of animal food they ate. Their broken skulls and smashed bones indicate that they sometimes were the victims of cannibals—fellow cannibals, probably. Burned bones, charred stones, and actual hearths prove that they used fire. Just when they became clever enough to make it rather than simply keep it burning is something we shall probably never find out. It may very well be that the art of fire making originated in more than one place. And it may have been learned, lost, and then relearned again. This may also be true about other skills and arts.

Of one thing we can be certain, and that is that life then was nasty, brutish, and short, as it was to be for hundreds of centuries to come, especially during the cold periods.

The time scale involved is so great that we may get a distorted picture of what conditions were actually like then. It would be wrong to think that nothing was permanent in the sense that we use that word. The comings and goings of the ice sheets were so slow that generations of men could live and die without seeing any perceptible change in them. Our notion of "permanent," as applied to the number of years that buildings can last, that institutions, communities, or states can remain intact, is so very short in comparison with prehistoric time that it is not in the same class. The Holocene covers only about 10,000 years, which may seem like a great deal of time to us, for it embraces all of mankind's ancient, medieval, and modern history. But in comparison with the 700,000 years or more that man has lived in Europe, it is only a moment. And in comparison with the enormously long periods of geological time, it is only a flash in the dark night of the past.

We mark our days with clocks, our years with calendars, our lives with years, our history with centuries, but millennia are needed to measure prehistory. The long-ago people who dwelt in a valley which was free of ice before the next glacier moved in may have remained there for 10,000 years or more. We know from excavated evidence that some sites were occupied even longer than that. A French cave, Arcy-sur-Cure, was lived in for 140,000 years.

THE FIRST European settlers had the world at their disposal even if they did not know what to do with its potential treasures. They could have had all the untouched gold in mountain streams for the taking, but apparently they did not bother with it even for use as ornament, for this imperishable bright metal has not been found among the earliest artifacts. There were so many game animals available for food then that it was not finding but killing them that was the chief task. The waters were teeming with fish, but these very ancient people had neither boats nor fishhooks. Cords and nets are made of such perishable material that we have no way of knowing whether or not they were used at that time. Shellfish, of course, have long been eaten by man wherever they were available. A hungry man will consume anything that seems to be edible, and easily obtained clams, oysters, limpets, mussels, and crabs, which could be smashed open by a stone, formed part of the diet of the first Europeans who lived near the sea. It should be noted, though, that "a diet in which shellfish are the mainstay, is normally associated with a low level of attainment, and shellfish occupied only a subsidiary place in communities which fished and hunted with vigor" (Ryder, 1963, p. 301).

We think that the first Europeans were able to speak, but we have no knowledge of their language. If they buried their dead we have found no evidence of it. If they had thoughts about life beyond death or stirrings of religious ideas, all trace of them has vanished.

These earliest people are not to be confused with the cave painters, the pottery makers, or the metal users, all of whom came much later. We are still back in the beginning of man's career. Viewed through the mists of time, the first European settlers seem indistinct and far away. But they cannot be ignored, for we owe them a great deal. They were the Prometheans who brought us fire, the mentors who taught us how to live in the wilderness and survive, the toolmakers who showed us how to make useful implements. They left no monuments, no art, no words; yet they live on, buried deep not only in the earth but in our unconscious minds.

There, where dreams originate and strange notions spring forth unbidden, the primeval men are hidden inside us, curled up at the base of the brain. From that dark corner of the mind they urge us to be like them, to scorn convention, to forgo unessential earthly possessions, and to live free and untrammeled in a simpler world. But they bring us their fears, too—the fear of falling from high places, the fear of darkness and night, the fear of the unknown.

We cannot escape their heritage and must take it as it has come down to us with the good and the bad mixed together. They deserve neither credit nor blame for the way they lived. Unthinkingly, they molded a way of existence that enabled them to survive. And only the strongest and the most intelligent ones did survive to transmit their genes to future generations and eventually to us.

THEY GAVE US the will and the stubborn courage to keep going even when the going was hard. From them comes the unflagging spirit that has kept the human race alive in a world where countless other species have become extinct.

We owe much to these dimly perceived creatures of the forests and the plains. And we owe them not only our lives but also our deft fingers; most of all we owe them our inventive brains. Everything we possess that is beyond the range of the cleverest animal comes originally from these earliest men who were still trying to get away from the beast-in-the-jungle phase themselves.

*Flint implement
from Saint-Acheul [Joly]*

PHASE THREE

7. A Strange Appearance
and a Disappearance:
The Neandertals Come and Go

VERY FEW human remains for the period from 500,000 to
100,000 years ago have been discovered, so the fossil record
for that remote era is regrettably incomplete. But somewhere before the end of that long stretch of time a new type
of man appeared—the Neandertal, *Homo neanderthalensis*.
(Modern German spelling omits the "h" that is still retained
in the taxonomic name.)

The Neandertals were eventually dispersed over large
areas of Europe, Asia, and Africa. But that does not mean
that their remains are common. G. H. R. von Koenigswald
(1964, p. 67) dramatized the scarcity of all human fossils
when he said: "What in more than a hundred years has
been discovered of Neandertal Man fills but a small church-
yard. What is known of pre-Neandertal Man can be placed
on two middle-sized tables, and what might belong to our
Tertiary ancestors I can put on the palm of my hand."

Neandertal Man became known to science in August
1856 when a nearly complete skeleton was dug up in the
Neander Valley a few miles east of Düsseldorf, Germany.
This was the first fossil man to be identified as such. Others
had been found earlier—in southeast Wales in 1823, near
Liége, Belgium, in 1829, and at Gibraltar in 1848—but no
one then realized how very old they were. Fortunately, the
top of the skull and some of the bones discovered in the
Neander Valley cave were turned over to a local school-
teacher who had the good sense to send them to an anatomist in Bonn.

It was a curious coincidence that the first Neandertal to
be identified as a new type of ancient man came from a

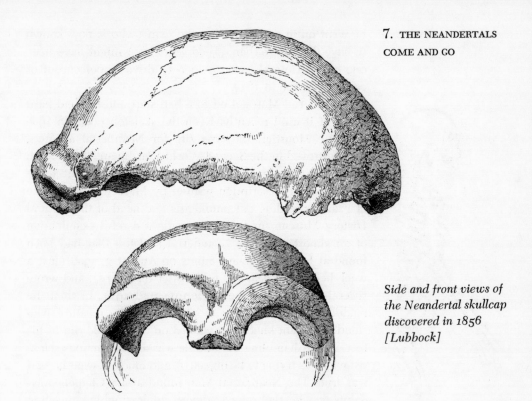

*Side and front views of
the Neandertal skullcap
discovered in 1856
[Lubbock]*

valley with a name that means "new man." It was called that
after Joachim Neumann, a local celebrity who wrote hymns
and liked to use a Greek version of his name: Neander.

The great antiquity of the bones found in the Neander
Valley, however, was not accepted by scholars of the day.
This was before Darwin's *Origin of Species* was published
in 1859, and the Bible was still the unquestioned authority
for anything in the remote past. The idea that Neandertal
Man might be older than Noah—or than Adam too, for that
matter—met with determined opposition even in scientific
circles. Rudolf Virchow, a noted German pathologist who
was interested in anthropology, said that the bones were
not old at all, that they were quite modern and had been
altered by disease. Oddly enough, he was right about disease, for later and better-informed anatomical examination
showed that this Neandertal had suffered from crippling
arthritis, a rather common ailment among his contemporaries. Another German scientist agreed with Virchow and
diagnosed the disease as rickets. The curved leg bones, he
said, had been bent by a lifetime of horseback riding. And

83

he went on to speculate that the man (who is now known to have died more than 30,000 years ago) might have been one of the Cossacks who helped to drive Napoleon out of eastern Europe in 1814.

Neandertal Man got off to a bad start and has had hard going of it until recently. Even the skeleton taken in 1908 from Le Moustier, the type site for Neandertal artifacts, was destroyed in the Second World War by an Allied bomb that hit the Berlin museum where it was kept. But worst of all was the description written by Marcellin Boule, one of France's leading paleontologists and head of the Natural History Museum in Paris. He made a careful examination of an almost complete Neandertal skeleton that had been found at La Chapelle-aux-Saints on August 3, 1908 (just a week before the nearby Le Moustier discovery), and wrote several reports on it between 1911 and 1913. In them he made Neandertal Man a monstrous apelike creature who stood with bent knees and walked on the outside rim of his feet with a shambling gait. Boule was a conscientious scientist who was trying to be objective, and much of what he said was true. The Neandertal Man found at La Chapelle-aux-Saints *was* beetle-browed, almost chinless, with a receding forehead and a big face on which a large, broad nose and a prognathous jaw were prominent. He was short in stature —only a few inches more than five feet tall—so his thick, stocky, heavily muscled body must have made his face seem even larger than it actually was. Certainly he was far different from the ideal of masculine perfection (Caucasian style) which the sculptured figures of Periclean Greece have impressed upon us.

But it was not Boule's technical descriptions that fixed the brutish picture of Neandertal Man upon the public's mind. That was done by journalistic accounts which overemphasized the more sensational aspects of the reports. Before long, Boule's Neandertal began to resemble the Hollywood version of Frankenstein's monster, and it has remained a repulsive figure ever since. The grotesque, oversized statue of a cave man that stands near the prehistoric museum in Les Ezies-de-Tayac perpetuates Boule's descriptions.

We know now that he was mistaken in many important aspects, for re-examinations of the Chapelle-aux-Saints skel-

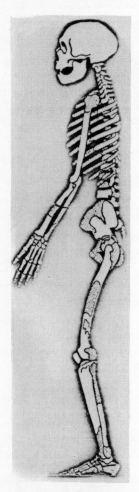

Above: the Neandertal skeleton of Chapelle-aux-Saints as reconstructed by Boule. Opposite page: skeleton of a modern Australian aborigine

84

eton made in 1955 and 1957 show that the Neandertal man whose flesh had once covered it was the victim of a severe case of Osteoarthritis Deformans which had distorted his vertical column so badly that he could not be considered a typical, healthy specimen of his kind. One of the examining teams reported (Straus and Cave, 1957, p. 358) that "there is no valid reason for the assumption that the posture of Neanderthal man . . . differed significantly from that of present-day men."

Other anatomists, after inspecting the bones, came up with the same opinion, disqualifying Boule's findings and finally rehabilitating the unjustly disparaged Neandertal. Since then he has been looked at with kinder eyes and, in scientific circles at least, is no longer thought of as an ungainly, shambling brute. In the popular mind, however, he is still the ugly creature that Boule made of him. To many people, the word "Neandertal" means dim-witted, clumsy, and brutish. It will take time for them to learn the truth about *Homo sapiens neanderthalensis* and admit him to the proud ranks of sapient men.

His physical characteristics—basically—are in his favor. We now know that a Neandertal footprint made in the soft clay on the floor of an Italian cave shows that his feet were very much like ours. And, more important, the Neandertal cranial capacity was amazingly large, 1,300–1,650 cc. in comparison with a range of 1,100–1,700 cc. for modern European males. The Neandertal brain, however, was less highly convoluted.

Culturally, the Neandertals had come a long way from earlier men. The circumstances in which the Chapelle-aux-Saints skeleton were found show that it had been carefully buried in a stone-lined grave in a small cave with flint tools placed near the body. Another Neandertal burial at La Ferrassie, in the same part of France, is an even better example of the way these early people honored their dead. Here the six skeletons, interred in a rock shelter, may have been members of the same family. The adult male and female were placed head to head while the small children were buried near them in separate graves. One was a foetus, but the Neandertals considered it human enough to give it proper burial. Some of the graves were covered by flat

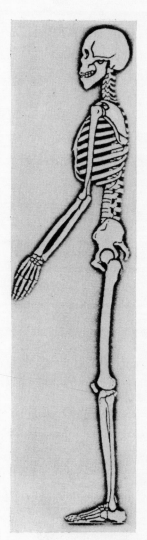

stones while two of the children's contained worked flints. The skeleton in the Neandertal type site, Le Moustier, had been buried with its head pillowed on a pile of flints. And a skull discovered in a hidden cave at Monte Circeo, Italy, was encircled by white stones. There are still other examples of Neandertal ceremonial burials, many of them in the Middle East.

The most remarkable of them was made public in 1968 when Mme. Arlette Leroi-Gourhan announced that pollen analysis of soil taken from the grave of an adult male Neandertal buried in Shanidar Cave in northern Iraq showed that the corpse had been laid to rest on a bier of pine boughs strewn with wild flowers (*New York Times*, June 13).

IN EUROPE, the discoveries made in rapid succession during the four years after 1908 in La Chapelle-aux-Saints, Le Moustier, and La Ferrassie caused a surge of interest in Neandertal Man, who had been a rather neglected and shadowy figure before that. It was at this time that some scientists conceived the notion that the Neandertals were so different from modern men that there was no connection between them. It had previously been thought that the Neandertals were probably ancestral to *Homo sapiens*; now the Neandertals were thrust aside as a separate species that had become a dead-end product in the evolutionary scheme. This was easy to do because more modern-looking human remains had long ago been found (1868) in Les Eyzies' Cro-Magnon rock shelter (see Chapter 9).

But even those who felt that the Neandertals were not much more than brutish half-men had to admit that their deliberately planned and carefully executed burials showed that they were more advanced than their predecessors, for earlier men apparently abandoned the dead bodies of their fellows just as animals do. With the much-maligned Neandertals, man moved a step upward on the evolutionary scale.

The upper portion of Dardé's statue of primeval man at Les Eyzies-de-Tayac

THE Neandertals were skilled hunters who regularly went after big game like mammoths and rhinoceroses. They also had to drive off or kill ferocious cave lions, bears, and hyenas that fought with them for the occupancy of their underground shelters. And they lived in such close association

86

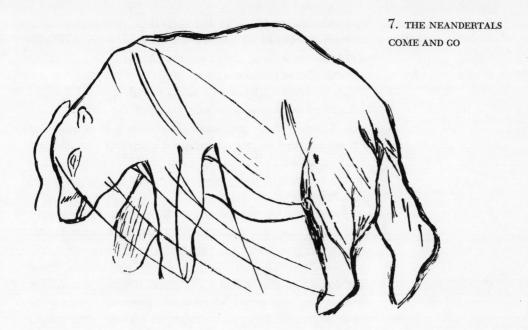

with cave bears that they made a cult of them, a cult which has continued into modern times in northern Europe and Japan.

Along with ceremonial burial practices, the rituals associated with the slaying of the cave bear show that Neandertal Man was calling upon magic to solve the problems of his life. So far as we know, he was the first in the long succession of early men to do so.

The practice of ritual magic consists of doing—or refraining from doing—certain things which are thought to affect the future and so bring about a desired result or prevent a harmful one. Since the Neandertals faced endless problems of obtaining food and keeping invading animals away from their shelters, the bear had a double meaning for them. While alive, he was a constant threat to the occupancy of the caves they both wanted; when dead, his huge carcass provided enough meat to feed a number of people for days.

The bear was thus a major factor in the lives of the Neandertal cave dwellers. Large and dangerous animals encountered in the field could be avoided, but this one might wander into a family's home at any moment. Worse still, after hibernating all winter in the deep interior of a cavern,

A cave bear depicted by the Neandertals' successors at Les Combarelles [After Breuil]

87

he would stir to life with the arrival of spring and come lumbering forward to surprise the human occupants who might not even have suspected that he had been sleeping in the depths of their own cave.

These caves had been formed by underground streams that carved out tortuous passages through the soft limestone rock. Some of them are hundreds—or even thousands—of feet long. Many have a complicated system of branches, so that a hibernating bear could easily have been hidden in a remote recess which the men living near the entrance did not know existed.

But the Neandertals eventually learned how to deal with cave bears. Big and powerful as *Ursus spelaeus* was, the odds were against him, for man had a weapon no other animal possessed. This was fire, the bright red, searing flame that dances on the end of a dry stick. It was a formidable defense, one that could be used to illuminate the dark interior of a cave and also to repel an animal which might suddenly loom up in the flickering light of the torch. Burned ends of sticks, found in the Tana della Basua cave near Toirana, Italy, show that they had been so used (Blanc, 1958, pp. 167–74, 267–69).

After a few thousand years of experience in dealing with cave bears, Neandertal men became masters of the situation. They perfected their hunting techniques so well that they may even have looked upon a hibernating bear as a dependable source of food. When they located a sleeping bear all they had to do was mark the location of the cave; then they could return at some future time when game was scarce—or when the winter weather was worse than usual—to claim the meat dinner that was peacefully snoring away.

If this seems unfair it must be remembered that it was a matter of survival. And it was always a desperate encounter between animals fighting for their lives. An aroused bear, even though drowsy, was a formidable adversary. Eight feet high when standing up and weighing 1,500 pounds, he could—and doubtless often did—crush his adversaries.

Fortunately, these winter cave-hunting expeditions could be prepared in advance. And not only wooden spears, stones, and torches were made ready; magic was also called upon to help. We do not know just what that magic was, but we have some evidences of it. Prayers, incantations, ceremonial processions, and dances were probably part of the proceedings. Perhaps skulls and hides from previous bear hunts were also used to bring about a successful conclusion to the one about to be undertaken.

In some European caverns bear skulls have been found set up in niches or arranged in ways which show that man had placed them there. Most interesting is Drachenloch, a long, narrow cave 8,150 feet up in the Swiss Alps. One of its many bear skulls had a femur thrust through the curve of the cheekbone. And in the cavern floor was a stone-lined pit covered by a large flat rock. Under the rock were seven bear skulls neatly stacked up to face the entrance to the cave.

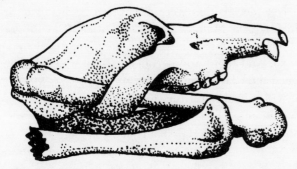

The Drachenloch cave-bear skull with a femur thrust through the curve of the cheekbone

To the Neandertals the cave bear was not only a dependable supply of meat in wintertime, he was also a totem to be admired, venerated, and perhaps worshiped. Despite this, the big animal did badly in his encounters with men. Cave bears were originally so numerous that tons of their bones have been carted away in modern times to be ground up for fertilizer. And many caves still have scratches made by bears' claws on the soft limestone walls.

THE EARLY Neandertals lived in a fairly warm climate, so they probably spent most of their time outdoors and did not have to worry about clothes. Later Neandertals had to move into caves and rock shelters when Europe again grew cold. They may have used these protective sites only in winter and then have become temporary nomads again in summer. No trace of their garments remains, but since they could not weave cloth, we assume that they must have used animal skins.

The human body has remarkable resistance to cold once it is conditioned to it. Darwin commented on this when he visited the Alacaluf Indians in Tierra del Fuego in 1832. Modern observers have noted that the Sherpas, who live high up in the Himalayas, also can stand exposure to amazingly low temperatures. It has been suggested that the Neandertals' short, compact bodies were well adapted to cold-climate living. They were, in fact, built somewhat like modern Eskimos.

THE Chapelle-aux-Saints Neandertal which Boule described more than half a century ago has been called the "Classic" or extreme type in order to differentiate the hulking, clumsy creatures who lived in western Europe from the "Progressive" Neandertals that were discovered in the 1930's in the Skūhl Cave on Mount Carmel, Palestine. The Progressive Neandertals are more like modern men, some of them amazingly so. And there are of course, all sorts of variations in between the Classic and the Progressive types. More specimens will probably turn up to fill missing gaps in Neandertal evolution.

Since the Neandertals flourished for more than 100,000 years—a period ten times longer than our whole modern era, the Holocene—they had plenty of time for mutation and specialization. Strangely enough, the Classic Neandertals of western Europe became more and more highly specialized—and they kept developing more strongly pronounced facial features.

The most remarkable thing about the Neandertals is not their long existence but their apparently sudden end. Sudden, of course, does not mean instantaneous; it took several thousand years for them to become extinct. This happened sometime between 40,000 and 30,000 years ago, when Europe was again entering a cold phase. They were replaced—and not only in Europe, but everywhere—by *Homo sapiens,* modern man.

The big question is: how and why did they vanish? Did they die off of their own accord? Or were they exterminated by *Homo sapiens* newcomers just as later European invaders killed the natives in Australia and North America? Or were they absorbed into the *Homo sapiens* stock and are therefore our ancestors?

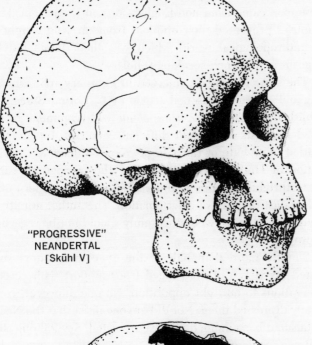

"PROGRESSIVE"
NEANDERTAL
[Skūhl V]

*Note that the Classic
Neandertal has more
pronounced supraorbital
ridges and less chin
than the Progressive one*

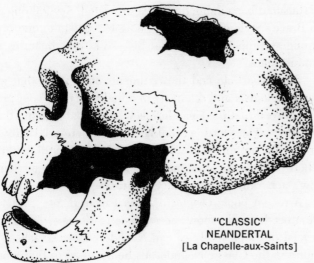

"CLASSIC"
NEANDERTAL
[La Chapelle-aux-Saints]

This last idea was first thought of in the nineteenth century, when "evolution was in the air—evolution from a
simian ancestor" (Keith, 1925, p. 223). But it was rejected
after the La Chapelle-aux-Saints, Le Moustier, and La Ferrassie discoveries, and remained dormant for many years. It
was not entirely abandoned, however, for Gustav Schwalbe,   91

Aleš Hrdlička, Franz Weidenreich, and H. Weinert clung to the otherwise unpopular notion. Perhaps the fact that these men came from non-English- or non-French-speaking countries prevented their opinions from carrying weight in an anthropological world which was then dominated by English- and French-speaking scholars.

The basic idea again emerged in February 1964 when a long and carefully reasoned article by C. Loring Brace was published in *Current Anthropology* with comment by 17 noted scientists from eight different countries. Intriguingly entitled "The Fate of the 'Classic' Neanderthals: A Consideration of Hominid Catastrophism," the monograph came out forthrightly for the Neandertal ancestry of modern man and against the idea of extermination. The author admitted, though, that his "viewpoint certainly should not be regarded as proven."

Slightly more than half of the 17 commentators supported his views; others ranged from support with certain reservations to outright opposition. No one, however, completely dismissed them. Nor did anyone insist that the Neandertals had been deliberately exterminated. Several objected to Brace's style of writing as being too polemic; one of his strongest supporters said that his use of certain terms was "unfortunate."

But the article and the comments on it show that most anthropologists and scientists in allied fields are now pretty well agreed that the Neandertals were probably man's direct ancestors. The word "probably" is used here advisedly, for practically nothing is absolutely certain in this still fluid area where today's theories may—or may not—become tomorrow's generally accepted facts.

A recent book, *Origins of Man* (1966, p. 151), by John Buettner-Janusch, shows acceptance of Brace's views: "The crucial question really is, can Neandertal faces such as are found in the Classic Neandertals be assigned to the population that is our own direct ancestor? We believe the answer is yes. . . . We reject the notion that the species *Homo sapiens* met a separate Neandertal species and wiped it out, but we do not reject the notion that populations moved from the Near East and the Mediterranean into northwestern Europe. . . . There was probably considerable mixture of genes as the result of the migrations."

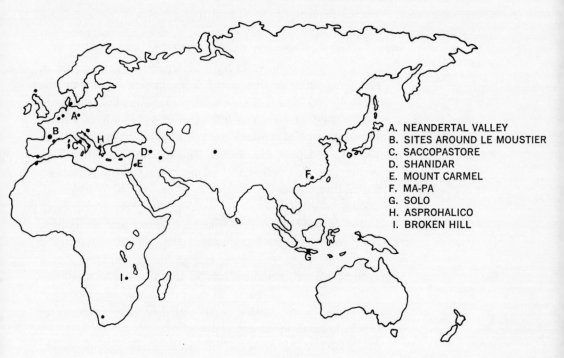

A. NEANDERTAL VALLEY
B. SITES AROUND LE MOUSTIER
C. SACCOPASTORE
D. SHANIDAR
E. MOUNT CARMEL
F. MA-PA
G. SOLO
H. ASPROHALICO
I. BROKEN HILL

Opinion about the fate of the Classic Neandertals, however, is still a moot question among some specialists. One of them, anatomist Michael Day, author of *Guide to Fossil Men* (1965, p. 41), says cautiously: "It is uncertain whether they [the Neandertals] became extinct because of the invasion of more advanced hominids, or became assimilated by the evolving population of modern man, or directly gave rise to modern man."

This brings us right back to where we began. Only the discovery of more Neandertal remains can provide enough evidence to convince everyone.

One of the best reasons for us to believe that the Neandertals were absorbed into *Homo sapiens* stock is that they disappeared throughout the entire world. Some of their more salient features, such as beetle brows, can be seen occasionally in living people, but as a species the Neandertals vanished as completely as the dinosaurs did. If they had been deliberately exterminated by *Homo sapiens* some pockets of them would surely have been left in remote places where no one else wanted to live. But there are no such pockets. The only Neandertal survivals are in ourselves.

Some of the more important Neandertal sites

93

Buried deep inside us are all that remains of these ancient people.

Clark and Piggott (1965, p. 65) have suggested that "modern man is likely to have emerged more than once in different parts of the world from human stocks at the Neanderthaloid stage. Cromagnon man and his cousins in Europe and western Asia thus represent only one of a number of groups of modern men to appear during the latter part of the Upper Pleistocene. The special claim they have on our attention is that they alone supported the Advanced Paleolithic culture on which the future of Old World civilization was to depend. In seeking the precise origins of *Homo sapiens* we are confronted by the usual difficulties, the scarcity of fossil traces and the imprecise dating of several of these. . . . It is reasonable to think of *Homo sapiens,* as we encounter him in his Advanced Paleolithic setting, as the outcome of a progressive development through an unspecialized Neanderthaloid stage from primitive Pithecanthropine antecedents."

Whatever the cause of the Neandertals' disappearance, they vanished from the scene, and their hunting grounds and rock shelters were taken over by *Homo sapiens,* the triumphantly successful species to which we all belong.

A good example of an occupational site with relics that date from Mousterian times which are overlaid by later ones is in Greece near the Albanian border. There, Asprokhalico, "the shelter of white stones," was the dwelling place of Neandertal hunters who slew the woolly rhinoceros and the mammoth. The location is a particularly favorable one, for some freak of climate makes it warmer than it could be expected to be. Like Les Eyzies in France, this Greek site was inhabited for long periods of time and can be considered as one of Europe's earliest prehistoric communities.

8. Neandertal Tools and Techniques

It is fortunate for us that the later Neandertals lived in caves, cliff overhangs, and rock shelters, particularly in the limestone country of France, for conditions there were just right for preserving their bone and antler implements. These, and their practically imperishable flints, were deposited in layers that can be dated. Since the earliest Neandertals, who lived in a warmer climate, dwelt outdoors most of the time, nearly all the artifacts they made of organic materials have vanished.

It has been said that the Neandertals created no art, but that is not quite true. First of all, it is entirely possible that they decorated their persons or their wooden or leather goods, but these, of course, have not survived. We know nothing about their clothing except that large numbers of Mousterian side-scrapers indicate that they dressed hides. It has also been observed that the teeth found in some of their remains show signs of having been used to chew animal skins. A polished mammoth bone discovered in Hungary is evidence that they went to the trouble of shaping objects for purely ornamental purposes.

We do, however, have a good-sized piece of stone that at least is a striving toward art. This was found at La Ferrassie, where it covered the child's grave described in the previous chapter. It is a crude thing, so crude that the layman might pass it by without noticing its significance. Its discoverer, Denis Peyrony, saw that a number of cupules had been hollowed out on its underside. Nearly all of them were in pairs, perhaps to symbolize women's breasts or the mother concept inherent in them. The making of such cupules runs through prehistory, but these are the earliest yet found. Peyrony said of them: "Whatever the interpretation given, we are here in the presence of something completely new: evidence of graphic expression in the Mousterian era, whereas up till now we had thought its oldest manifestations were in the Aurignacian."

The mourner who painstakingly scraped out these little holes in a rock that was intended to be a gravestone was, so far as we know, the founder of all art, the originator of symbols, and the world's first person to erect a carved monument to the dead. The thoughts and emotions that motivated him are very human. With him, man definitely left the most primitive stage. His deft fingers were shaping not only practical objects but something that was intended to appeal to the mind, the heart, and the spirit.

WHEN it came to flint implements, the Neandertals made some improvements over what had been done before, but their work does not mark any noteworthy advance.

Kenneth Oakley (1961a, p. 56) says of their tools: "Typical Mousterian industries include small discoidal cores and two main types of flake-tool, usually with plain striking-platforms and finely retouched edges; the side-scraper, sometimes D-shaped, and the triangular point with one or both edges dressed for use as a knife."

A Mousterian point

Many animal bones of various kinds occur in Mousterian deposits, but they are nearly all fragments, broken to get at the marrow. The Neandertals sometimes used bone splinters as tools without bothering to shape them further. And they employed large bones as platforms and small ones as pressure-flakers when they finished flint edges. Otherwise they seem to have made little use of bones and antlers. That was to come later, when men had learned more about the many ways these raw materials could be employed.

Hand-sized round limestone balls have been found in Neandertal sites. These may have been suspended on cords and hurled as bolas to entangle an animal's feet. Some prehistorians, though, believe that they were only convenient missiles for throwing. The fire-charred, rounded stones occurring in Neandertal deposits were probably water heaters that were put into a liquid-filled rawhide container. Pottery had not yet been invented.

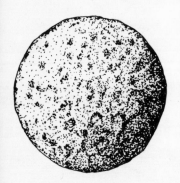

A Mousterian lime-stone ball

The outdoor shelters used all year by the first warm-weather Neandertals and in summer by the later ones were doubtless made of wood covered by skins or leaves, all of which have long since vanished. Only the caves and rock-protected sites have preserved material that tells us how these ancient men lived.

Before this time, early European settlers had retreated when the massive ice sheets moved down from the north. But the Neandertals, with clothing, caves, and fire, were brave and hardy enough to stay on through the bitter winters.

Records compiled for the last 80,000 years show that the European climate was then quite cool or very cold. Somehow the Neandertals managed to live through it. It has been suggested that low temperatures were finally responsible for their disappearance, but it seems unlikely that men who had been conditioned for tens of thousands of years to cold weather would be killed off by a sudden drop to even lower temperatures.

It may very well be that the Classic Neandertals isolated in western Europe became more and more specialized because of their geographical separation from people with advanced features. Progressive Neandertals, who came from the Middle East, may have interbred with these western Europeans and so have improved the stock. Interbreeding, invasion, and migration could all have helped to break the deadlock that was retarding the Classic Neandertals.

MOUSTERIAN implements show us that the Neandertals had developed the skill and forethought needed to strike off flint flakes that would have a desired shape and size. The hand-axe people had been interested primarily in the core-tool that emerged from their rather haphazard and clumsy chipping. But the Neandertals carried the process a step further to produce not only the flakes they wanted but better core-tools as well.

Much of their earlier work was doubtless done by trial-and-error methods that caused a great deal of spoilage, but the Neandertals eventually learned some of the finer techniques needed for chipping flint into desired forms.

These early men certainly must have cut, scratched, and injured themselves not only by working flint but in other ways as well. Sores of all kinds festered and may have led to blood poisoning and death. The pathological record told by Neandertal bones is not good. Badly infected teeth can be seen in disease-ridden sockets. And arthritis, brought on from constant exposure to damp and cold, was a common ailment that shows up in many malformed Neandertal bones.

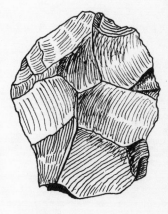

A Mousterian disk

A Mousterian side-scraper

97

It has been estimated that Neandertal Man had an average life-span of less than 30 years, which is not even half what it is now. But the Neandertals shortened the lives of their fellow men by deliberately killing and eating them—a practice which had come down to them from earlier days. Whether they ate their contemporaries for food or for ritual purposes does not matter; they were killing off a sparse population at a time when every healthy person was desperately needed to perpetuate the species. Yet evidences of cannibalism are fairly common. Two Neandertal skulls found in Italy, at Saccopastore in 1929 and 1935 and at Monte Circeo in 1939, both had the underparts broken open to remove the brains.

Some anthropologists, however, are reluctant to admit that such mutilation is definite proof of cannibalism. According to them, the removal of the brains may have been purely ceremonial with no thought of using them for food. It has also been suggested that the foramen magnum opening was enlarged so the skull could be mounted on a stick. The wood, of course, would long since have rotted away without leaving a trace.

The Monte Circeo skull. Note that the foramen magnum has been broken open to remove the brain

But we have more than broken-open skulls to indicate cannibalistic practices among early men. One example is at Krapina, Yugoslavia, where a rock shelter was excavated during the years from 1899 to 1905. The numerous cracked and scattered bones of at least 13 human beings discovered there—and the fact that some of the bones had been charred —all point to the probability that they are the remains of a huge cannibal feast which had taken place in the shelter during Neandertal times.

The Krapina bones have other and more important meanings, for some of them are nearer in shape to those of modern man than they are to the Classic Neandertal.

Neandertal Man's place in the taxonomic scheme is still a matter of dispute. Ernst Mayr (1963, p. 337) summed up this uncertain standing when he said: "The facts that are so far available do not permit a clear-cut decision on the question whether Neanderthal was a sub-species or a separate species. It seems to me, however, that on the whole they are in better agreement with the subspecies hypothesis. It would seem best for the time being to postulate that Neanderthal (*sensu stricto*) was a northern and western subspecies of

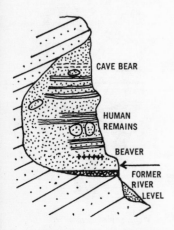

The Krapina rock shelter

CAVE BEAR

HUMAN REMAINS

BEAVER

FORMER RIVER LEVEL

98

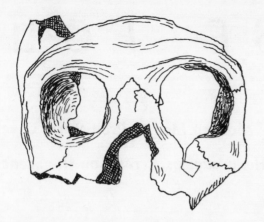

*One of the better-
preserved Krapina skulls*

Homo sapiens (*sensu lato*), which was an incipient species but probably never reached species level prior to its extinction."

In 1964 Bernard G. Campbell, the British taxonomist, classified Neandertal Man as a subspecies of *Homo sapiens* and called him *Homo sapiens neanderthalensis*. With this demotion to a lower-case letter, Neandertal Man at last achieved a capital rank.

The Neandertals—especially the unlucky Classic ones who were caught in an evolutionary dead-end trap—were certainly not handsome as we now define attractiveness in human appearance. Nor were they outstanding in accomplishment, in inventiveness, or in creativity of any remarkable kind. Like all people, some of them were doubtless brighter, quicker, and better-looking than others. Since they are long dead, there is no reason to speak badly of them. If *Homo sapiens* refrains from mass suicide, he may evolve into a still higher type, and then that new man will look back at us as bloodthirsty savages, brutal killers, and unintelligent beings who were reckless enough to endanger their own world.

PHASE FOUR

9. Modern Men in Prehistoric Caves:

Homo sapiens Arrives on the Scene

So FAR, all the physical objects that have to do with European prehistory can be seen only in museums, but the material from the earliest periods is of little interest to most laymen, for it consists largely of stones and bones. The stones are cruder than those that were shaped later, they are less varied in form, and they may seem monotonously repetitive to anyone who is not trained to understand their significance. Few laymen want to look at any kind of bones except skulls, and even skulls mean little to someone who doesn't know what features to look for. It should be noted that many of the bones—especially the important ones—displayed in museums are plaster reproductions. The precious originals are locked up and are shown only to qualified scholars. Plaster casts of artifacts and art objects are also used in museums which don't possess the originals. There is nothing wrong with this, but it is regrettable that the casts are often so poorly made that they misrepresent the real objects.

With the coming of the period when *Homo sapiens* took over, prehistory becomes much more interesting. The earlier men were too far away in time and cultural development to leave anything that seems meaningful to us, but the more modern men who replaced them created many things we can appreciate. Their artifacts occupy more space in museums because there are more varieties of them; their art reveals a great deal about their personalities, and, in the more recent periods, these people seem nearer to us, not only in time but in their ways of living, of thinking, and of recording what they saw in the world around them. They could not write, but they could draw, paint, and make sculptures, and what they left speaks to us across the ages.

Cro-Magnon is a generic term for the first clearly recognizable examples of full-fledged *Homo sapiens*. The word is almost as well known as Neandertal, perhaps because people who have been imbued with the notion that the Neandertals were repulsive brutes would prefer to have the more seemly Cro-Magnons for ancestors. Actually, of course, they may have to accept both.

There is no doubt that Cro-Magnon Man was a more advanced type than his predecessors. Ashley Montagu (1957, p. 130) has called him the Apollo of prehistoric men because he has so often been described as tall, handsome, with regular features, a high forehead, a prominent chin, small teeth, a thin skull, delicate face bones, and, most important of all, without the heavy brow ridges that characterize the Classic Neandertals. The modern European, northern type, had at last arrived. W. W. Howells (1959, p. 208) has said that Cro-Magnon Men were members "of the White, or Caucasoid, racial stock, because the features of their skulls and facial skeletons all have that stamp. The one actual painting of a man so far known, a small bas-relief at Angles-sur-Anglin, gives us a White man (actually a lightish purple, but the effect is 'white') with black hair and a black beard."

The original Angles-sur-Anglin bas-relief was painted in color although much of the pigment has faded or chipped off. Sculpture, painting, and engraving were used in this very early portrait of a Magdalenian man

The first one of these stylishly acceptable ancestors was recognized as such in the spring of 1868, when earth was being moved to make way for a railroad in Périgord that was to run through Les Eyzies-de-Tayac. Louis Lartet describes the excavations (1875, p. 66): "The workmen . . . soon came upon broken bones, worked flints, and, lastly, human skulls." More digging revealed "four black beds of ashes, one on [top of] the other, the lowest of which contained the stump of the tusk of an elephant." Lartet said that the ancient cave was nearly filled up with fallen rocks and accumulated debris and had been abandoned in prehistoric times so that everything in it was undisturbed.

Five skeletons and some bits of foetal and infant bones were taken from this rock shelter, which was locally called Cro-Magnon. The people who dwelt there had lived sometime between 30,000 and 20,000 years ago.

Even the most skeptical anatomists of the time had to admit that the skulls, especially the fully developed one of a man who had died when he was about 50 years old, were in every way modern. As has often been said, if a Cro-Magnon man were dressed in present-day clothes, he could mingle with us and be taken for one of our contemporaries. His only trouble would be in communication, for no one would be able to speak with him, and he naturally could not write because he lived long before writing was invented.

His hometown, Les Eyzies, is an underrated place. If it were given its proper value in mankind's progress toward civilization, it would rank far higher than it does, for it played a pioneer role in the development of villages. And villages, of course, led to cities, where civilization began and matured.

This woodcut, which appeared in Lartet's Reliquiae Aquitanicae *in 1875, shows the Cro-Magnon site (at left) as it was when the railroad through Les Eyzies-de-Tayac was first built*

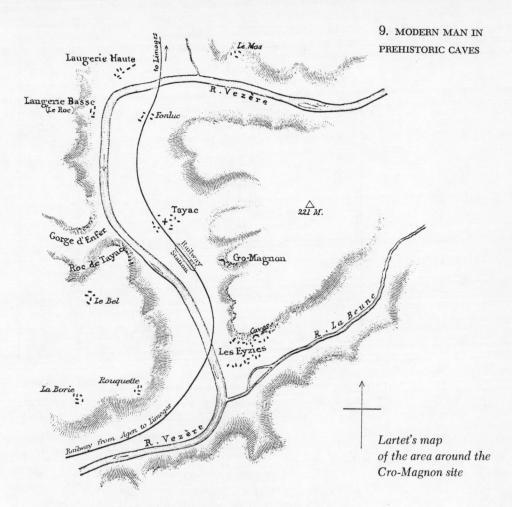

*Lartet's map
of the area around the
Cro-Magnon site*

Anyone who visits the modern French town can see why
the area around Les Eyzies was a favored location in prehistoric times. Here the Vézère River, a tributary of the Dordogne, flows through the pleasant valley it has carved out
of limestone rock, leaving high cliffs along its shores. These
cliffs are honeycombed with caves and in many places jut
out over the level ground below to provide overhangs which
were used as shelters. The depths of the long, winding
caves that run far into the limestone *causses* were not lived
in but were used as shrines for practicing the magic rituals
of the hunt.

This valley was a concentration point for game in those
days, with all kinds of animals passing through it, so there
was nearly always an ample supply of food. Water, too, was   103

The many sites of prehistoric interest near Les Eyzies. The circle is an enlargement of the area within five miles of the town

plentiful and near at hand. So were wood for fuel and flint for making implements. The numerous caves and rock shelters are clustered so closely together that it is easy to stroll from one to another. In some cases, they are so near to each other that the nextdoor neighbor was within voice range.

At Les Eyzies, all the essentials needed to make a self-supporting permanent community were at hand. To people who had been hungry nomads for generations, this well-sheltered, bountiful valley must have been a veritable paradise. (Perhaps the idea of the Garden of Eden came from the memory of places like this.)

Les Eyzies became a loosely organized settlement where people got to know each other. The benefits that come from close social contact gave rise to a new kind of man—the community dweller, who is a step farther advanced than the members of a roaming family group or of a nomadic tribe. He has a place he can call home, and he has neighbors who can be depended upon for help in obtaining food, for mutual defense, and for essential service in times of dire emergency like childbirth, illness, injury, or death.

104   Les Eyzies, of course, was not the only one of these early

prehistoric communities, and it is certainly not the oldest one, but it is important to us because its natural surroundings have remained almost unchanged, while its art and artifacts have been remarkably well preserved. If prehistoric men of this period were to return, they would probably feel more at home here than anywhere else.

The area around Les Eyzies is dotted with so many important finds that some of the best-known names for Upper Paleolithic sites come from it. The terms Mousterian, Périgordian, Gravettian, Tayacian, Micoquian, and Magdalenian were derived from locales in this neighborhood. Les Eyzies is called the capital of prehistory because of its central position in this artifact-rich region.

The Cro-Magnon site is no longer in existence. The garage belonging to the hotel of that name covers the place from which the celebrated bones were taken. Four layers of ashes, flint tools, reindeer, mammoth, bison, and horse bones, an elephant tusk, and many sea shells, some of them perforated for stringing, were associated with the human skeletons found here. Since Les Eyzies is more than a hundred miles from the nearest ocean, the Cro-Magnons evidently traveled or traded with people who did.

THE Cro-Magnon rock shelter plays a major role in prehistory because it made the world aware of the fact that mod-

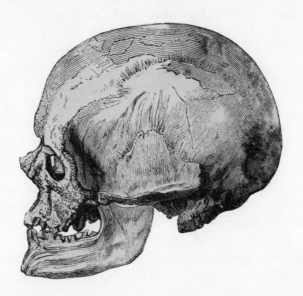

The skull of the "Old Man" of Cro-Magnon. He was less than 50 years old when he died [Joly]

105

*A prehistoric rock
shelter at Les Eyzies as
it looks today. The holes
were cut into the walls to
support timbers of dwellings
in medieval times*

ern men have been around for tens of thousands of years.
Yet other examples of *Homo sapiens* had been discovered
long before 1868. In 1822 a headless skeleton, stained red
with ochre, had been found in the Paviland Cave in southeast Wales. With it were the bones of extinct animals, shells,
flint tools, and ornaments made of bone and ivory. Dean
William Buckland, who was Reader of Geology at Oxford,
examined the find, and then, to make sure that it did not
disturb orthodox belief in the Bible, declared that the animals had been swept into the cave by the Flood, but that
the body of the man had been deliberately buried there
during the Roman occupation of England. That it was
buried was true enough, but everything about it showed
that it had been placed in the ground in Paleolithic times.
The Dean, who seems to have been consistent in his errors,
also said that the skeleton was a woman's. It therefore became known as the Red Lady of Paviland. Actually, it was
the skeleton of a man about 25 years old. The bones of the
masculine Red Lady were sent to Oxford, where they remained in the University Museum for many decades until
their true antiquity was at last recognized.

Another early discovery of human bones that were
roughly contemporary with those found in the Cro-Magnon
rock shelter took place in Aurignac in the lower Pyrenees in

106

1860. There, in a cave behind a huge stone slab, were 17 human skeletons. By the time the French geologist Édouard Lartet could reach the site, the bones had been given proper Christian burial in the local graveyard. (It is now known that these remains were not Paleolithic but Neolithic.) Deep in the undisturbed floor of the cave, however, Lartet dug up fragments of Paleolithic human bones and objects made out of ivory, antler, bone, and sea shells. This site gave the name Aurignacian to the period when the Cro-Magnons lived.

The skeletons of the men found at Aurignac and Cro-Magnon are by no means the earliest examples of *Homo sapiens* yet known. The remains taken from the Skūhl Cave in Mount Carmel, Palestine, in the 1930's are fairly modern in form and are far older than the French discoveries. In France, the Combe Capelle skull, which was dug up in Périgord in 1909, is supposed to be the earliest representative of *Homo sapiens* yet found in Europe. (It was destroyed during the Second World War in the same bombing explosion that wrecked the German museum where the Neandertal remains from Le Moustier were stored.) Combe Capelle antedated Cro-Magnon by several thousand years and had a somewhat Neandertaloid jaw.

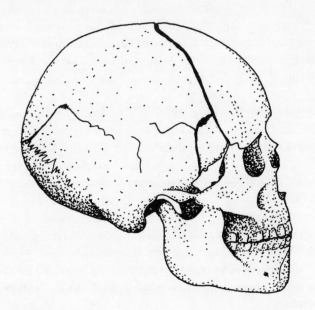

The Combe Capelle skull, which is believed to be the earliest one of a Homo sapiens *yet found in Europe*

107

A Magdalenian burial at St. Germain-la-Rivière. Now in the Les Eyzies Museum

Other discoveries of skeletons with relatively modern features were made between 1872 and 1901 in the Grimaldi Caves on the Riviera coast between Monaco and the Italian border. Two of these, a middle-aged woman and a teen-age boy, who had been buried together, were once thought by some anatomists to have certain Negroid traits. More recently, however, opinion has changed, partly because the skulls had been so badly restored that it is difficult to tell what they were originally like.

Numerous Cro-Magnon remains have been found throughout Europe from southern England to Russia. (Scandinavia was not regularly inhabited until the great icecap covering it melted.)

THE many discoveries made in the mid-nineteenth century publicized ancient man so well that when Sir John Lubbock (later Lord Avebury) published his *Prehistoric Times* in 1865 it became a best-seller. Lubbock originated the terms Paleolithic and Neolithic. The word prehistoric had been invented in 1851 by Daniel Wilson for the title of his book, *The Archeology and Prehistoric Annals of Scotland.*

Prehistory was on the way in the 1860's, marching in step with Darwin and his supporters. Earth taken from excavation after excavation was burying the men who still insisted that the Bible was the only reliable guide to the antiquity of man.

108

WITH THE Neandertal and Cro-Magnon discoveries, the mists that had obscured the existence of early men began to disappear. Many years were to pass before the prior existence of *Homo erectus* and his australopithecine predecessors would become known, but the groundwork for the study of prehistory was being laid.

Oddly enough, the Cro-Magnon find did not silence the nineteenth-century detractors of Darwin's theory of evolution. They argued that if man had remained unchanged for some thousands of years, then there was no reason to believe that he had ever evolved from a lower form.

As a matter of fact, man's form has changed in certain slight ways since the Combe Capelle and Cro-Magnon people lived. C. L. Brace and Ashley Montagu (1965, p. 255*f.*) point out what recent evolution has done: skeletal robustness and the indications for muscularity have been decreased; so has that part of the face related to the jaws and the teeth. Third molars ("wisdom teeth") often do not appear in the people of central Europe, and the edge-to-edge bite that is still characteristic of the few remaining hunting and food-gathering men has been replaced by the overbite in which the lower front teeth bite behind the upper ones. This occurred in the Middle East after the introduction of metal tools and the development of agriculture some 10,000 years ago but did not take place in England until after the Norman Conquest of 1066.

They then go on to explain that "as the amount of protein in the diet decreased and the starch and carbohydrate content increased, the amount of chewing for the purpose of increasing the digestibility of the food became relatively greater. Unlike meat, starches and carbohydrates start the process of digestion in the mouth where thorough mixture with salivary enzymes commences their conversion into simple sugars that can then be handled by the stomach.

"The food-producing revolution did not immediately result in the loss of the edge-to-edge bite since it took several thousand years before the full possibilities of the change in subsistence began to be realized. With a sedentary existence, the production of food surpluses, and the accumulation of tangible possessions that this made possible, inven-

109

tion and technological progress occurred at an ever-increasing rate. The development of metallurgy culminating in the Bronze and later Iron Ages finally gave people a tool-kit which effectively put teeth as manipulating tools out of business, and it is not surprising to observe the cessation of incisor wear and the gradual appearance of partial overbites making their appearance with the beginning of the Bronze Age."

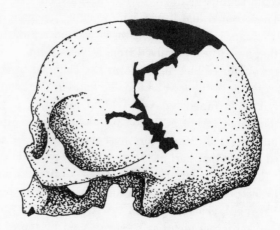

*The Chancelade skull.
Found more than five
feet underground in a rock
shelter near Périgueux,
it had been powdered over
with red oxide of iron*

THE PERIOD from 40,000 to 30,000 years ago, when Europe was going through the Göttweig Interstadial and the weather was fairly warm, was a formative one for the evolution of mankind. This was when the Cro-Magnon people first made their appearance—and the Classic Neandertals disappeared. It was also a time when differing forms of *Homo sapiens* were complicating matters. Not only the so-called "Negroid" skeletons of the Grimaldi Caves showed variations from the standard Cro-Magnon pattern, but a somewhat later man, the Chancelade, who lived in France when the weather turned cold again, had what were once believed to be Eskimo features. More recent thinking on these apparent variants, however, tends to put them all together as one people with local minor differences in their skeletal forms—the same kinds of differences that can be noted among men of today.

The human population of the world was then steadily increasing in numbers and spreading out into new territory.

And this was also the time when men who were isolated

from each other by geographical barriers such as mountains and seas were developing the bodily and facial differences that makes a modern southern Italian unlike a northern German, or a Spaniard unlike an Alpine villager. Jacquetta Hawkes described this formative period when she said (1963, p. 54): "Sun and frost, forest and plain, humidity and dryness, height and latitude, diet and water content, a variable inheritance from the remoter past and the chance movements of peoples, all united during these millenia to give our single species the differences of height and proportion, of facial structure and skin colour, of shade and texture of hair, which make the rich variety of mankind. No other species save our own domesticated dog has so remarkable a range of form while yet remaining one species."

It would be a mistake to designate all the people who succeeded the Neandertals as Cro-Magnons simply because a few of their skeletons were found in a French rock shelter which had that local name. A better descriptive term for these fully developed representatives of *Homo sapiens* would be "men," for that is what they were, men in every sense of the word. Unfortunately, "men" has been used to characterize all kinds of early humanoid creatures. Let us therefore coin a new expression for these post-Neandertals and call them "Modernmen."

THESE Modernmen, *Homo sapiens* all, were shaping themselves into three major and three or more minor racial groups in certain areas of the world. Their individual origins are still obscure but may someday be clarified by more findings.

Europe was being inhabited by the Caucasoids, Asia by the Mongoloids, Africa by the Negroids, while minor races like the Bushmen were also in Africa, the Australoids in the continent that gave them that name, and a multiorigined people who were to be called the Polynesians were just beginning to spread out through the islands of the Pacific. The Western Hemisphere was still unsettled.

This was a time for origins, for reshapings, for new combinations, and for the beginning of what was to be. We know a great deal about this period so far as its artifacts are concerned, but all too little about what was happening to its people. Skeletal remains tell us nothing about skin

111

color, and unless some bits of hair remain—which they seldom do on truly ancient skulls—nothing about that either.
Eye color is presumably lost forever. So are the shapes of
breasts, buttocks, and other forms of flesh.

Scientists, however, are constantly inventing new ways
to find out things that seemed irretrievably lost. Perhaps
they—with the help of some fortunate archeological finds—
will someday be able to tell us more about the physical
features of our early ancestors.

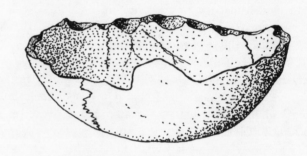

*A human skull used as
a drinking cup. It
was one of four found in
a row at Le Placard*

10. Early *Homo sapiens* Tools and Cultures

Homo sapiens, who had probably come from the Middle East—or Africa, or both—began to occupy all of the European continent that was free from ice. This took time, several thousand years, in fact. And the numerous skeletons that have been found show that there was a great deal of variation among the new people. The Neandertals, in western Europe at least, had been of fairly uniform stock, but their successors were a mixed lot. In animal-breeding terms they would be called mongrels. Whatever their origins, the newcomers are the ancestors of all modern Europeans and also of the millions who left that part of the world to settle in other lands.

What is called the Cro-Magnon type still persists today, particularly in southern France, Spain, parts of Germany, southern Sweden, and North Africa. The Guanchos of the Canary Islands preserve Cro-Magnon features better than anyone else.

Homo sapiens improved the Neandertal flint implements and learned how to make better use of such material as bone, antler, shell, and wood. But they carried on the hunting and food-gathering tradition, for agriculture was as yet unknown.

Yet they lived in a fairly advanced society. Those who managed to survive the diseases and dangers of childhood grew up to be strong and healthy. The family was the essential group, and the number of people involved with each other was small. Except on special occasions, a person might never come in contact with more than a few score of his fellow men. These special occasions, however, were important, for it was then that marriages were made and new blood was brought into a group that would otherwise become too inbred. These gatherings may have been held for animal drives or to settle long-standing disputes.

The words "may have" are used advisedly here. Except for the few hints given in their pictures and statues, we have 113 very little valid information about these talented people who are best remembered for their art. We cannot compare them to living primitive people, which is always risky; in the case of the superbly gifted cave artists, it would be unfair.

It seems reasonable to assume that the women ordinarily stayed home to take care of the children, gather edible plants, and cook the meat which the men brought home from the hunt. Footprints in some of the caves show that these people danced, and during the dance they presumably sang, chanted, clapped hands, and hammered on things that would make a noise.

The cave painters have left us so many indications of their existence that we tend to feel that we know more about them than we actually do. (We do have more information about them than we have about any earlier people.) But it is very easy to misinterpret their art and artifacts. It is entirely possible that some of our best "guesses" are absurdly wrong. Yet we have no choice but to be guided by our best-informed experts. What they say today may be disproved tomorrow, but that has always been true and doubtless always will be. Fallibility is an inevitable human trait.

ONE OF the things we do know about this society is that it was dominated by a tribal chieftain and a shaman, whose province was magic and medicine. He was the liaison between the people and the spirits, and he communicated with the uneasy dead. He specialized in curses and spells, which he supposedly could inflict or cure. Since his followers believed in him implicitly, his power was practically unlimited. Carleton Coon says of him (1954, p. 105): "His profession, not prostitution, is the oldest. From the shaman is descended a long line of specialists, including priests, diagnosticians, surgeons, teachers, and scholars."

The shaman was the first intellectual. He was the man of ideas, of dreams, of words, of art. The chieftain was the man of action, the hunter, the soldier, the keeper of his people's physical well-being, and their protector from attack. Both leaders had their followers: the chieftain, his lieutenants and simple huntsmen; the shaman, his acolytes as well as a number of artists, singers, dancers, and tellers of tales.

In small groups the chieftain and the shaman may have been the same person, but in larger ones the offices were

probably divided because very different types of men were needed for each task. The basic structure of society was being formed at this time. In essence, it has changed very little since then.

In all things, the group, the unit, the tribe was important, while the individual was necessarily subordinate, for the individual must die, but the group can be expected to live

The famous sorcerer of Les Trois Frères in the Pyrenees—a shaman in animal guise

115

on. The fate of the individual represented mortality, while the continuance of the group stood for immortality. Both were the shaman's province, and he presided at the rites of passage which mark a person's progress from birth to death. Others in the tribe could spend their time in daily activities without having to devote any thought to the larger issues, but the shaman was always concerned with matters that were beyond the ordinary man's ken. Since magic was his major preoccupation, he naturally took over everything that had to do with it. This meant that art came under his influence because it was closely associated with the magic of the hunt.

Although some recent interpretation of prehistoric cave paintings questions the long-held idea that their sole purpose was to bring about a successful conclusion to the pursuit of game, there seems to be no doubt that magic of some kind was tied up with all early art. But the probable motivations are less important to us than the pictures on the walls of the caves. They tell us more about the people who made them than stone implements or other artifacts can.

The Neandertals had used only the mouths of the caves, but the deep interiors were now being explored to find suitable places to be decorated. Dark, seldom-visited chambers and small passages were sought out, for the artists wanted to make sure that their pictures would not be disturbed. The main reason that so many prehistoric pictures are still in existence is the fact that they were kept out of sight for many thousands of years. Countless others that were put in more vulnerable positions have long since vanished; some have faded away even in our time.

Plan of the cave La Cullavera near Santander, Spain. The cave is four-fifths of a mile long; important sites are at B and C

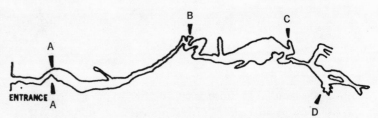

THE Neandertals' successors lived all over Europe, but it was only in a small area of southern France and northern Spain that they produced great quantities of the art that has made them famous. A few engravings have turned up in England, Holland, Switzerland, and other places, but they are not

116

as good as the Franco-Cantabrian pictures. They show the influence of what was going on in the great central core of artistic activity, but they are derivative and—in the true sense of the word—provincial.

Cave painting required a sheltered wall for the pictures, but small figures made of bone, ivory, stone, or clay could be made anywhere. These cult statues antedate the painted caves and were widely disseminated throughout Europe. Most of them depict females, often with grossly exaggerated sexual features. The face is nearly always slighted and is sometimes left blank. Although there is no reason to believe that prehistoric women were steatopygous, a number of these figures are. The fact that they often have no feet and are portrayed with legs ending in a point may simply mean that they were stuck into the ground to preside over household shrines.

They are fertility figures, but they express the desire for more progeny not only for man but also for the game animals on which he depended for food. They do not represent individual women but are generalizations of the idea of conception, of birth, of the endlessly repeated cycle of life. Fleshly as they may seem to be, they stand for a great spiritual idea as well, for with them begins man's longest enduring religious theme, the Mother Goddess, a concept that is still with us today. The madonna-and-child images that are sold in stores or stand in millions of homes and countless churches throughout the world are the direct descendants of those ancient figurines.

It may seem odd to call the early Mother Goddess statues the embodiment of a spiritual idea, for with few exceptions they are grotesque, sprawling representations of women with huge breasts, distended bellies, enormous thighs, and emphasized pubic triangles that symbolize the carnal aspects of sex rather than the female principle in its more unworldly guise. But they stand for life, for breeding and multiplying, for filling the earth with people and making their place upon it secure and supreme. Since prehistoric Europe was thinly populated it is easy to see why its inhabitants wanted to reinforce their ranks. But out of the basic idea of the Great Mother came other concepts, some of which are among man's finest. Compassion, charity, affection, and generosity all stem from her.

The Venus of Willendorf. Discovered in Austria in 1908, this four-inch figure has become one of the best-known works of art made by early man

117

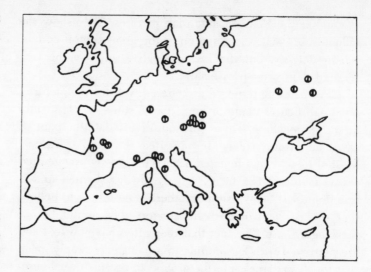

*Sites where prehistoric
Mother Goddess figures
have been found in Europe*

The word "cave dweller" is somewhat of a misnomer, for these people lived in rock shelters more often than they did in caves, and when they did occupy a cave they stayed near the entrance, where ventilation was better and smoke from the campfire could easily get out. On fine days they used the terrace just outside the entrance as a gathering place where they could sit in the sun while the women did their housework and the men shaped tools while they planned the next hunt.

The rock shelters were more open, but stone walls or skins stretched on poles were used to cover the sides. No traces of these temporary protective devices remain, but the men who could paint pictures on the walls of their caves were surely advanced enough to think of such simple things.

Life in these prehistoric communities must have been rather pleasant. Cleanliness was a virtue that had not yet been discovered, and only those persons whose bodies were strong enough to overcome wounds and diseases could recover without help from medicine, although it is possible that the shamans and the older women knew of herbs and other natural healing substances which may have had some value. But if life was uncertain—and short—it was free. And the people who dwelt in these cave communities had reached a phase of human existence where discovery was on the march and the future beckoned to men who were steadily improving their lot.

118

Jacquetta Hawkes (1963, p. 133) describes how these people lived: "It is easy, and surely permissible, to picture the formation of hunting parties, visiting by courtship parties, and large gatherings round fires where meat from the communal hunt was being roasted. Sometimes medicine men, artists and other leaders, perhaps horned, masked and clad in pelts, must have made solemn entries to carry out their hunting and fertility rites at the images deep in the rock. At certain times, perhaps at mid-winter to turn back the sun, perhaps in the early spring for the fertility of the game animals, there may have been ceremonies drawing hunters from afar for their celebration. During the hard, bright winter nights there must have been fires making wavering patches of light at point after point along the limestone cliffs."

In the Dordogne, Les Eyzies was the chief center around which many other prehistoric communities were located. Lascaux is only a few hours' walk from there, and other decorated caves are even closer at hand. The painted caves near Angoulême and Cahors are not too far for a determined walker to reach, and even those in the Pyrenees and northern Spain were accessible to anyone who wanted to make a special trip to them. One assumes that visitors who came to examine the art were welcome.

There can be no doubt that these prehistoric artists saw each other's work. The similarity of style shows that. And this is important, for creative people always benefit from being able to exchange ideas. Lascaux has been called the Sistine Chapel of prehistoric art. Les Eyzies can be said to have been like Renaissance Florence, where artists flourished because they could communicate with each other. The Italians had patrons; so did the cave artists, for they were backed by the powerful shamans who needed their help.

The pictures and sculptures created in France and northern Spain from 30,000 to 10,000 years ago were, so far as we know, the very beginning of representative art, the first of man's strivings to express himself in other ways than spoken or chanted language. These works are older than any produced anywhere else. Compared with them, the earliest Mesopotamian, Egyptian, and Chinese art is recent, while archaic Greek art is practically modern.

PHASE FOUR DURING THE 30,000- to 20,000-year-long period between the passing of the Neandertals and the invention of agriculture, several different cultures arose in western Europe. There has been much dispute among leading authorities about suitable names for these cultures and for their probable duration. Current thinking about this is explained by William Howells (1954–63, pp. 94–95): "In the old days, archeologists used to talk about 'periods' of the European Upper Paleolithic . . . Aurignacian, Solutrean, and Magdalenian. Nowadays they think of somewhat different populations . . . with different cultures, partly existing at the same time and partly succeeding one another in Europe or parts of Europe, as new immigrants or influences arrived, or as changes took place on the spot. The main series of events is the same, and the old terms still have some meaning. But the archaeologists today see much more complicated groupings, as they work out finer distinctions of stonework, and as they plot these all on the map, observing how they are related to one another in layers in the ground at a great many different ancient living sites.

"As things now stand, there were two early traditions, one called Périgordian (comprising the Châtelperronian and Gravettian) and the other Aurignacian, each of these made up of rather complicated successions in themselves. The former Solutrean 'period' seems to have been instead a relatively short florescence of some older ideas, perhaps of African derivation, which were especially developed both in eastern Europe and in Spain; this outburst of striking stonework was relatively short. The latest phase in the west of Europe was the Magdalenian; but if you are considering the final stages of Europe as a whole, the picture is more varied, with several related or legatee local cultures to the north and east, all running on to the end of the Paleolithic."

But many of the old terms are still in use. The chart on the next page shows the succession of cultures involved. Compare them with what Dr. Howells has to say.

To complicate things, local cultures are sometimes mentioned. Creswellian, for instance, is British; it corresponds to the late Aurignacian and extends into the Magdalenian. Sauveterrian, Tardenoisian, and Maglemosian are Meso-

120

Years Ago		*Years Ago*		
	Mesolithic			
	↑			
ca. 12,000	Azilian			
16,000 *to* 10,000	Magdalenian			
17,000	Solutrean			
		28,000 *to* 20,000	Gravettian	⎫ Périgordian
30,000	Aurignacian	35,000	Châtelperronian	⎭
	Homo sapiens arrives			
before 35,000 *or* 40,000	Mousterian			

SUCCESSION OF EUROPEAN PALEOLITHIC CULTURES

lithic and will be treated in the chapter on that period.

The major cultures are divided and subdivided; Magdalenian has six divisions and two subdivisions; so has Périgordian, while Aurignacian is almost as complex. Someday the time structure of these cultures may be agreed upon; they will then be easier to understand. Meanwhile, we must put up with inconveniences in a body of knowledge that is constantly growing and undergoing changes as it grows.

DURING this time men learned to strike better-shaped and much longer flakes from the flint nuclei that were the raw material for their tools. And pressure flaking, which is done by snapping off small pieces along the edges with a pointed bit of bone, made it possible for skilled workers to devise new shapes and modify old ones.

European skill in shaping flint reached the height of its development during Solutrean times when the famous laurel-leaf points were made. These long, beautifully shaped and finished blades are believed by some prehistorians to have been used as spearheads, but they seem to be too fragile and valuable for that. The Solutreans were noted for their slaughter of wild horses by rounding them up and then driving them over a steep cliff to fall to their deaths. The long rocky spur at Solutré, near Macon in central France, gave the Solutreans their name. In the field below it are the   121 bones of tens of thousands of horses which supplied food for feasts there for thousands of years. The laurel-leaf blades, which have been found among the broken-up bones, may have been used as sharp knives to cut up the flesh. There are keen edges on both sides, but one of these could easily have been covered with a bit of hide to protect the hand while slicing.

The Magdalenians, who were expert workers in bone, ivory, and antler, developed a new implement which we call a harpoon, although it was not intended for use on aquatic animals. A number of projecting points assured its staying firmly in place when it was driven deep into the flesh of a reindeer or other large land creature. Like the modern harpoon, it may have had a line tied to it; in fact, it may even have been detachable from the shaft that propelled it. Notched spear-throwers helped to increase its range and force. It was an effective weapon, but except for its ability to remain in the wound it was not much of an improvement over the ordinary spear. European hunters had yet to discover the greater range and superiority of the bow and arrow. This was apparently an African invention which did not reach Europe until Mesolithic times.

Large rib bones were especially favored because they could be used as spatulas, spreaders, and snow cutters, among other things. Flat shoulder bones made good shovels as they had for ages past, but disks were cut from them now to serve as buttons or amulets. Some were decorated with engravings. Splinters of bone were used as awls or punches, and, when very slim, as pins or needles.

Since reindeer were plentiful at this time, their heavy antlers made good working material. One of the most interesting types of objects made from them were what the French call *bâtons de commandements*. These were often beautifully carved or decorated with engravings, and they were distinguished by the fact that they had one or more holes bored through them. They were first discovered in 1833 and were given their name shortly after that. It was an inspired guess, for although all sorts of practical uses for them have been suggested, it seems most likely that they were wands for the shamans to wield in ritual ceremonies.

Their rodlike form suggests sexual symbolism. Giedion makes this plain when he says (1962, pp. 227–28): "All

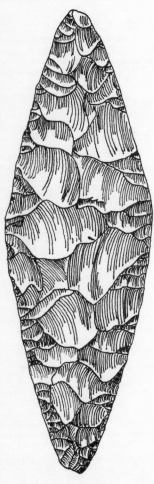

A Solutrean laurel leaf. These thin, finely wrought, sharp bits of flint represent European implement making at its best

122

This bâton de commande-ment *from La Madeleine was acquired a century ago by the British Museum*

straight lines betokened the phallus; all circles the vagina. . . . In . . . the perforated staff, the *bâton de commandement* . . . it is not impossible that we have here a representation of bisexuality; of the desire and demand for fertility raised to its highest power."

Also found among Magdalenian ceremonial objects are perforated oval plaques that resemble Australian bull-roarers. One of these, when attached to a string and twirled around in the air, makes a strange whirring sound that must have been very impressive to a naïve audience. Obviously, this was the voice of a god—or of an ancestor—which only the shaman could interpret.

IN eastern Europe, where wood was scarce and mammoths plentiful, their massive bones were used as supports in house building, with hides stretched over them to serve as exterior walls. Mammoth tusks supplied ivory from which figurines could be carved. Several of them found near Buret and Maltà in Siberia portray men—or women—in fur garments with trousers and hoods.

A bone disk, perhaps used as a button.
From Laugerie-Basse

Since these figurines are artists' concepts, they may or may not represent prehistoric costumes literally. Fortunately, we have the real thing. It was also found in Russia in a burial made ages ago in ground that has been frozen ever since. The perfectly preserved skeleton of a 55-year-old man that was taken from the grave wore fur trousers and a shirt decorated with rows of mammoth-ivory beads. His wrists were adorned with thin mammoth-ivory bracelets and strands of Arctic-fox teeth hung from his neck. A large scraper, a flint knife, and a pendant with a drilled hole in it accompanied the corpse. Since the burial is believed to be about 33,000 years old, this is the most ancient clothed body yet found.

123

The frozen soil of Siberia has not only preserved man in its icy grip but long-extinct animals as well. More than 20 frozen mammoths have been found in various states of completeness. When an unusually warm season causes the ice to melt, the prehistoric corpses seldom get a chance to decay because wolves and other carnivores begin to devour the still-edible flesh as soon as it appears. The tender lower section of the trunk is a favored morsel; so is the top of the head, since it is likely to show above the ice first.

The best-preserved specimen of a frozen mammoth, which was found in a crevasse near Beresovka in the early years of this century, has been mounted and is on display in a Russian museum.

Mammoth-bone figurine from Siberia, showing a fur garment

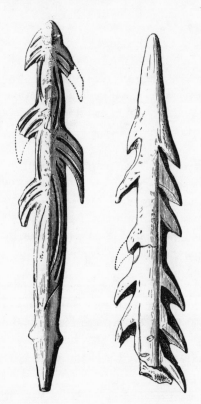

Harpoon heads from Périgord [Dawkins]

124

11. The Modern World Discovers
Paleolithic Art

NOTHING TELLS US as much about prehistoric men as their
art does. It gives us an insight into their thinking, shows us
what fauna and flora were contemporary with them, and
tells us something about their ways of living, their magic
rituals, and their sexual practices. What we have, of course,
is only a small part of the immense body of art that was
created in those far-off times because everything made of
organic material has perished, and much of the supposedly
enduring art is slowly fading, decaying, or being destroyed
by men. The Second World War took its toll; other acts of
violence may obliterate still more.

Fortunately, we have so much of it that we have not yet
absorbed it all. Work on interpreting it goes on year after
year, opening up new vistas and hinting at still farther ones
beyond them. Discoveries are constantly being made in the
field, and it is not impossible that one rivaling Lascaux in
importance may occur any day. Museum displays and
superbly illustrated books are making it possible for the
public to see what was long buried in the ground in remote
and often inaccessible places. Most of the original material,
however, is still in Europe; very little has been brought to
America.

Our knowledge of prehistoric art is very recent. Men
did not find out that their far-removed ancestors had created
works of art until the 1830's, when a notary named Brouillet,
who was exploring the Chaffaud Cave south of Poiters,
found a flat piece of bone with two deer engraved on it. No
one had any idea of its great antiquity. It was attributed to
the Celts and in 1851 was sent to the Cluny Museum in
Paris, where it remained until 1887 when it was deposited
in the Musée des Antiquités in Saint-Germain-en-Laye. It
was about this time that the *bâton de commandement* mentioned in Chapter 10 was found in the cave of Le Veyrier

125

*First Paleolithic picture
to be identified as such—
the Chaffaud deer*

Bâton de commandement
from Le Veyrier [Dawkins]

south of Geneva. Since this had only a floral pattern engraved on it, it attracted even less attention than the Chaffaud artifact, which had interesting pictures of animals.

When Édouard Lartet and his son Louis made even more important discoveries during the 1860's in the Pyrenees and Périgord, they too were largely ignored. Then when Lartet printed detailed accounts of his findings, the English proved to be more interested than the French in his artifacts. Some of them were acquired by the British Museum, and in 1865 Sir John Lubbock (Lord Avebury) used a few as illustrations in his pioneering book, *Prehistoric Times*. In 1887 the British Museum obtained several more fine pieces.

All these, however, were small objects made of bone, ivory, antler, or stone. The French call such things *art mobilier* because they can be moved whereas wall paintings are fixed in place. Mobiliary art usually lacks color and seems rather unimpressive to nonspecialists. The public continued to ignore it; so did most savants. More and more such specimens were found, but they were stored in museums or in the cabinets of private collectors.

The great cave paintings, which were to attract worldwide attention, remained undiscovered for another generation. Many were hidden in caverns that were as yet unknown; some went unnoticed in the deep interiors of partially explored caves; still others were buried under many feet of the debris that had accumulated during the ages. Yet some were in easily accessible places and had been seen by countless visitors who did not realize what they were. Sometimes they scratched their names or initials on them. One cave, Rouffignac, which is only a few miles west of Lascaux, had been mapped in 1759. The names of people who explored it in the eighteenth century can be seen on

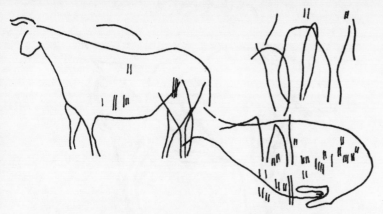

its walls and ceilings. They obviously paid no attention to the ancient pictures and probably mistook them for the drawings of children or local peasants.

It was not until 1956 that proper notice was given to the numerous engravings and paintings of mammoths, rhinoceroses, horses, and other animals in the cave. Then bitter controversy arose about the authenticity of some of them. The Abbé Henri Breuil, a noted expert on prehistoric art, cleared them and so did a majority of well-qualified scholars, but the matter has never been settled to everyone's satisfaction.

Only those who have visited the painted caves know how difficult it is to make out some of the pictures. Usually the guide has to point out their details. Some, especially those in Lascaux, are brilliantly clear, but they are exceptions.

IN 1878 a schoolmaster named L. Chiron made the first find of prehistoric murals. He was going by boat down the Ardèche River when, at a point a few miles above its junction with the Rhône (between Aiguèze and Pont-Saint-Esprit), he noticed a small cave just above the water level. In it he saw some engravings of animals that were visible by daylight. Farther inside were still more. Some were hard to make out, but there was no doubt that the outlines of horses, deer, a large bull, and numerous mammoths were cut into the rock walls.

Chiron was so impressed by what he had found that he returned to photograph some of the animal pictures. But he was unable to interest anyone in them, so his discovery went unnoticed for years.

The first Paleolithic wall engravings to be identified. From the Grotte Chabot

One of the
Altamira bison

The engravings in the Grotte Chabot, compared to some of the later discoveries, were in no way remarkable— and they were in a remote cave that could be reached only by taking a boat down the tortuous canyon of the Ardèche. It is therefore not surprising that they were neglected for so long.

Only a year later came one of the greatest discoveries of prehistoric art, yet it too received a hostile reception, for no one would believe that such fine pictures could be far older than the earliest art of Mesopotamia, Egypt, China, India, Greece, and Rome.

They were the now-famous paintings of Altamira, which were found in an easily reached cave on the northern coast of Spain less than 20 miles west of Santander. The existence of the cave had been noted in 1868 when a hunter's dog vanished into the ground in pursuit of a fox. By an odd coincidence, the great Lascaux cave was also discovered by a dog in 1940. Apparently European man's oldest friend was guiding him back to the long-ago past they had shared in common.

The paintings in Altamira were not noticed when the cave was first entered in 1868, and some years later, when Marcelino de Sautuola, a local landowner, was searching the cavern floor for prehistoric objects, he did not bother to examine the walls or ceilings carefully. In 1878 he went to Paris to visit the exposition that was being held there and saw some of the *art mobilier* that was being displayed. This inspired him to return to the cave the next year; this time he took his seven-year-old daughter Maria with him. It was fortunate that he did because the little girl could easily

128

enter a low-ceilinged chamber near the entrance (the floor has since been deepened). After a few minutes she came running out, calling to her father, *"Papá, mira toros pintados!"* ("Come see the painted bulls!")

De Sautuola scrambled into the low-ceilinged chamber and directed his lamp's rays upward where the child was excitedly pointing. Above him he saw a number of engraved and painted animals, mostly bison. But among them were three does, three wild boars, two horses, and a wolf. These were not ordinary cave paintings; they happen to be among the best ever found, for they are large, beautifully drawn, and colored in red, brown, and black. And they are the first Paleolithic paintings recognized as such by modern man. The animal pictures discovered in the Chabot cave are line engravings without color.

In 1880 de Sautuola published a pamphlet entitled *"Breves apuntes sobre algunos objetos prehistóricos de la provincia de Santander."* It contained the first printed illustrations ever made of Paleolithic paintings, but, as was so common in those days, this important work met with indifference and hostility. Its author died in 1888, unrecognized for his great discovery.

More years had to pass before a skeptical world could be convinced that there was such a thing as Paleolithic painting. Then, in the spring of 1895, a farmer who lived less than two miles south of the noted prehistoric community of Les Eyzies was enlarging a shallow rock shelter to make a storage place and noticed that the long-accumulated debris had buried a small opening in the rock wall.

On April 11 several small boys crawled inside the narrow passageway. The lights they were carrying soon illuminated some engravings. Emile Rivière, who was noted for his prehistoric discoveries at Menton in 1872, was invited to explore the newly found La Mouthe Cave. He did so and found many more engravings and some paintings, all of which had certainly been sealed up for thousands of years.

La Mouthe, more than Altamira, which had been opened for some years before its paintings were found, helped to break down the stubborn resistance to the idea that highly developed Paleolithic art could exist. Then one discovery after another finally convinced scholars and the public. In 1896, the Pair-non-Pair Cave near Bordeaux was found;

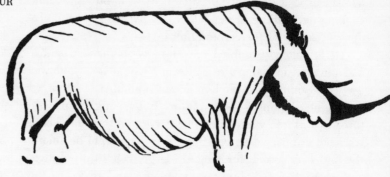

Rhinoceros tichorhinus
*drawn in crayon on
the walls of
Font-de-Gaume*

in 1897, Marsoulas in the Pyrenees; in 1901, Les Combarelles and Font-de-Gaume, both near Les Eyzies. Still other discoveries were made until more than a hundred European decorated caves had been opened up.

Most of them are in France, some are in Spain, and a few are in Italy, while isolated examples exist in central and eastern Europe. England has none, nor have the Low Countries or Scandinavia. Scandinavia could not, for ice covered the northern part of the continent when most of the caverns were being decorated. England and the Low Countries have interesting caves that were used by prehistoric men, but no mural art has been found in them. Mobiliary art has a somewhat wider range.

So far as we know, only Europe has caves that were decorated in Paleolithic times. Those in other parts of the world—Africa, India, and Mexico, for instance, are all much later. There seems to be no doubt that art began in Europe, probably somewhere in southern France or northern Spain. Since no political boundaries existed then, the prehistoric men who lived in the Franco-Cantabrian area were all the same people. Resemblances can be noted in pictures that are geographically distant from each other. And no artist, of course, ever signed his work; he couldn't, because writing hadn't yet been invented. He did not even use a symbol—like Whistler's butterfly—to identify what he had done. Art belonged to the tribe, not to the person who created it. The association of the individual artist with his work is a rather modern idea that apparently came in with the Greeks in historic times.

130

THE QUESTION most visitors to the painted caves ask is: "How old are the paintings?" Since their creators made no attempt to indicate which picture was made before which, the question is not always easy to answer. But they did unwittingly leave many clues.

For one thing, a new picture is often engraved or painted over an older one. Sometimes the superimposition is so complicated that it is difficult to tell one picture from another. But the superimposition is helpful in establishing the relative date of the pictures, especially with paintings, because a pigment that overlies another one is obviously later. Matters are not so simple with engravings because their lines, which were cut into the rock with a sharp bit of flint, may be of the same depth; in such cases it is hard to determine which line was incised first.

Fortunately, there are other methods that can be used to establish priority. When an engraved line cuts through a painting, the pigment was certainly put there first, and vice versa. With engravings alone, a very careful inspection of

*Superimposition—
engraved figures on a
stalagmite in Teyjat*

131

the depth and width of the lines can sometimes help to determine which are earlier.

In caves that contain objects with carbon in it, it has been possible to establish absolute dates by the radiocarbon method. But the dates indicate occupation rather than the exact time at which the paintings were made. Since some of the caves were used over a period of thousands of years, the date determined may be far removed from the one wanted. A radiocarbon date for some organic material found in Lascaux, for instance, shows that people were in the cavern as recently as $8,720 \pm 100$ or even $8,060 \pm 75$ years ago. Yet the style of the paintings shows that they are far older. A probable date of $15,516 \pm 900$ has been assigned to them, although the Abbé Henri Breuil believed that they were about 7,000 years older than that.

More dates are being established every year. Before long we should have a reasonably accurate chronology of early man. Meanwhile we must put up with our present-day estimates.

The caves show us that man was far advanced enough some 15,000 or more years ago to create splendid works of art that are fit to rank with the world's finest. Certainly any museum would be proud to have one of them. But no museum does, for if they are of any size and importance they cannot safely be moved and therefore have to be left in place. If you want to see them you will have to go where they are still *in situ*.

No reproductions, no matter how good, can do the originals full justice. There are many reasons for this; modern color pictures have to be printed on flat sheets of paper, while the paintings are nearly always on curved surfaces; the even lighting needed for camera work is very different from the dim and usually directional light in the caves; and pictures that can be printed in a book are necessarily much smaller than the big ones on the cave walls. *Art mobilier* and sculpture can be reproduced exceedingly well; rupestral painting cannot. And this is not only a matter of color; texture too is important, and a color plate can hardly even hint at that.

The paintings give us a vivid glimpse of the world in
which these prehistoric men lived. And it is not only the

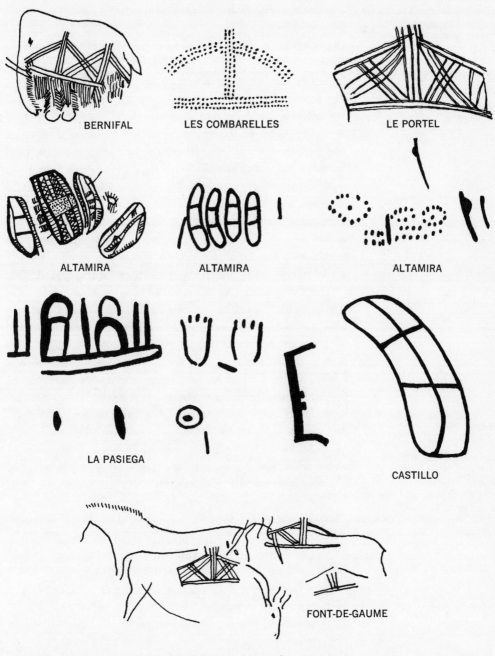

BERNIFAL

LES COMBARELLES

LE PORTEL

ALTAMIRA

ALTAMIRA

ALTAMIRA

LA PASIEGA

CASTILLO

FONT-DE-GAUME

pictures that tell us what that world was like; other attempts at communication exist. Some of these are abstract symbols called tectiforms, claviforms, blazons, and various other names that describe their shapes. It is difficult—and perhaps

Tectiforms and other abstract marks from France and Spain

133

impossible—for us to interpret them, for they were devised by people who are so far removed from us in their ways of thinking that it is hard for us to sense what they were trying to say. But an attempt is being made to understand them. Whether the probable meanings so far deduced are correct one cannot yet say. But work has begun, and the results are certainly worth following.

In addition to the meaning of these symbolic devices, the positioning and superimpositioning of the animal and human figures on the cave walls seem to have an important significance of their own. Mme. Annette Laming-Empéraire foresaw this and outlined the problem in her book on Lascaux in 1959 (pp. 172ff.). She also said that detailed inventories of the figures and their positions in the caves would have to be drawn up in order to reveal whatever intent there might be in the way they were located. Her call for the need for inventories, of course, went far beyond the immediate problem of the figures in Lascaux and applied to those in the other painted caves as well.

Dr. Laming-Empéraire amplified these ideas in a later book, *The Meaning of Paleolithic Wall Art* (1962). Meanwhile, André Leroi-Gourhan, who is now the director of the Musée de l'Homme in Paris, was working along parallel lines. He made a statistical study of more than 2,000 animal pictures in some 60 caves and came up with the following:

1. More than 85 per cent of the pictures of bison, wild cattle, and horses (all large animals and major sources of food) occur in the middle of a painted panel or in the most important chamber of a cave.
2. Pictures of deer, ibex, or mammoths do not occur in such central or important positions.
3. Rhinoceroses, lions, and bears are in the most remote parts of the caves and not in central positions.
4. More than 80 per cent of the human female figures, both representational and abstract, are in the central portions, while 70 per cent of the male symbols are not.

Having established these facts about the locations of the pictures and abstractions, he then goes on to interpret the probable significance of the more common symbols found in the caves. He believes that triangles, ovals, and rectangles stand for the female sex organ and that straight lines, barbed lines, rows of dots, and other narrow signs represent the male organ. He extends this interpretation of what might be called the prevalence of sex organs in paleolithic art to include wounds on animals as symbols of female sex organs.

He divides the 20,000 years of Paleolithic art into four major periods: primitive—Style I, 30,000 to 25,000 B.C., and Style II, 25,000 to 18,000 B.C.; archaic—Style III, 18,000 to 13,000 B.C.; and classic, Style IV—13,000 to 9000 B.C.

His book, *Préhistoire de l'art occidental,* 1965 (American edition, *Treasures of Prehistoric Art,* 1967), contains pages of tables, charts, and diagrams intended to support his thesis. His work goes farther than anyone else's in trying to find a meaning in cave art. It has not, however, met with universal acceptance among prehistorians, some of whom question his theories. But it is a pioneer thesis that must be taken into account in any future studies of the subject.

Until Leroi-Gourhan gave us at least a glimpse of the possibilities of meaning in Paleolithic art we had to look at the pictures without any comprehension of what they might be beyond the fact that they portrayed animals—and sometimes men and women. But we were unable to see any meaning in them so far as their creators' interests were concerned. Now it seems that these prehistoric men were more advanced than had been thought. Dr. Laming-Empéraire (1959, p. 200) says of them: "The mentality of Paleolithic man was far more complex than is generally supposed and . . . the scope of his artistic inspiration extended far beyond a daily preoccupation with the hunt and its quarry. If these paintings and engravings do indeed illustrate myths of very great antiquity, they may represent man's first attempt to express his vision of the world and the relationship of one living creature with another."

*Houselike tectiforms
from Font-de-Gaume*

12. When and Where
the Paintings Were Made

IT SEEMS LIKELY that mobiliary art was carved or engraved at the mouths of the caves, either in broad daylight or by the light of a campfire—or both. The tools used were small sharp pieces of flint. Rock sculpture had to be done by laboriously hammering away small chips by repeated blows with stones that could be held in the hand. In some cases, a bit of flint with a good cutting edge was used to scrape away the soft limestone. Clay figures were molded by hand just as they are now.

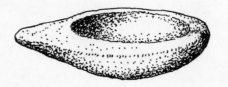

One of the stone lamps used by the cave artists. From La Mouthe

The mural paintings, except when placed near the cave entrance—which they seldom were—had to be executed by artificial light. A number of crude stone lamps have been found (there were dozens in the Dead Man's Shaft at Lascaux). In some caves, disk-shaped concretions with saucerlike depressions occur naturally. Lamps were also made of shells or animal skulls. Anything hollow that was fireproof, leakproof, and not too fragile would do. When these containers were filled with animal fat, to which a tuft of dried vegetable fiber was added for a wick, a serviceable lamp was ready. Modern experiments show that they produce only a feeble light, that they smoke badly, and that they soon have to be refilled. Some kind of co-operative effort was needed to keep the underground enterprise going, so teams of apprentices may have been organized to bring fresh fuel, food, and water to the men who were working in the deep interiors of the caves. In poorly ventilated areas, and especially in narrow passages with only one outlet, the air must have been quickly filled with smoke.

Was it ordinary smoke? Or did the shamans know how to put hallucinating drugs in the lamps to induce trances and compel the artists to work for long, half-conscious hours in oxygen-starved surroundings? So far we do not know, but chemical analysis of what is left in the shallow saucers might conceivably cast some light on the subject. And did the shamans also use drugs during the religious ceremonies that took place in the caves?

Whether or not drugs were used on the underground artists, they certainly had to work under miserable conditions. Darkness, smoke, lack of fresh air, eternal dampness, cold, awkward, cramped positions, possible rockfalls or floods, encounters with cave bears, and the chance of getting lost in the maze of twisting tunnels were some of the unpleasant circumstances that were routine for Paleolithic painters. It is a wonder that the pictures—of the animals at least—are as sane and normal as they are. The pictures of people seldom were, as will be seen.

THE TECHNIQUES were simple. Engravings were incised in the rock with pointed flint burins, some of which have been found near the pictures they made. Occasionally the engraved outlines were filled in with color. Many of the paintings consist only of black or red lines drawn on the rock surface. Others are more elaborate, but the palette was necessarily limited. Besides black and red, yellow was also used. Brown appears as a mixture, although perhaps not a deliberate one.

These were the original colors, but chemical changes may have altered some of the pigments so that they now seem purple, violet, mauve, and white in certain places. And almost everywhere, especially near the cave entrances, where light, moving air, and temperature changes could get at them, the colors have faded and are fading still.

The pigments were made by pounding or grinding mineral oxides in hollow stones or on the shoulder blade-bones of large animals. When the material was reduced to a fine powder it was mixed with fat, blood, or urine to produce a thick paint that would adhere to the walls.

The figure to be painted was first sketched on the rock

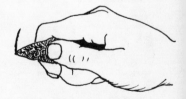

Scratching a line on rock with a flint burin

137

surface with a pointed flint that left scratched outlines. Later, crayons made of solid pigments were used. Some of them have been found. We also have some small, flat stones on which preliminary sketches were made.

It is possible that some of these prehistoric artists had what is called eidetic ability, which would have enabled them to project the image of a previously observed object on a blank surface and then trace its outlines accurately. A modern study of eidetics was made in 1933 by the German scholar, E. R. Jaensch.

This remarkable ability is now quite rare, but it may have been commoner in ancient times. Some of the Cretan artists are believed to have had it. If the early cave artists did, it must have been exceedingly useful and would go far to explain why these early painters, who lived before the traditions of art had yet crystallized, were able to do such good work in depicting the animals that were contemporary with them.

AT LASCAUX, color was at first applied by dabbing large dots of pigment on the surface and then filling in the space between the dots. This early method was followed by a more advanced one in which extensive areas were covered by applying the pigment with pads of moss or lichen. Details were then added by brushes made out of tufts of hair. Sticks with the ends slashed or hammered out to produce fibers also served as brushes. Sometimes color was blown on by using hollow bones or reeds as air guns.

What we know about Paleolithic art techniques has been established by analyzing the paintings and the few remaining tools. We cannot be certain that we are right, but artists who have examined the pictures agree that they could have been made in the ways described. No contemporary drawings exist that show the cave painters at work, nor is it likely that any will ever be discovered, because they concentrated on their work and not on themselves. They were truly dedicated, perhaps more so than any artists who have lived since.

Ochre crayons used by the cave artists

Not art but magic of some kind was what mattered. The cave painters did not hesitate to put one picture on top of another, and sometimes they retouched the older ones. What they did was surely not accidental or casual. There must have been a purpose to it.

138

Closely connected with superimposition is the more primary problem of why the first picture was placed just where it was. Leroi-Gourhan has showed that certain kinds of pictures were nearly always put in certain well-agreed-upon positions. Was it felt that one spot possessed more magic, more power than another? If so, then it was obviously better to put more pictures in the same desirable location even if they had to be placed over those already there.

The pictures range in size from quite small ones (usually engravings) to very large ones, which are nearly always paintings. Some in Lascaux are more than life-size. They have been drawn freely by expert hands, and everything about them shows that their creators knew their subjects extremely well. Most of us are so used to glancing quickly at men and animals that we do not know what it is to study intensively the shape, motion, and behavior of living creatures. But Paleolithic hunters did this professionally. They waited long hours in ambush; they noted and remembered the places where their quarry gathered or passed by; and because they had been doing this ever since they were old enough to be allowed to hunt, they knew the beasts they were after better than any hunter with a gun does now. They were more expert than their modern counterparts because they lived, dreamed, talked about, and gave their undivided attention to the creatures that meant so much to them. In those days men and animals were linked together by a powerful psychic bond. The beasts that were hunted were more than prey, more than food; they took on a mystical quality that was associated with art, religion, and sex. We have divorced ourselves from that world now and are perhaps the poorer for it. It had a oneness, an integration that we lack.

Palle Lauring (1957, p. 25) said of the Paleolithic hunter that he "must have eyes like a lynx, ears like a cat, and a nose like a wolf: he must know the tracks of animals in the grass, the habits of the deer at sunrise and at midday, the watering places, the rhythms of nature. And the hunter does not go through the same seasonal round year after year; he can never be sure that the same situation will repeat itself, can never be certain that wolves and bears will react as he expects. He needs a cool head, steady nerves, and a swift and unerring eye. A hunting culture never grows indolent, except when made to degenerate by contact with higher cultures."

Every observer of wild animals knows that when the animals remain absolutely still they blend into their background so perfectly that it is almost impossible to see them until they move. Prehistoric hunters had to learn how to separate these forms from the surrounding foliage, grass, rocks, and protective shadows. To do this he had to know exactly what the creature he was seeking looked like—its size, its color, and the details of its anatomy.

Sometimes, when he was not certain that what he thought he saw was real or not, the hunter noticed that natural inanimate forms could be deceptively lifelike. Stones, branches of trees, or just insubstantial shadows could take on what seemed to be the shape of an animal. From these observations he learned that such images could be formed in his own mind. He undoubtedly dreamed about animals at night; now he discovered that he could conjure them up when he was wide awake. While he waited in ambush he may have scratched pictures of them in the dust. And he may have used such pictures to teach young boys what animals in the field looked like. Some ingenious shaman may have decided to make more permanent use of such talents by having the earth-drawing artist put his pictures on the well-protected walls of caves.

*Human faces carved
by wind (Corsica)
and by water (Brittany)*

Anyone with a good visual imagination can see pictures in natural objects. Clouds often provide such inspiration. "Sometime we see a cloud that's dragonish," said Shakespeare in *Antony and Cleopatra*. And Hamlet jested with Polonius about a cloud "that's almost in the shape of a camel," only to change it capriciously a moment later to a weasel and then to a whale. The Rorschach test uses shapeless blobs of ink to bring out hidden impulses of the subconscious mind. A modern painter may create images he had not purposely intended to record. At all levels the human mind is a clever deviser of imaginary shapes, and sometimes it gets inspiration from natural objects. Campfire flames must have supplied prehistoric men with dancing images as they still do for us.

A walk along a beach will provide many objects that resemble men or beasts. Boulders and cliffs may have been

140

shaped by wind or water into lifelike forms. The pink granite coast of northern Brittany has great sea-carved rocks that look like giant pigs, squids, and other animals. Men's faces appear there, as they also do in the wind-eroded rocks of Corsica.

Natural objects like these must have given prehistoric men the idea that they too could create such images. In some cases they took a piece of material that already had a somewhat lifelike shape and then worked on it to make it seem even more real. What they did, of course, applies to two-dimensional figures as well as to sculpture in the round.

Shadow shapes made by the sun or a fire can be outlined by a bit of charcoal. Millions of such pictures may have been drawn in unprotected places where they were soon washed away by the rain before man found out that he could preserve them by putting them on a sheltered wall inside a cave.

It could not have taken him long to learn how to apply color to the outlines on the cave walls, for he had been putting pigments on impermanent materials like wood, bark, and leather as well as on his own skin. Since all these substances have perished we know nothing about painting before the cave murals were made. Only they remain to show us the near-beginnings of art.

These early hunter-artists were true pioneers who had no body of older work to guide them, so they had to make their own rules and establish their own conventions. Most of their figures are drawn in profile, as were those in the much later Egyptian art. It is easy to see why, for it is far simpler to render a face or a figure in profile than it is from any other point of view. The next easiest is the straight frontal view, which is sometimes found in prehistoric art. Hardest of all is any kind of angle view.

Two-dimensional pictures introduce problems of perspective and apparent distortion. Paleolithic artists had an ingenious way of handling this. They presented the body of an animal in profile with the horns and hooves shown frontally. Breuil called this "twisted" perspective. The modern observer gets used to it so quickly that he soon takes it for granted. There is no reason why he shouldn't, for it is an agreed-upon convention just as linear perspective is, which came in during the fifteenth century A.D. Before then, artists

used other tricks. The Egyptians, for instance, would show a pool laid out flat with trees growing out straight from the four sides while a human figure stood outside to dip a jar into the water.

The cave painters had little or no interest in backgrounds. Sometimes there is a line or lines which may or may not indicate the horizon. Plants and leaves sometimes appear but as ornaments complete in themselves rather than as backgrounds.

Composition, as we know it, did not exist in prehistoric art. The axis to balance the right and left sides of a picture was then unknown. So was the horizontal as such. Circular forms rather than angular predominated, while the right angle itself did not exist except by accident. But pictures did not just happen, they were planned. The artists who planned them, however, had rules that were unlike ours, rules which we are just beginning to understand. And it must always be remembered that the cave murals were created over very long periods of time and usually by many people. Nevertheless, there is order in them, even if we do not immediately grasp it.

We can look and admire, for the pictures were made by men who were not very unlike us. What we see is not alien. There is a human quality to it that should appeal to us.

142

One thing that is quite understandable is the way that Paleolithic artists indicated movement. The positions of the animals' legs show that they are almost never standing still. Sometimes they are crouching and getting ready to spring, or they are running full speed, leaping, or falling. Lascaux has a frieze of swimming deer and a picture of a horse falling from a height. In the later art of the Spanish rock shelters almost every figure is shown in violent motion.

Our sophisticated modern eyes, trained by looking at futurist paintings like Giacomo Balla's dog with multiple tails and feet, may see movement in Paleolithic pictures where the artist did not intend it. This is particularly true of the boar on the Altamira ceiling. He seems to have eight feet and, therefore, like Balla's dog, might be supposed to be running. But a more careful examination shows that a later boar has been painted over an earlier one, thus adding four feet to the four that were already there.

The eight-legged boar of Altamira

*Balla's "Dog on a Leash"
[Buffalo Fine Arts Academy;
George F. Goodyear]*

Reindeer bone inscribed 35,000 years ago in Czechoslovakia and believed to be a lunar calendar

The Tuc d'Audoubert clay bisons [Collection Musée de l'Homme]

PALEOLITHIC PAINTING, at its best, is very good and could be placed alongside most modern pictures and not suffer by comparison with them. Paleolithic sculpture, however, seems less successful. It can be argued that its makers had nothing but stone tools to work with, but so did many other people who managed to carve beautifully shaped statues out of solid rock long before the superiority of metal tools was known.

Paleolithic sculptors had a far longer tradition behind them than Paleolithic engravers and painters did, for men had been handling flint for hundreds of thousands of years and had become quite adept at making it take the form they wanted it to. After that long experience, shaping stone—and fairly soft stone—should have been easy. Yet most Paleolithic bas-reliefs are crudely made, and free-standing statues were never attempted except in miniature form. Even the two clay-modeled bisons in the Tuc d'Audoubert Cave are only two feet long.

Large and impressive bas-relief friezes do exist. One of the best is the rock shelter of Cap Blanc in Périgord. Here the figures are nearly life-size. There are six horses, some small bison, and what seems to be a reindeer or a bull. Weathering has damaged some of the carvings so badly that it is hard to make them out, yet traces of color remain to show that they were once brightly painted, just as nearly all sculptures were for thousands of years to come.

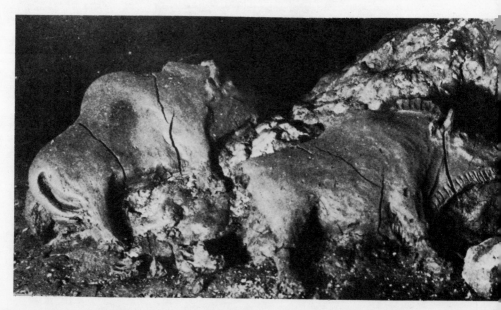

The bas-reliefs of humans found in the nearby rock shelter of Laussel are more crudely carved than the animals of Cap Blanc, but they are of great interest. The one of a woman holding a cow horn has the exaggerated sexual features of the Venus figurines that have been found all over Europe.

Most large Paleolithic statues are rather static, but many of the small ones vividly depict action and motion. The sculptors were masters at carving tiny animals in bone or ivory; they could also engrave them well. Their figures usually portray animals realistically, but some reduce the basic shapes to abstract forms. The deeply carved bones found at Isturitz in the Pyrenees are probably more than merely decorative; their geometric patterns surely have some meaning.

Certain pieces of bone incised with lines or checkmarks seem to be tallies of some kind. The theory that they may be careful records of the phases of the moon was advanced by Alexander Marshack in an article in *Science* for November 6, 1964. He believes that countless numbers of such records exist and that they preserve lunar observations made over thousands of years. Compare this with the suggestion made by Gerald S. Hawkins in *Nature* on October 26, 1963, and in his book, *Stonehenge Decoded,* in 1965. He maintains that Neolithic Stonehenge was a cleverly designed astronomical observatory that specialized in predicting eclipses. Only time and further study can prove or disprove the idea that man learned astronomy before he learned how to write.

PALEOLITHIC MAN was further advanced in his art than in anything else that has come down to us. He may have been equally skilled in music, the dance, and in poetry, but whatever he accomplished in those areas is forever lost. The value of his pictorial and sculptured art, however, is beyond question.

S. Giedion, in his book *The Eternal Present: the Beginnings of Art* (1962, p. 538), says: "The complete freedom and independence of vision of primeval art has never since been attained. . . . Whether one looks at the Hall of the Hieroglyphs of Pech-Merle, with its intertwining figurations, or at the Altamira ceiling, with its powerful sequence

12. WHEN AND WHERE THE PAINTINGS WERE MADE

One of the deeply carved Isturitz bones

The Venus of Laussel [Collection Musée de l'Homme]

*The two-horned
"unicorn" of Lascaux
[French Government
Tourist Office]*

of animals intimately associated with indecipherable symbols, the space conception of primeval art remains the same. It is not chaos. It approaches rather to the order of the stars, which move about in endless space, unconfined and universal in their relations."

13. Subjects and Techniques

SINCE THE CHIEF SOURCE of Paleolithic people's food was obtained by hunting the wild animals that were then plentiful in Europe, it is not surprising that the commonest subjects in their art are the creatures they were concerned with most. Sometimes the artists created imaginary beasts. One of the most famous is the so-called unicorn (with two horns) that stands just inside the entrance to Lascaux.

Pictures of human beings are not only scarce, they are notably inferior to those of animals. They are so much inferior, in fact, that it seems as though they were deliberately made that way. An artist who can draw a horse well can surely draw a man reasonably well—if he wants to. Some taboo or other mental barrier may have prevented the Paleolithic artists from doing justice to the human face or figure.

The pictures of animals are more or less realistic, the portraits of humans somewhat less so. Abstract patterns appear in the cave paintings and even more often in mobiliary art. Some abstract figures apparently have definite meanings, particularly the tectiforms, claviforms, and other marks mentioned in Chapter 11. The word "tectiform" comes from the Greek root that means builder. It was adopted because some of these symbols seem to represent huts or tents. They also might represent traps or snares. Leroi-Gourhan believes that they are female sex symbols. Claviform comes from the Latin word meaning club. This, he says, is a male sex symbol.

These abstract figures are forerunners of the written word, for they are obviously intended to convey a direct meaning and are evidence of man's efforts to communicate with other men, or with gods.

The cave pictures may seem easier to understand, but they, too, have their mysteries. There is certainly much more to them than there appears to be. A few—very few—portray scenes. One of these is in the Shaft of the Dead Man

147

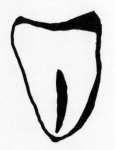

*A vulva incised in rock
at La Ferrasie*

Jolly satyr of Le Portel

at Lascaux; another is the ritual scene at Les Trois Frères; while there is a multifigured combat in the Addaura Cave near Palermo, Sicily. All these have men in them, but there are others in which only animals appear. Some show them in action like the one of the swimming deer at Lascaux. The two clay figures of bison in the Tuc d'Audoubert Cave are about to couple.

Prehistoric people had no inhibitions about sex in animals or men. Human sex organs are often carved on the walls of caves; bone or ivory phalluses are common, and the Venus figurines nearly always have the sexual features emphasized. Depictions of human beings coupling are rare, but they exist. They may occur more often in abstract forms that we have not yet learned to interpret.

Almost without exception, the women portrayed in prehistoric art are mature and notably stout. Since such corpulent women could not have gotten around easily in times when quick movement was needed for survival, they were either carefully guarded priestesses or unreal idealizations of creatures that the artists would liked to have had as sexual partners.

Male figures occur, but they are scarce, and they seldom emphasize sexual characteristics. There is one in the Pyrenees cave Le Portel, however, which shows a bearded man painted on the wall with a protuberent stalagmite serving as an erect penis.

This trick of incorporating an existing natural form into a work of art was fairly common. One of the best examples is the figure of a wounded bison engraved on the floor of the Pyrenees cave Niaux. Here the artist has made use of a small hole produced by water dropping from the ceiling to

*The Niaux bison with a
water hole for an eye*

148

serve as an eye for the beast that was drawn around it. Other holes represent wounds from which engraved barbed darts project.

Rounded rocks were sometimes made to represent the hindquarters of large animals. The uneven surfaces of the ceiling in Altamira gives an extra dimension to the animals painted on it. In Pech-Merle two big stalagmites with long streamers of calcite hanging from them look so much like mammoths that they may have inspired the artists who decorated the cave to make others like them.

Pech-Merle also has figures made by running a finger through the soft clay on the ceiling. These are called meanders because the lines wander casually around like a river flowing through level ground. Other examples of them can be seen in Baume-Latrone and Gargas.

Some of the figures in the caves were evidently put there to insure success in the hunt. The Montespan Cave in the Pyrenees has the clay figure of a bear about three feet long. It never had a head because the hide of a bear complete with skull was stretched over it. Pieces of a bear skull were found lying between the paws when the statue was discovered. This artificial bear was apparently used as a target in a ritualistic ceremony, and the clay is still riddled with holes made by the spears that were hurled at it.

Montespan also has a wall panel of a hunting scene in which an engraved horse is penetrated with javelin marks.

This clay figure in Montespan was covered with a bear's hide and used as a target for spears. When found, a bear skull was lying between the forepaws [Collection Musée de l'Homme]

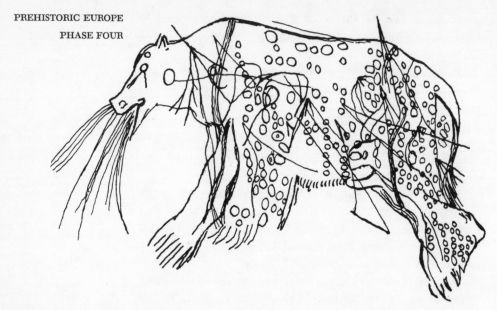

*Engraving of a wounded
bear spitting blood,
in Les Trois Frères
[After Breuil]*

Nearby, in Les Trois Frères, are two engraved bears which have been stabbed so many times that they are vomiting blood.

Marks left by their spears are not the only personal evidence left by the prehistoric men who visited these caves. Their footprints are still there, sharp and clear, perfectly preserved in the clay floor that is protected from time and the elements. Niaux, Pech-Merle, and Aldène all have such footprints. And in Pech-Merle there are also the marks of a staff or cane made in the floor when some prehistoric visitor walked in.

Many caves have human hands imprinted or silhouetted on the walls. The desire to leave such marks seems to be universal, for they are also found in Africa, Australia, New Guinea, Yucatan, and the American West. In the French Pyrenees, Gargas has so many that it is sometimes called the Cave of the Hands. Both meanders and hands are believed to be very early in the evolution of prehistoric art, for it did not take much skill to produce them. A hand dipped in color and pressed on the wall will leave a clear imprint, while pigment blown from the mouth, either directly or, better still, through a hollow bone or reed, will leave a nicely outlined silhouette.

*Outlines of a hand made
by blowing pigment on it,
in Castillo*

Many of the hand marks made by primitive people

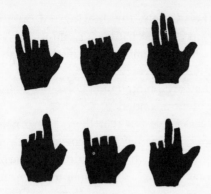

throughout the world show that some of their makers'
fingers were missing, wholly or in part. We have no way of
telling whether such mutilation was accidental or deliberate,
but we do know that purposeful mutilation has been widely
practiced among the various savage and semisavage tribes
of the world. Sometimes it was done to the fingers of infants,
sometimes to those who were about to undergo the rites of
puberty, and perhaps most often to those who wanted to
make an offering of thanks to their gods for a favor granted
or a danger averted.

*Positive impressions
of mutilated hands,
in Gargas*

This does not mean that we can take it for granted that
all prehistoric men thought and acted in the same way.
They may have, and they may not have. But there are plenty
of mutilations in the ancient handprints in the caves. Speaking of Gargas, where there are more than 150 such prints,
Geoffrey Grigson says (1957, p. 152) that the mutilations
are of different kinds: "The top portions are missing on
some hands from four fingers, on some from three fingers up
to the forefinger, on some from little finger and third finger,
on others from second finger and third."

A LINK between small and large, between *art mobilier* and
the cave murals, is the hand-sized stone on which prehistoric
draftsmen engraved drawings. Perhaps one particular stone
had some special magic, for they often put one sketch on
top of another until the surface is covered by a wild tangle
of twisted lines that make no sense to the casual observer.
But there is a whole gallery of art there with the pictures
stacked together like a pile of transparent paper with drawings on each sheet. Such papers, of course, can easily be

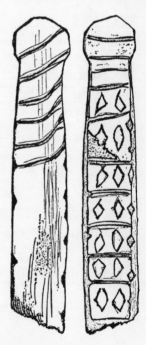

*In 1875 Lartet
thought that these were
tally-sticks [Lartet]*

151

A realistic-looking bird engraved on a piece of antler, from Isturitz

separated. Fortunately, the drawings on the stone can too, although it takes some patience to do it. The stone is photographed; then a number of prints are made, and each desired drawing is preserved on one of these, while all the unwanted lines are painted out. The same technique is used for unscrambling meanders.

It has been suggested that there are so many drawings on the stones because they were covered with blood or pigment before each sketch was made. The sharp flint burins would then cut through the temporary covering and leave indelible marks on the surface of the stone. The artist therefore never saw the tangled lines underneath. If this method was used, we have inherited the jumble and have to sort it out by restoring the original drawings one by one.

These sketch stones, with their multiple drawings, should not be confused with the engravings on *art mobilier*. They ordinarily contain only one picture.

THERE CAN BE no doubt that the sketch stones—and *art mobilier* too—had special meanings. Basically they must contain messages that are similar to those on the much larger cave murals. It is possible though that the miniature

Part of the frieze in the great mammoth chapel of Pech-Merle [French Government Tourist Office]

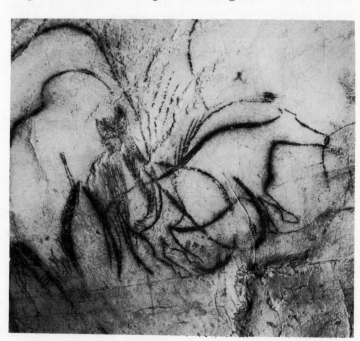

pictures differ in essence from the bigger and more formal ones. They are more likely to deal with homelier themes and more personal expressions.

Leroi-Gourhan has made a statistical study of the frequency with which various animals were portrayed in *art mobilier*. Ranking in this order, they are: horses, bison, reindeer, ibex, does, cattle, male deer, humans, bear, and fish. Far behind these are felines, birds, mammoths, and rhinoceroses. Direct representations of human female sex organs outnumber male nearly seven to one.

A comparison of this with Leroi-Gourhan's analysis of areas where such animals were placed in cave art (see p. 134) shows certain correlations. Bison and horses take top positions in both lists; cattle rank high; so do human sex organs.

Much more work has been done on cave painting than on *art mobilier*. This highly interesting field still awaits a patient researcher who may come up with some revealing and important information about prehistoric man's ways of thinking and of expressing his thoughts in tangible form. Many questions remain unanswered. Which animals, for

The head of a wild horse, in Montespan. To make pictures as lively as this, the artist had to observe his subject closely

The decorated end of a spear-thrower made of reindeer antler. The now headless animals are believed to be ibexes. From Les Trois Frères [Collection Musée de l'Homme]

153

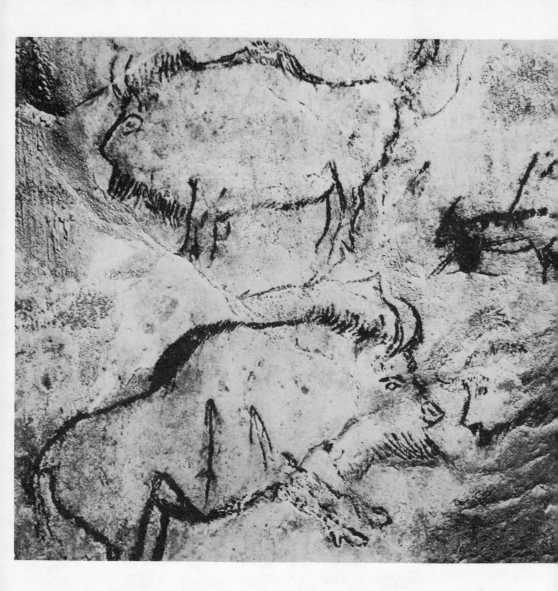

Bison in the "Black Hall" of Niaux. The lower one is wounded; so is the ibex at the right [French Government Tourist Office]

instance, were sculptured most often in the round? And on what substances? Which have bored holes associated with them? How many are associated with human beings? And in what way? These and other questions come readily to mind. Some of the answers should prove to be significant. The direct sexual connotations alone will be more numerous than those found in parietal art, as even a cursory examination of them shows.

Major field discoveries in prehistoric art have been

tapering off in recent years. More time now needs to be spent in making a careful study of what we already have. There may be unexpected treasure lying neglected on museum shelves. Pioneers in interpretation are needed now.

13. SUBJECTS
AND TECHNIQUES

A bone pendant from Chancelade, one of the many pictures that need interpretation

14. Prehistoric Men, Women, and Monsters

PALEOLITHIC PORTRAYALS of people are rare, but they are not as scarce as they were once thought to be. More and more of them have been found. Most were engraved on pieces of stone, ivory, or bone; some were incised on cave walls. Sculptured human figures are fairly plentiful, but painted ones are not. As of this writing, no large and important paintings of people have yet been discovered. The schematic figure in the Dead Man's Shaft at Lascaux is the best known. Humans, however, do become much more common as subjects in the later prehistoric art of eastern Spain.

Some odd questions arise about the people who appear in Paleolithic pictures. A good many of the men seem to be smooth-shaven. How did they manage this at a time when metals were as yet unknown? Did they use sharp flakes of flint or obsidian? Their hair has been roughly trimmed, and the women have carefully arranged headdresses.

Hybrid animals followed by a man disguised as a bison. From Les Trois Frères [After Breuil]

The way their faces are drawn makes them look more like animals than people. Some look like birds. Was there a taboo against making people look like people? And if so,

156

why was it sometimes—especially near Angles-sur-Anglin—ignored?

It is possible that what seem to be human faces are not real faces at all but masks. In some cases there is no doubt that they are. The famous sorcerer of Les Trois Frères has a human body with a prominent penis, but his face is covered by a furry mask surmounted by antlers and animal-like ears, while a long tail that looks like a horse's protrudes from his rear. In the same cave is a betailed, ithyphallic shaman wearing a bison's head. He is prancing behind two reindeer while he plays some kind of mouth-held stringed instrument with what appears to be a bow. (African Bushmen still do this.) Close examination of the reindeer associated with the shaman shows that they are as odd as he is, for one has human forefeet while the other has a bison's head turned backward to look at the shaman who is approaching her swollen vulva. A third human figure in this cave has a bison's head, a man's hind legs, and a huge penis that is shaped like a bull's.

The most celebrated scene in prehistoric art—the mural in the Dead Man's Shaft of Lascaux [Collection Musée de l'Homme]

157

Other masked—or presumably masked—figures occur in prehistoric art. Perhaps the most celebrated of them is the prostrate victim in the Dead Man's Shaft at Lascaux. This schematically drawn, ithyphallic corpse has a beaked head that makes it look somewhat like the bird that is perched atop a rod stuck into the ground nearby. Some anthropologists believe that this is an early example of totemism.

In addition to the obviously masked figures and those which are hybrids of men and animals, many grotesque human faces appear in prehistoric art. Because of the artists' inhibitions about portraying human beings realistically, we have only a dim idea of what their subjects were actually like. Fortunately, however, at least one fairly realistic portrait has been found—the painted bas-relief recently discovered in the rock shelter near Angles-sur-Anglin. It presents the profile of a young man with a black beard, short hair, and the kind of upturned stubby nose that so often appears in prehistoric pictures of people. This most ancient of all fairly representational portraits has certain features which indicate that it was intended to record the face of an individual and not merely to be a generalized type. The subject's friends may have thought it was a good likeness. Perhaps it was. See illustration on page 101.

Although most prehistoric pictures of human beings make them look ugly by our standards, there are some exceptions. A notable one is the tiny ivory head of a young girl found at Brassempouy in southwestern France in the 1890's. Nearly all such feminine portrayals represent women

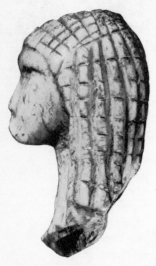

La Dame de Brassempouy
[Musée des Antiquités
Nationales, Saint-
German-en-Laye]

of a mature age, but this one is unmistakably youthful and attractive even though her face is sketchily done and has no mouth. But her stubborn little jaw shows great determination, and her elaborate headdress is one of the first we have to show us what prehistoric women did with their hair. This girl who lived so long ago seems to be a person and not just a symbol, although she may have been that too.

Apparently there was a prehistoric portrait artist—or school of portrait artists—near Angles-sur-Anglin, where the realistic picture of the young man was found, for a number of engraved stones with figures of people scratched on them have been discovered in the nearby grotto called La Marche. They are more realistic than most prehistoric

pictures of human beings. Like the young man, they all have

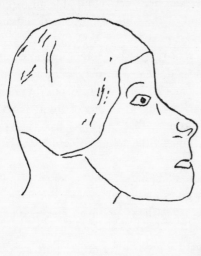

Some of the many realistic portraits of human beings found in the grotto of La Marche [After Lwoff]

prognathous noses that are so long and pointed that they look like snouts. They were all made about the same time, approximately 14,000 years ago. Sometimes the human portraits went beyond bestialization and travesty to become wispy, unreal figures that the French appropriately call *fantômes*.

159

Prehistorians have searched their minds for an explanation of this singling out of the human face for denigration, mockery, and fantastic distortion. Some say that they were not supposed to represent people but totem ancestors, god-spirits, or perhaps local deities who may once have been men and were commemorated for their deeds by having their images put on cave walls or on bits of stone, ivory, or bone. It is possible, of course, that they may have been any one or all of these things. But why caricature the dead heroes?

There is a widespread belief among modern primitive people that a portrait gives an enemy great power over the person represented in it. Perhaps prehistoric men had the same idea.

The argument that the prehistoric artists portrayed humans badly because they lacked experience in sketching them does not make much sense because other creatures like birds, fish, snakes, wolves, lions, and rhinoceroses were seldom depicted, but when they were, they were very well drawn. And they were never ridiculed. Did the artists believe that the beasts of the field and forests were superior to the bare-skinned, slow-moving, and highly vulnerable bipeds who hunted them? Or had the shamans convinced their followers that they were such poor things that they deserved to have their insignificance perpetuated?

ALTAMIRA

LOS CASARES

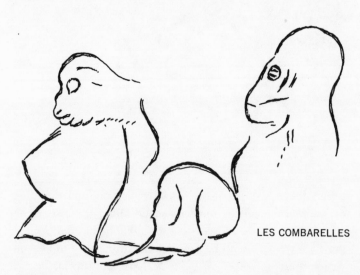

LES COMBARELLES

160

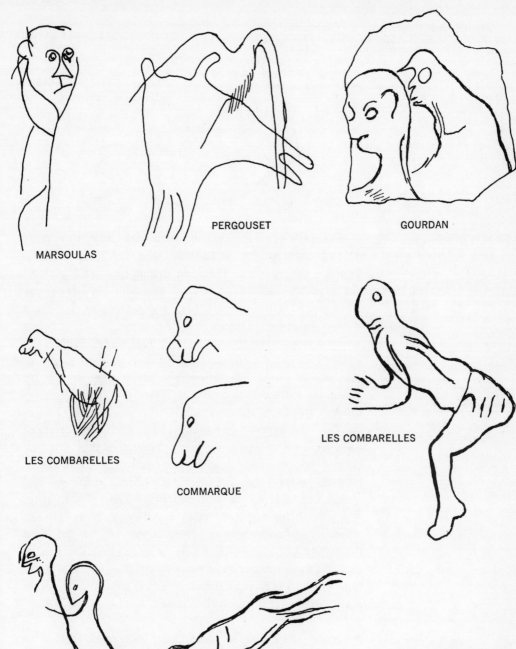

MARSOULAS

PERGOUSET

GOURDAN

LES COMBARELLES

COMMARQUE

LES COMBARELLES

LOS CASARES

Human beings satirized, bestialized, distorted, and made into phantoms

161

Two very feminine figures, carved on the walls of La Madeleine, are associated with pictures of a horse and a bison

Generally speaking, women come out better than men. At Angles-sur-Anglin, for instance, there is a frieze of three Venuses in bas-relief. They are incomplete—and perhaps always were—but they are very real and very feminine. They consist only of bellies, legs, and sex organs, but there is no mistaking what they represent.

Even more seductive are the two bas-reliefs found on the walls of La Madelaine in 1952. (Leroi-Gourhan (1965, p. 289) says of them: "The attitudes in which these women are posed are extraordinary for Paleolithic art; they express a careless freedom which is unique for the period." Unfortunately, the figures have weathered so badly that parts of them have fallen away. But the outstretched legs, pendant breasts, and reclining postures are still intact. They anticipate the graceful statues made by the Greeks of the classical period and embody the sentiments that Keats was to write about the figures on Attic vases, for they are truly "forever panting and forever young." The sculptor who carved these bas-reliefs had conceived a way of portraying the human form that was thousands of years in advance of the still-unborn Mesopotamian and Egyptian artists who were to represent people in stiff and formal poses.

FEMALES, both human and animal, are often shown in Paleolithic art with their bellies distended by pregnancy. Fertility in animals meant more food; in humans, more people. There was a constant need for both.

There has been much dispute in recent times as to whether primitive people know that there is a connection between intercourse and birth. Bronislaw Malinowski has

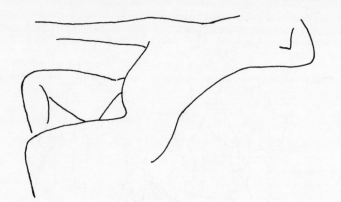

said that the Trobriand Islanders, whom he studied at first
hand, did not realize that there is. But that does not mean
that all primitive people are equally ignorant of biological
cause and effect.

Since Paleolithic art has so much sexual significance,
perhaps that, rather than hunting magic, was its primary
motivating force. Many of the portrayals of men show them
with the penis in erection. The shaman who whips himself
into a frenzy may very well bring on sexual excitement. He
may also have induced it in his followers. Although modern
soldiers deny that going into battle causes an erection, late
prehistoric art often depicts active warriors in ithyphallic
stances, but that may be a convention intended to demon-
strate virility.

One remarkable example of erection in the midst of violence occurs in a scene engraved on the walls of the Addaura cave near Palermo, Sicily. It shows several standing
figures with beaked faces (masks?) intently watching two
naked men who are wrestling while bound together with
cords which are so arranged that they will cause strangulation when pulled tightly. Both wrestlers have erections,
although it has been suggested that they may be wearing
penis sheaths like those now used by certain New Guinea
tribesmen.

The Addaura picture is full of action, full of mystery, full
of many odd things not easy for us to understand. Like the
painting in the Shaft of the Dead Man at Lascaux, this is
one of the few prehistoric pictures that tell a story. Both, in
fact, are among the world's first documentaries. Unfortunately, their meaning is not clear to us, although we can at 163

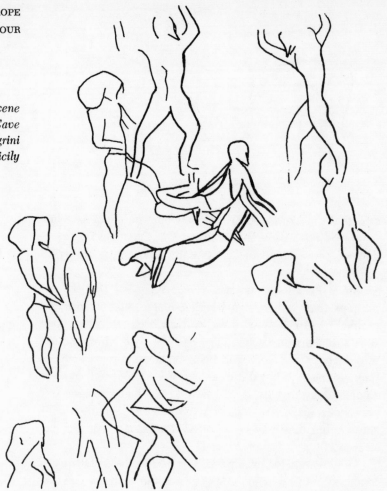

*The engraved scene
in the Addaura Cave
on Monte Pellegrini
near Palermo, Sicily*

least sense part of their significance, for they obviously have
to do with violence.

The Addaura engraving tells us what every hangman
knows—that strangulation will bring on an erection. Wilhelm Stekel, in his book *Sadism and Masochism* (1929, II,
pp. 357*ff.*), makes some interesting comments on this.

THE PREHISTORIC ARTISTS did not always use complete figures
to express sexual ideas; sometimes representation or symbolization of the genital organs was enough. The phallus is
fairly common, but the vulva is commoner still. It appears
164   on cave walls realistically and also as an abstract character.

(See the chart in Leroi-Gourhan, 1965, p. 453, figure 780.) It is possible too that all sorts of sexual symbols were devised and combined with other things so successfully that their meaning has been lost. Many of the symbols are easy to interpret, but it may very well be that we have overlooked some of the subtler ones.

The more we learn about prehistoric art the more we realize that it came from the depths of the unconscious mind. We also have to realize that many thousands of years ago the unconscious mind may have differed from ours. We have burdened it with civilization's fears, desires, ambitions, antagonisms, and other emotions which primeval men had not yet encountered. Basically they were undoubtedly very much like us, but we are so far removed from them that we live in a world that has little in common with theirs. We have broken the links with animals that meant so much to them; made the hunt into a pastime; shut ourselves away from the cold with central heating; insulated ourselves from the hot breath of summer with air conditioning; and turned over the duties of guardianship to professional police and soldiers. But the men who lived nearer the beginning of time were still close to the natural world. Their reaction to it was more direct, and they were surely better than we are in dealing with it. Just as the dog has a keener sense of smell than we have, the pigeon a better sense of direction, and the bat a far superior sense of locating things, so may those ancient men have possessed powers that we do not even know exist. Since those powers are hopelessly beyond our ken it is idle to try to guess what they might be. It is enough to admit to ourselves that the painters who worked for thousands of years in the dark caves may have known more than we do about now forgotten things that were as real to them as radio and sonar are to us.

Their ideas about sex probably were—in some ways at least—very different from ours. Giedion hints at this when he says (1962, p. 89): "The vulva . . . appears constantly, generally alone, but sometimes in combination with the animal whose increase is desired. Such representations of female organs certainly have nothing to do with human sexual instincts, nor do the much rarer representations of male organs."

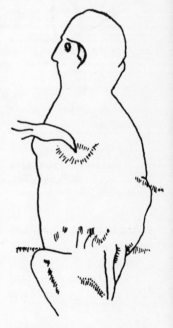

A strange-looking human figure, perhaps hooded, in Le Gabillou

165

PHASE FOUR   OUR VISUAL ARTISTS come closer to paralleling prehistoric thought than any other kinds of creators do, and they have been doing so for a long time. More than 400 years ago Hieronymus Bosch and Pieter Bruegel were painting pictures the shamans would have admired for their vivid portrayals of misshapen monsters mixing with misshapen men. In more recent times Francisco Goya, William Blake, Odilon Redon, James Ensor, Paul Klee, Max Ernst, Salvador Dali, Yves Tanguy, and Pablo Picasso have pictured the farther reaches of the imagination. And now artists everywhere are producing abstractions, distortions, and terrorizations that are even farther out. We, of this generation, are in a better position to understand and appreciate prehistoric art than any of our predecessors were, for we are used to seeing pictures and sculpture that do not attempt to portray visual reality but try rather to express their creators' inmost thoughts. In that we have come full circle and have left the Greek artists of the classical period on the other side.

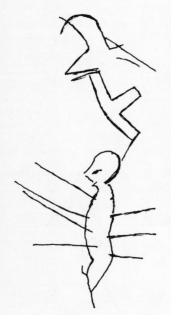

A man, penetrated by spears, and with two tectiforms above him, in Pech-Merle

Masked men, clad in furs and dancing. Engraved on a bâton de commandement *found in the Abri Mège of Teyjat*

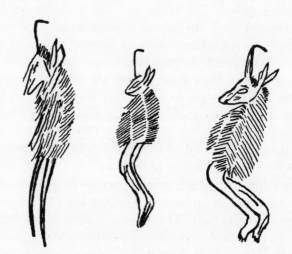

166

15. The Prehistoric Cave-Sanctuaries

WHEN ALTAMIRA was discovered in 1879 people were not yet ready to accept the idea that prehistoric men could create great works of art. Nor could anyone see the Altamira paintings without going to Spain. They were not published until 1906, when they appeared in an expensive limited edition financed by the Prince of Monaco.

Before 1906 the few people who made the trip to Santillana (near Santander) had to visit Altamira under primitive conditions. Even now the lighting is not as good as it is in some of the French sites, and the local guides stress the Painted Hall near the entrance and slight the other less impressive but still very interesting areas.

The Painted Hall, however, rates high in any consideration of Paleolithic art. On its ceiling are more than a score of large, once brightly colored but now somewhat faded images of bison, boars, horses, deer, and even a wolf. The cave has a few human figures, but most of them are hard to make out. So are some of the superimposed animals. But about a dozen of the paintings, mostly those of bison, are strong and clear. They are masterpieces that would rank high in any art.

An examination of the part of the ceiling where the animals are concentrated, which is about 60 by 30 feet, shows that the artists used natural configurations in the rock as part of their design. The most attractive pictures are in polychrome, which after the passage of thousands of years is still notable for its color.

A careful study of the great mural and the areas near it brings out countless small details of overpainted older figures and reveals tectiforms, claviforms, hands, and some indistinct shapes that are difficult to identify. This tangled complex, with its overlays and underlays, obviously took many generations to create. Radiocarbon dating indicates that the artists were at work in the cave about 15,500 ± 700 years ago. How long it took to complete all the decorations

167

can only be guessed at. The style suggests that the work was done over not too long a period, but in prehistoric terms this can mean centuries rather than years. The cave also has some meanders, which are presumably very early.

Altamira has many tectiforms, some of them quite elaborate. And in a few of the deeper passages, natural rock projections have been made to look like masked faces.

Paolo Graziosi (1960, p. 176) said of the animals on the ceiling of the Painted Hall that "in some figures . . . through a subtle application of tones and shading and a skillful blending of colours, chiaroscuro reaches a perfection unequalled by any other primitive form of art. . . . The figure develops with perfect balance and emerges alive and concrete from the surface of the rock. The hair, beard, and fur of the bison have an almost tangible reality, now soft, now velvety, now harsh. Details are emphasized carefully by means of engraved lines. . . . The bison's bulging muscles vibrate under their many-coloured coats, and great folds of skin hang from the throats, breasts, and hips. The few colours that make up the palette of Altamira are combined with taste, and a full scale of shades, from the most delicate to the most vivid, was formed by blending them."

LASCAUX was discovered on September 12, 1940 during the German occupation of France. Work on the cave could not be started until after the war, but there was no doubt that a major cache of great art had been found. Steps were immediately taken to safeguard the underground treasures.

In Chapter 11 it was pointed out that both Altamira and Lascaux were discovered when dogs disappeared into obscure-looking holes in the ground. Most caves, even the Franco-Cantabrian painted ones, are conventional openings into cliffs or steep hillsides, but Lascaux lies under the soil of a slightly sloping bit of woodland. (Pech-Merle is similarly located.)

On this September day four young boys were exploring the countryside near the little town of Montignac, which is about 15 miles northeast of Les Eyzies. When their dog vanished, they noted that he had fallen into a hole that had been made some years before when a storm uprooted a fir tree. One of the lads went down into the hole and found himself in a cave that no one knew existed. Since it had

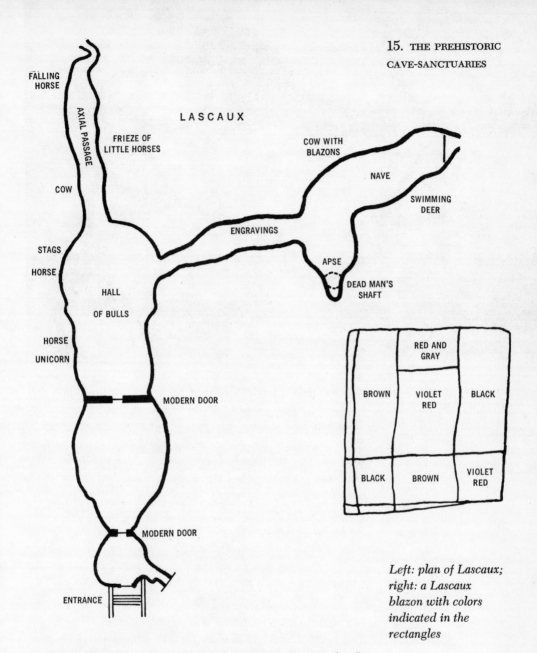

LASCAUX

FALLING HORSE

AXIAL PASSAGE

FRIEZE OF LITTLE HORSES

COW WITH BLAZONS

NAVE

COW

ENGRAVINGS

SWIMMING DEER

STAGS

HORSE

APSE

HALL

OF BULLS

DEAD MAN'S SHAFT

HORSE

UNICORN

MODERN DOOR

MODERN DOOR

ENTRANCE

BROWN	RED AND GRAY	BLACK
	VIOLET RED	
BLACK	BROWN	VIOLET RED

Left: plan of Lascaux; right: a Lascaux blazon with colors indicated in the rectangles

been completely sealed off, its contents were exactly the same as they had been when the last man left it in prehistoric times.

The boys kept their secret for a few days and then told their schoolmaster about what they had discovered. He promptly got in touch with the Abbé Henri Breuil, who happened to be at Brive, which is only 25 miles away. Once

169

that noted prehistorian arrived on the scene on September 21, Lascaux was sure to get the world attention it deserved.

Breuil had injured his eye, and he was soon to go to Spain, Portugal, and Africa, so he could not remain in Lascaux to copy the newly found pictures, important as they were. He suggested that the Abbé A. Glory do the work, a task that was to take many years. (The pictures have also been photographed in color.) Meanwhile, the public could not be admitted to the cave until huge, hermetically sealed doors and an air-conditioning system were installed to keep the atmosphere inside as constant as possible. When the public was allowed to enter, visitors flocked to the cave by the thousands, and Lascaux soon became one of the leading tourist attractions of France. After a few years, fungus-covered spots began to appear on the paintings, apparently caused by the breath or body exudations of the visitors. In order to save the murals, Lascaux was closed on April 16, 1963.

SEEING the paintings in Lascaux is a great experience, comparable to visiting one of the leading museums of the world. In a way it is more than that, more like entering Rem-

170

brandt's studio immediately after the artist had left it for the last time. And, to make the parallel more exact, all his pictures, finished and unfinished, would have to be there.

Most painted caves require a guide to point out the details of the decorations, for they are often obscure, confusingly tangled together, or badly faded. There are superimpositions in Lascaux, and some difficult-to-see engravings, but the general effect of the cave is overwhelming. Everything is sharp and clear; the colors sparkle; the huge beasts are all recognizable; and one feels that here, more than anywhere else, Paleolithic art reached its greatest perfection.

The cave is entered through the great Hall of the Bulls, a low-ceilinged chamber about 100 feet long by 33 feet wide. Its walls and irregularly shaped roof are covered with paintings of wild bulls (aurochs), horses, deer, and other large animals. To the left of the entrance stands the strange-looking misnamed "Unicorn," an imaginary creature with a gravid belly, sides marked by big oval spots, and a non-classifiable animalian head from which two long, straight horns project. Efforts have been made to compare its head with that of the Tibetan antelope (Panthalops), but this seems far-fetched. Its creator may have been illustrating a dream rather than anything real.

From the Hall of the Bulls two long, narrow passages lead off, one straight ahead and the other, larger one to the

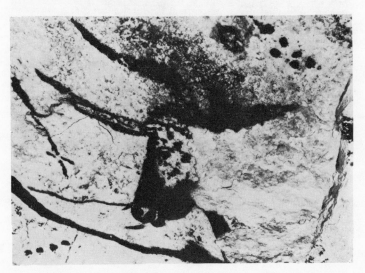

This shows how pigment-covered slabs have fallen from the paintings in Lascaux's Hall of Bulls [French Government Tourist Office]

171

right. The left one has the famous falling horse at the end of it; the right one has engravings as well as paintings, and near the end is the picture of the swimming deer. Just before that is the Shaft of the Dead Man. Since this can be seen only by going down into a deep pit by ladder, the public was not admitted to it even when the cave was open to visitors. In ancient times, however, many people descended into the narrow shaft, for its upper edge is worn smooth by the passage of their bodies.

On the wall near the bottom of the pit is painted the most famous of the few scenes ever depicted in Paleolithic art. A huge bison with a spear through his hindquarters is

The painted roof of Lascaux's Axial Passage [French Government Tourist Office]

172

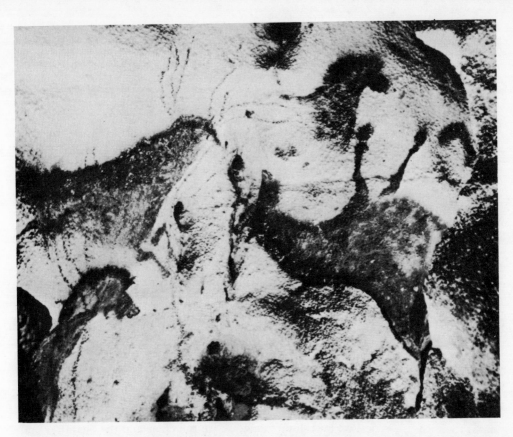

disembowled but is still standing with his head bent side-ways. Lying on the ground in front of him is the stiffly drawn body of a man with an erect penis. A broken neck or backbone would cause the erection, but it may be the customary indication intended to show the sex of the person portrayed. A bird perched on a pole stands nearby, while what may be a spear-thrower lies on the ground. To the left is a two-horned rhinoceros that seems to be casually wan-dering away. Since it is painted in a very different style it may have had nothing to do with the hunting accident. The man's head has a pointed beak that is very much like the bird's. (See illustration on page 157.)

Lascaux is rich with the abstract symbols of Paleolithic art. Among them are a few called blazons, which are fairly large rectangles, engraved or painted or both. The care lav-ished on making them seems to indicate that they are of special importance. Their position in the cave and their as-

The falling horse at the end of the Axial Passage [French Government Tourist Office]

173

sociation with certain kinds of animals may offer clues to their meaning.

Although most of the Lascaux paintings are in very fine condition, they are by no means perfect. Even when they were first discovered it was noticed that good-sized pieces of the pigment-covered walls had fallen away. And there was a certain amount of water damage. But the over-all impression made by this outstanding cave-sanctuary is overwhelming. The emotional impact produced by these age-old paintings is like that caused by the Sistine Chapel, to which this much earlier decorated temple is often compared.

ALTAMIRA AND LASCAUX are the most celebrated painted caves yet discovered, but there are many others that are almost as interesting. Pech-Merle, which is near Cahors and only about 75 miles southeast of Les Eyzies, is one of the best. Geoffrey Grigson (1957, p. 89) has said that it is "strong, deep-coloured, dramatic, enormous, one of the few painted caves of the dimensions of a cathedral. . . . Inside this cathedral I have felt . . . as if I were making my roundabout secret way by clerestory gallery, by passages between the walls and in the walls, by openings, and by newels, past Gothic stalactites and diaper work and mouldings and stony foliage . . . to the choir and the chantries and the Galilee and the extravagant Lady Chapel."

As this description indicates, Pech-Merle is as famous for its beautiful calcite formations as it is for its Paleolithic art. Its decorations were made over a long period, for it has many early meanders. In a tangle of scrawled lines on the

The pig-tailed meander woman of Pech-Merle

174

ceiling of what is known as the Hall of the Hieroglyphs are mammoths, bison, an ibex, and other creatures. Almost lost among them are three large figures of women with long, pendant breasts. Two have no heads, but the one that has also has a pigtail. This may be one of the world's first representations of human hair, perhaps even earlier than the headdress of the lovely maiden of Brassempouy.

The prehistoric people who used Pech-Merle left many evidences of their presence. There are footprints clearly impressed on the floor; hands are painted on the walls; and in the new gallery, Le Combel, where stalactites that look like women's breasts hang from the ceiling, Paleolithic artists noted the resemblance and touched the points with red pigment to emphasive the similarity.

Great numbers of cave bears lived in Pech-Merle in ancient times. Their bones and skulls once littered the floor of a chamber called the ossuary, while the scratches their nails made on the limestone walls can still be seen.

Pech-Merle is known for many things, but it is perhaps most famous for the two checkered horses that are painted on a smooth stone slab which stands upright near the present entrance. Silhouettes of human hands are associated

The checkered horses of Pech-Merle [Collection Musée de l'Homme]

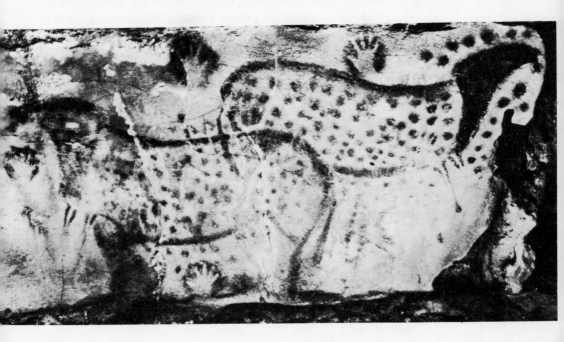

with them, and one of the animals has a barely visible fish superimposed upon its back.

Altamira, Lascaux, and Pech-Merle are only introductory to a list of decorated caves that are worth visiting. Some of the others are:

FRANCE

Dordogne
Cap Blanc (rock shelter with large sculptures) · Les Combarelles (engravings) · Cougnac · Font-de-Gaume · La Mouthe · Rouffignac

Pyrenees
Gargas · Mas d'Azil · Niaux

French caves open only to specialists who must make arrangements in advance:
Montespan · Le Portel · Les Trois Frères · Le Tuc d'Audoubert

SPAIN

Candamo · Castillo · Pasiega · Pindal

As to museums, the great exhibit of prehistoric objects in the Musée de l'Homme in Paris has many fine sculptures and first-rate examples of *art mobilier*. There is an even better collection at Saint-Germain-en-Laye, just outside Paris. The museums in Toulouse and Périgueux have interesting exhibits, as do the small museums in Les Eyzies, Cabrerets, Montauban, and Solutré.

An engraved fish from Spain's Cave of Pindal

16. Later Developments in Prehistoric Art

ART, WHICH BEGAN IN France and Spain and had been practiced there for thousands of years, began to decline in quality. For some mysterious reason the artists lost their interest and their skill. A new kind of mural decoration made its appearance in eastern Spain. The paintings were not placed far inside caves but under shallow rock shelters where they were exposed to outdoor air and sunlight. Fortunately, the Spanish climate is warm and dry, so many murals of this late period are still in good condition.

This late art of eastern Spain is sometimes called Levantine, which is confusing because the word is ordinarily associated with the countries at the eastern end of the Mediterranean. The murals are also called Capsian, which is even more inappropriate because Capsian is derived from Gafsa in Tunisia and is better used to describe North African art.

The content of the pictures gives some clues to their date, for bows and arrows often appear in them. And the numerous human figures are wearing either short skirts or trousers and what seem to be garters. The people are highly stylized and sometimes almost abstract. It is obvious that the murals are much later than those painted in Paleolithic times. Recent attempts to date them indicate that they were made during the period from 12,000 to 7,000 years ago, and that the more abstract ones are even later.

A few of the animals portrayed show the influence of Paleolithic art, for twisted perspective is occasionally used. According to Breuil (1951–59, p. 190), "they have the same graceful silhouette, the same lithe, accurate outlines." Action scenes, which were rare in Paleolithic times, are common here, and they often involve humans. War, which was never depicted in Paleolithic art, is a popular subject, although few men are involved in these skirmishes because the population of Europe was still small, too small to permit major wars. Violent action runs through the pictures; the people are always on the go, and in many cases seem

The bow and arrow make their appearance in art. From Cogul, Lerida; Spain

177

frenetic in their leaps, bounds, gesticulations, and strange posturings.

Not only bows and arrows, but other clues indicate that a strong African influence was at work. Spain is a natural link between the Franco-Cantabrian area and northern Africa. The Tassili rock pictures found in the Sahara are later than the ones made in eastern Spain, but it is entirely possible that earlier African pictures than these had some effect on the Spanish ones. As it is, there is curious similarity between the two in their stark silhouettes, their emphasis on motion, and their choice of subjects. This tradition continued in Africa until fairly recent times, as Bushmen and South African paintings attest.

The whole subject of prehistoric eastern Spanish art has been neglected. It is exceedingly interesting and undoubtedly full of meaning that might cast some light on primitive peoples' ways of thinking, but the literature on it is slight—and is even slighter in English.

One fascinating aspect of this art is the fact that it has many abstract symbols. The later figures of men and beasts become more and more schematic until they lose all connection with reality.

Abstract human figures from eastern Spain. From top to bottom: Cueva del Mediodia dei Arabi; La Sierpe; Covatilla de San Juan

178

*Lively human figures
from eastern Spain.
From top to bottom:
Valltorta; Cueva de los
Caballos; Els Secans;
Gasulla*

179

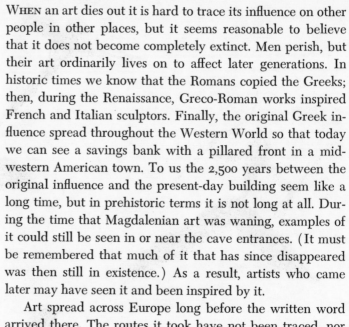

WHEN an art dies out it is hard to trace its influence on other people in other places, but it seems reasonable to believe that it does not become completely extinct. Men perish, but their art ordinarily lives on to affect later generations. In historic times we know that the Romans copied the Greeks; then, during the Renaissance, Greco-Roman works inspired French and Italian sculptors. Finally, the original Greek influence spread throughout the Western World so that today we can see a savings bank with a pillared front in a midwestern American town. To us the 2,500 years between the original influence and the present-day building seem like a long time, but in prehistoric terms it is not long at all. During the time that Magdalenian art was waning, examples of it could still be seen in or near the cave entrances. (It must be remembered that much of it that has since disappeared was then still in existence.) As a result, artists who came later may have seen it and been inspired by it.

Art spread across Europe long before the written word arrived there. The routes it took have not been traced, nor can it be proved that the later work was a heritage from the painted caves of Paleolithic times. But there are certain resemblances in style and subject matter. Research needs to be done in this field just as it needs to be done in trade routes and the migration of symbols.

EXCEPT FOR a few places in Sicily and the south, Italy has little Paleolithic art. The engravings in the Addaura Cave at Monte Pellegrino have already been mentioned. The Levanzo Cave, which is on a small island off the western coast of Sicily, has some strange-looking engravings of quasi-human beings who have hammer heads, as do some creatures portrayed in the Tassili paintings recently found in the Sahara (Lhote, 1958–59, pp. 104–5). Are they masked faces or are they pure fantasies? Whatever they are, it is odd that two widely separated ancient peoples should have such similar grotesque concepts. The Levanzo figures are the only ones of their kind that have yet been discovered in Europe, but others like them occur fairly often in the art of the Sahara.

The numerous outdoor rock carvings found in the Camonica Valley in northern Italy were probably made during the 2,000 years before the beginning of the Christian Era and therefore are not truly prehistoric. But it is interesting to note that they are very much like the older art of eastern Spain in their grouping of figures and in their schematization. So are the late rock carvings of Scandinavia.

Holland and Belgium, according to S. J. de Laet (1958, p. 32), have no prehistoric murals, "although a large number of Belgian caves are very suitable for painted or

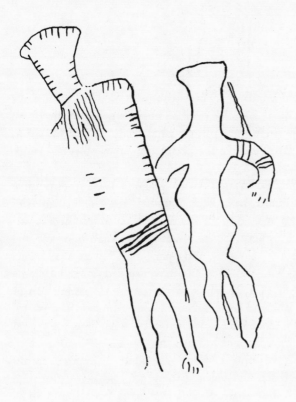

Opposite page: honey gatherers attacked by bees. Above: hunting scene from Camonica Valley; at left: the Levanzo hammer-headed figures; below: hammer-headed figure from Tassili

181

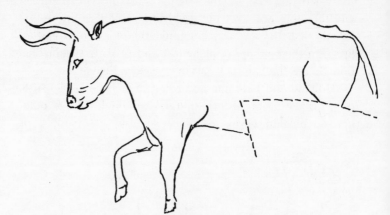

*Aurochs engraved on a
rock slab found in the
Trou de Châleux, Belgium*

engraved decoration." These countries do, however, have some excellent mobiliary art. The small engraving of an aurochs found in the Trou de Châleux is as well drawn as anything discovered in the prehistoric art centers of France or Spain.

England also has no cave art, and only two rather crudely scratched figures have been found there. The British Isles were still connected to the continent then so that access was easy, but life there was so much harder than it was in the Dordogne, the Pyrenees, and Spain, that few settlers came, and those who did may not have stayed long. Grahame Clark (1939, p. 178) has said that the total population of southern England at this time (when the north was still covered by glacial ice) was probably less than 2,000 and may even have been as few as 250.

This scanty populace had to spend all its energies in obtaining food for survival and therefore had very little time for art. The few small objects that have been found show obvious affinities with what was going on in France and Spain, but they are poorly made provincial offshoots of the main stem of Paleolithic art.

Since Scandinavia and all of northern Europe were still covered by vast sheets of ice at this time no one could live there. South of the huge continental glaciers, however, mobiliary art had been made for some time. Small Venus figurines had been carved for tens of thousands of years there and were now being replaced by engravings and other types of sculptures. Isolated examples of such work, of widely

182

*Prehistoric English
engravings.
Above: a horse, Creswell
Crags, Derbyshire;
below: masked human figure,
Pin Hole Cave, Derbyshire
[British Museum]*

varying merit, have been found—in addition to the countries already mentioned—in Switzerland, Germany, Austria, Czechoslovakia, Hungary, Bulgaria, Poland, and Russia.

Cave paintings are scarcer. Clark and Piggott have commented on this (1965, p. 88): "The geographical distribution of cave art is more uneven than that of chattel art, and it is even more markedly concentrated in the west. If its absence from the south Russian plains is understandable enough, this hardly applies to Czechoslovakia, Hungary, Austria and south Germany where plenty of caves are known to have been occupied by Advanced Paleolithic man. This gap is emphasized by recent discoveries in the South Ural district of Russia, a notable centre of Advanced Paleolithic occupation. Here, in the Kapova cave near the south bend of the Bielaya river, an impressive group of paintings has been found, featuring stag, wild steppe-horse, mammoth and cave bear. The significance of this find of cave art, comparable in style with some of those from the Dordogne something like 2,500 miles to the west, is that it emphasizes both the broad homogeneity of the Gravettian culture and its essentially creative character."

Our knowledge about the locales of cave art can, of course, change any day if new finds are made—as they probably will be. And we must not forget that we have only a small fraction of the Paleolithic art that was produced, for the greatest part of it has disappeared. But we know what

183

to look for now and have developed refined technical skills that will help us in the search. It is even possible that we may someday be able to discover painted caves that have been completely buried without leaving any trace of the entrances that once led to them. There, deep inside a mass of undisturbed limestone rock, even finer collections of prehistoric paintings than those found at Altamira and Lascaux may be awaiting discovery.

Simple arithmetic shows that a vast amount of Paleolithic art must have been produced, for men kept working at it for more than 20,000 years. Egyptian art lasted for about 5,000 years, but nothing that man has ever undertaken continued for the enormous stretch of time that prehistoric art did. The artists were few in number, but they kept up their output for so many years that they must have turned out tremendous quantities of pictures and mobiliary art. It has been difficult even for time and weather to do away with everything that accumulated over such a long period of active production.

*A human figure
in animal guise.
From Gasulla, Spain*

184

17. The End of a Great Era

THE PERIOD FROM 40,000 to 10,000 years ago is noteworthy because it was then that mankind showed the first stirrings of the creative ability that was to make it supreme among all the living beings on earth. Neandertal Man had made many cultural advances, among which were respect for the dead, improved food-getting techniques, the use of clothing, more sophisticated tool-making, and the beginning of magic, which was the foundation of religious and spiritual ideas. But *Homo sapiens* rapidly showed signs of being far superior to all the creatures that had preceded him. Art was practically unknown to the Neandertals; *Homo sapiens* made sculpture, engraving, and painting part of his daily life and thus left us revealing records of his existence. Compared to him, all earlier men seem to be pale and shadowy figures that have little in common with us.

His art shows that he not only knew the animals around him exceedingly well but that he had the imagination to devise fantasy creatures which had no real existence. His pictures indicate that he practiced sexual acts with animals. Some people, however, prefer to believe that these are not literal portrayals but wish fulfillments.

Recent interpretation and statistical analysis give us new information about the relative importance assigned to various beasts. Portraits of people suggest that the artists either had a very low opinion of their fellow men or were barred by taboo from making anything but caricatures of them. Their drawings show that they had a good sense of humor. They also give us proof positive that some of their people —probably the shamans—wore masks and animal disguises. Statuary rather than paintings or drawings provide evidence that the Mother Goddess concept was in existence at least as early as the beginning of art.

Poor as these prehistoric representations of human beings are, they at least clothe the bones of their people with flesh. For the first time we can see—even though dimly   185

—what our remote ancestors looked like. Sometimes we even get hints of what they wore as clothes, headdresses, and ornaments.

We have been given this window into the ancient world by artists who cut it through the wall of time. The Neandertals may have been very much like the people who succeeded them, but we have no way of knowing, for they left us no pictorial records. Artifacts can tell a great deal, but art tells even more.

Due honor should be given to the nameless men who worked deep in the dark caves where flickering lamps were their only means of illumination. It should also be given to those who fashioned figures on bits of bone, ivory, and stone. They are our guides to a world that we have only recently discovered. Like gnomes working under the earth, they have provided a foundation for human history.

The true wonder of what Paleolithic artists accomplished is seldom appreciated even by people who have a good knowledge of art. For some inexplicable reason, this gestative period has been relegated to archeology rather than given an essential place in the history of art where it rightly belongs. Perhaps the fact that the paintings are permanently attached to the walls of caves in obscure parts of Europe has caused them to receive less attention than they deserve. Yet they foreshadowed the future. The cave artists, for instance, knew as much about perspective as the Egyptians did. Perhaps they knew even more, for they were not bound by the rigid conventions that the Egyptians were. Giedion has said (1962, p. 534) that the Egyptian artists were hampered by their unswerving allegiance to the "principle of the vertical and the horizontal," while the prehistoric painter had boundless freedom to do as he wished. His figures did not have to stand upright; he could mix large and small ones, and he could deliberately put his drawing on top of a more ancient one without feeling that he was doing it any harm. It had served its purpose, lived out its useful time, and would lose none of its magic by being covered by a new picture that brought more magic to the scene.

The Paleolithic artist anticipated a great deal that our twentieth-century painters think they originated. Like them, he tried to present what was in his mind rather than what

was in front of his eyes. He believed that inner vision is
what counts most, that images from the outer world must
always undergo a transformation when they pass through
the artist's mind.

And, in common with the modern painter, the prehistoric
one depended heavily on symbols. He felt that there was
magic in them, magic that he wanted to put into his work.
To the sensitive observer, what he did has much of that
magic still.

WE SEE prehistoric paintings under very different conditions
from the way they were supposed to be seen—if, indeed,
they were meant to be seen by human eyes at all. There is a
good possibility that they were not, that they were placed
far back in the dark interiors of deep caves where only the
gods could come to view them. Naturally, such superhuman
creatures did not require light to examine the pictures.

Even the mortals who saw the paintings when they were
still fresh on the walls had to look at them in very poor light.
That is how they were supposed to be seen, for dim and
flickering lamp or torchlight was the only kind of illumination that ever entered the caves in prehistoric times. This
was not considered a disadvantage. Much of the pictures'
power came from first catching sight of the great beasts as
they loomed up out of the shadows. Then they moved,
marched, and seemed to come alive. And the darkness
around them was filled with half-sensed, half-glimpsed
things that became momentarily visible when the tiny flames
on the hand-held lamps brought them out of the surrounding blackness and then let them fall back again.

The artists chose the locations of their paintings in such
light and planned everything accordingly. One was supposed to come upon the animals suddenly. When the startled
eyes beheld them, the hand would waver and make the
flame dance. In that uncertain light the monstrous beasts
must have seemed even more frightening than real ones encountered in the field.

Now we have brought powerful illumination into the
caves. Even the minor ones are seen in company with a
guide who carries a flashlight or an acetylene lamp. Bright-
ness is introduced into places that were intended to remain
forever dark. As a result we see the paintings very clearly, 187

perhaps too clearly, for they were not meant to be looked at in such brilliant light.

THE DEEP interiors of the painted caves are eternally silent except for the sound of water falling drop by drop or, in some places, rushing by in underground streams. In a few instances there are waterfalls. Away from the entrance the temperature is constant, summer and winter alike. Daylight never comes, and in that unending black night time seems to have no meaning. There the human mind is close to the dream state. No man-made cathedral, no matter how vast, how dim, how silent, provides so favorable a background for the summoning up of images from the unconscious mind. The setting is ideal for magic. Here the shaman could make his people believe anything he wanted to tell them. Here strange rites and rituals went on. Here everything worked together—shamans, artists, people, and the surrounding darkness all acted as a unified force to make magic real. And to them it was real, as real as the mighty beasts that looked down from the walls. The painted animals, already far older than any living creature and imbued with the magic that generations of men had bestowed upon them, presided over the scene for thousands of years before the ever-waiting darkness finally closed in.

The darkness did prevail. Despite what seems to have been a triumph of religion, power, magic, and art, the force that motivated this long-lived culture weakened, and all that it had produced slowly perished. We do not know why. Perhaps a change of climate was responsible. Perhaps an invasion of less advanced people destroyed this vital culture as it was to do thousands of years later with the Sumerians, the Mycenaens, the Egyptians, and the Minoans.

Archeological evidence shows us that this culture, which had endured longer than any other, did not die out quickly. The Magdalenians were replaced by the Azilians, the Sauveterrians, the Tardenoisians, and others. Paleolithic became Mesolithic, and implements and hunting and fishing techniques were improved, but the great accomplishments of the Paleolithic artists ended, and most of what they had done perished. Only a few of their pictures, safely sealed away in caves, survived to tell us that these gifted creators had ever lived.

Look upon their work and admire. Their pictures mark man's first breakthrough from the unimaginative existence of his savage forebears to a way of life in which there were values other than physical ones. These artists opened the way for culture in its finer sense. Every institution of learning, every library, and every museum in the world owes them a great debt. They made the best things in our lives possible.

PALEOLITHIC did not become Mesolithic overnight, nor did the changes occur at the same rate everywhere. At all times less advanced and more advanced people were contemporary, just as they are now. Savage and savant have always had to share the world.

MENTION must be made here of an important step in the distribution of the human race—man's first entry into the New World. The exact timing of his arrival has not yet been settled, but the date is steadily being pushed back as discovery after discovery is made.

The story begins with a mystery. In 1869, a geologist named C. J. King, who was working near Tuttleton, California, found a broken piece of polished stone, the handle of a pestle perhaps, embedded so solidly in gold-bearing gravel that he had trouble getting it out. Since the gravel, which was overlaid by lava, had been deposited in the Pliocene, the problem of dating the artifact becomes an exercise in improbability. Macgowan and Hester (1950–62, p. 178) point out that if all the circumstances surrounding the discovery are true "we have to face a staggering idea. We have to believe that a strain of *Homo sapiens* originated in the New World long before Java man. We have to believe that he acquired the skills of the New Stone Age far ahead of man in the Old World, and that he then disappeared. It is easier—but not too easy—to think that the lava flowed in recent times, after glacial waters had worked a pestle of early man into the gold-bearing gravels, which would push the seed-grinders of California far, far back in time. It is still easier to believe that King was out of his head." And it is, of course, quite possible that the geologist was mistaken. He also may have been the victim of a fraud. There are dozens of possibilities, nearly all of which are more acceptable than the known "facts." But King was a first-rate scientist who later organized and became the first director of the United States Geological Survey.

Leaving such sensational ideas aside, we are still not on firm ground when it comes to the earliest date for the arrival of the first people to settle in the Americas. We know that they were past the Neandertal stage, which means that they must have come here at some time after 35,000 or 40,000 years ago. This has long seemed to be reasonable enough, for until very recently no claims to such remote dates have been made.

Meanwhile, parts of a human skeleton and a projectile point were dug up in the mid-1960's in the state of Washington. The bones were broken and charred and may have been the remains of a cannibal feast. They were dated to 13,000 to 11,500 years ago, which makes them the oldest yet to be found in the Western Hemisphere. The discovery was called the Marmes Man after the name of the ranch on which the bones were found, and details were made public late in April 1968 (*New York Times,* April 30, 1968). Then, in August, a small, delicately shaped bone needle was found on the same site.

During the same year, another discovery was made in the Mohave Desert 15 miles northeast of Barstow, California (*Science,* May 31, 1968, and *New York Times,* June 1, 1968). Here some crudely chipped pieces of chalcedony that look like primitive pebble tools were dug out of an alluvial fan where they presumably had been deposited 40,000 or more years ago. Some scientists dismissed them as naturally formed stones like the eoliths that had attracted so much attention just before the turn of the century. But Louis S. B. Leakey, who had gained a world reputation identifying the very early tools made by man in Africa, supported the probable authenticity of the find. There the matter rests, but the last word on the Barstow stones has obviously not yet been said.

More possible evidence for man's being in the Americas in very early times comes from the southern end of Chile, where fragmented stones that resemble pebble tools have been found. With them were broken pieces of bone from mammoths and other extinct animals. Charcoal recovered with them dates back to 30,000 to 40,000 years ago (*New*

190

York Times, June 18, 1968). Only more excavation in this area will convince experts that the stones were man-made.

As of now, all that we know about the settling of the Americas is that bands of men crossed the land bridge over the Bering Straits at a time when the sea level was still low because so much water was still frozen in the huge glaciers that covered parts of North America and Europe. Others probably came the same way as long as the bridge was still passable. Then still others—but very few—may have arrived by sea over the centuries. Some could have been storm-tossed waifs who managed to survive the impossible voyage; others may have been hardy navigators who purposely crossed the Pacific or Atlantic Oceans in their frail craft. We have seen in recent years how easy it is to sail a very small boat across the Atlantic. But there is no definite proof of any very early crossings.

However, we do know that men reached South America 14,000 years ago and that a few went on to its southern tip sometime between 11,000 and 8,000 years ago. Most of the established dates for early men in the Americas center around 14,000 to 8,000 years ago. Perhaps the unlikely King and Barstow and Chilean "men" were isolated strays. And, of course, they may not be genuine.

As of this writing it seems that people from northern Asia were settling the Americas at the time when the Paleolithic period was reaching its end in Europe and the Mesolithic was replacing it in some areas. Neolithic cultures were just beginning to come into existence in the Middle East. It was a time of transition throughout the world. Movement, change, and improvement in living conditions mark this point in the evolution of human culture. And man was extending his habitat to take in the entire earth.

R. S. MacNeish offers some interesting dates for New World "firsts" (1965, p. 93). Based on Mexican culture, he says that "it would appear that ground stone mortars and pestles occurred before 7200 B.C., that the first domesticated plants appeared before 5000 B.C., that villages came into existence about 3500 B.C., pottery about 2300 B.C., ceremonialism about 1500 B.C., and polished axes at about 1200 B.C."

These dates are all later than comparable ones for the Old World.

PHASE FIVE

18. The Transition from the Old
to the New Stone Age

THE INTERVAL between Paleolithic and Neolithic culture is called Mesolithic (meso = middle). The term is in common use, but it does not meet with general favor. Even scientists who use the word may refer to the period as the "so-called Mesolithic." And V. Gordon Childe, who was largely responsible for popularizing the name, said (1958, p. 1) that Mesolithic cultures can be "termed Mesolithic, because in time—and only in time—they occupy a place between the latest Paleolithic and the oldest Neolithic cultures."

The word has never had unqualified approval because the transition period between hunting and agricultural cultures is not marked by any notable change in economy. The "so-called" Mesolithic people were hunters and food-gatherers just as their Paleolithic predecessors had been.

Braidwood and Reed (1957, p. 20) say that "the word 'Mesolithic' does have considerable focus in meaning *if* its usage is restricted to those archeological materials of northwestern Europe which indicate various cultural readaptations to the early post-glacial succession of environment in that area. . . . But whether such 'Mesolithic-ness' exists as a world-wide phenomenon, and whether it is different in kind from 'upper-Paleolithic-ness' are quite different matters. We suspect that from a purely subsistence level point of view, there is no difference in kind between the two."

The transition took place while Europe was undergoing a tremendous change in climate, and the huge ice sheets covering the northern part of the continent were beginning to disappear. The warming-up period, which started more than 12,000 years ago, did not go on steadily, but even with

192

several long colder intervals it eventually melted the enormous accumulation of glacial ice. Such ice can melt much faster than it forms.

As the ice receded, its rate of withdrawal built up to nearly a thousand feet a year, and the end of each summer's melting was marked by long lines of stones dropped at the retreating glacier's southern edge. These deposits of stones have enabled scientists to calculate the speed of the glacier's disappearance. The ground left bare became tundra, but only for a while, for forests replaced it as pioneer trees like birch, willow, and pine grew up. Then hazel, oak, elm, lime, elder, and beech took over until vast stretches of woodland covered much of Europe.

While this was happening, the sea level remained low. England was still attached to the continent, and what is now the North Sea was swampy ground. The Baltic Sea remained a fresh-water lake until the ocean finally flooded that great basin with salt water.

Skeleton found in a Maglemosian grave in Barum, Skåne, Sweden [Museum of National Antiquities, Stockholm]

Over a period of thousands of years the level of the ocean was steadily rising. The coastlines changed and so did the courses of rivers that had formerly run far out from what is now the edge of the continent. Land that Paleolithic men had occupied was flooded; some of it is now several hundred feet under water.

The warmer climate that was melting the ice also made drastic changes in Europe's wildlife. The mammoth, the woolly rhinoceros, the giant elk, and the musk ox became extinct, while the reindeer, which had once roamed as far south as the Pyrenees and the Riviera, now stayed all year in the colder northern sections where the weather was more to their liking. The disappearance of reindeer from southern and central Europe during the period from 11,500 to 7,500 B.C. was a serious loss to people who had been largely dependent upon their meat for food and on their antlers for the raw material they had made into many kinds of implements. It is believed that the departure of the vast reindeer herds and the consequent shortage of food reduced the human population of Europe. The ice, even as it vanished, took its final toll.

COMPARED TO the brilliant Magdalenians and the near-civilized Neolithic peoples who were to come, Mesolithic man seems inferior. But he did a great deal to improve the lot of the human race. It was he who gave us new methods of transportation—boats, sledges, and skis. And with boats came new and better ways of catching fish.

*Norwegian rock carving
of a man on skis*

Mesolithic men were the last of the people who were exclusively hunters. Their villages, which were often located on the seacoast to be near good fishing grounds, prepared the way for the larger communities that were soon to come.

We have no definite information about man's first efforts to move through or across water; they probably go so far back that they are forgotten. But hominids surely splashed around in shallow water even while they still had apelike features. Watching animals swim would give later men the idea of lying face down in the water and paddling with arms and legs. A floating log could serve as a support. A tree trunk hollowed out on one side by natural decay would bring about the next step. Then men did their own hollowing out and shaped the tree trunks as they wanted them to

These rock-carved figures of men fishing from a boat—found in Kville, Sweden—are much later than Mesolithic, as is the man on skis on the opposite page. We have no comparable pictures made then

be; in this way the dugout canoe was born. With it one could go almost anywhere as long as the water was fairly smooth and land was in sight.

A dugout canoe found in Pesse, Holland, has been dated by radiocarbon methods to be 9,000 years old. Canoes made of the bark of trees may be just as ancient, but no remains of such perishable light craft have been discovered.

Bundles of reeds were bound together to make the elongated shapes needed for water travel on the Nile. Inflated animal skins were used for the same purpose on the Tigris and the Euphrates, and hides were stretched over frameworks in the British Isles to make coracles and curraghs, which are so seaworthy in rough water that they are still used in some places. In the Far North, where immersion in bitter-cold water could be fatal, practically unsinkable and splash-proof kayaks were eventually developed from the skin-over-frames idea.

At some time and at some place a man stood up in one of these early vessels and noticed that his cloak, spread out wide while a strong breeze was blowing, acted as a sail that moved the boat across the water. Or he may have been transporting a leaf-clad tree, which would have served the same purpose. Boys at play on the water may have discovered the principle of the sail; then their elders took over the idea and adapted it to serious uses. The sail was to take

195

man to new places and eventually open up the world for him. And it was to be the principal motive power for water transportation until the steam engine replaced it in the nineteenth century. Except for short bursts of speed, oars could not compete with sails, for human arms tire while the wind keeps blowing day and night. Then, when mechanization made sailing obsolete, it took its place with the horse and was preserved as a popular outdoor sport.

WATERWAYS were the first roads, and they were in use long before men domesticated animals to draw sledges or pull wheeled vehicles. For the transportation of goods on land, men themselves hauled travois or other primitive load-carrying devices.

Rafts and dugouts developed into planked boats which gradually became larger and larger until they could be called ships. More seaworthy vessels made longer voyages possible. At first, however, water-borne traffic stayed close to shore and seldom ventured to move at night. Experience gave the sailors confidence and taught them where the safest routes were.

Since ships could transport far more cargo than the crew could carry if they tried to move it on land, merchandise and people were taken from one place to another by water. The ships also carried a hidden cargo—knowledge. The people who came ashore were unconsciously acting as missionaries who would plant new ideas in still backward lands. Ships were enormously important, far more important than any kind of land transport was until the railroads came in in the nineteenth century. And they were especially important while they were still so new that one of them, entering a harbor for the first time, could impress the people there with its novelty. To us, these vessels would be considered tiny, but they were then the largest things afloat, so the men on them must have seemed like powerful and supernatural beings, just as the Spaniards did when the Indians saw them for the first time.

BOATS AND SHIPS enabled men to go farther out to sea for fish. Paleolithic man had eaten the few fish he could catch, but Mesolithic man made food taken from the sea a major part of his diet. He had to because large animals were be-

196

coming scarce. The reindeer had gone off to the north of their own accord, but man himself may have been responsible for the extermination of other species. Increased population needed more food; more hunters and improved techniques killed off more animals, eventually making meat harder to obtain. Seafood temporarily filled the gap between hunting and agriculture.

Enough Mesolithic fishing gear has been found to give us a good idea of the methods used. And since much of the gear was recovered from bogs where the moist soil preserves organic material, we have dug up bits of nets, wooden fish traps, spears, and paddles.

Before men made pointed fishhooks they used gorges, which were pieces of stone roughly shaped like a double cone and tied in the middle to the line. These were covered with bait. When a fish swallowed one and got it well down into his stomach, quick work would bring him out of the water before he had a chance to spit the gorge out. This clumsy but fairly effective device is very old, so old that it was in use long before Mesolithic times. But man did not have to wait for the coming of metal to make fishhooks; he carved them out of bone and shell. Fish spears and harpoons were also in wide use.

A fishhook made of flint. Others were carved out of bone
[Danish National Museum]

THE MELTING of the glacial ice took a long time. "About 12,000 years elapsed between the maximum extent of the ice . . . and the final dissipation . . . when the world sea level reached its present *niveau* in about 4000 B.C." (Butzer, 1964, p. 406).

One might think that the warmer climate prevailing in Europe would inspire a rise in creativity and inventiveness, but things did not work out that way. Clark and Piggott summarize the cultural decline that took place (1965, p. 142): "In southwestern France, the centre of the most highly developed culture during Late Glacial times . . . the Azilian culture . . . was in almost every respect inferior to that of the Late Magdalenian which it immediately succeeded and from which it almost certainly sprang. The flint workers developed no new ideas of importance, and their small thumbnail scrapers compared ill with the splendid blade scrapers of their predecessors. The antler and bone industry was greatly diminished. The only significant form to survive

197

was the barbed harpoon-head, made from stag—rather than reindeer—antler and no longer picked out by vigorous incision. A few traces of incised lines and zig-zags on pointed bone objects and the rather pathetic lines and dots painted on river-worn pebbles, the most expressive of which suggest highly developed anthropomorphic forms, are the only sad remnants of the splendours of Magdalenian chattel art. Again, and even more revealingly, though the Azilians almost without exception occupied the self-same caves, they apparently gave up blazoning their walls and roofs with representations of their prey."

The later French cultures, Sauveterrian and Tardenoisian, were even poorer. Their flintworkers specialized in making ever smaller implements (microliths). These tiny bits of sharp flint were used as arrowheads, for the bow was in wide use by this time. The little arrowpoints indicate that they were used for killing small animals and birds. Apparently the skills developed by the mighty hunters who had slain mammoths and rhinoceroses were no longer needed, and the hunters themselves were gone with the huge creatures that had been their prey.

The Sauveterrians seem to have produced no art at all, and the Tardenoisians were equally unproductive. The Azilians left us large numbers of pebbles with enigmatic symbols painted on them. With them, art ceases to be representational and becomes purely schematic. Some of the pebbles have what may be figures of men or animals on them, but they are even more stylized than the markings that were carved or painted on rocks in eastern Spain, northern Italy, and Scandinavia by people who came later than the Mesolithic Azilians.

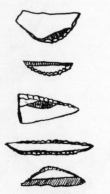

Tardenoisian microliths from Piscop, Seine-et-Oise

The cave of Mas d'Azil that gave this culture its name is a remarkable one, for a river runs through it, and a modern road follows the water's edge. This tunnel-cavern was occupied long before the Azilians took it over, and many Magdalenian objects have been found in it. Still in place in the rocks are mammoths' teeth and the bones of extinct animals.

The painted pebbles for which the Azilians are best known may have more significance than we, at present, are able to comprehend, for we cannot interpret the symbols on them. We do know, however, that ancient men did not create such characters idly. And it is not impossible that

198

Azilian painted figures from Mas d'Azil

they may be links with the tectiforms, claviforms, and blazons of Paleolithic times.

MESOLITHIC people had reached Denmark, and a big swamp there has given the name to one of the major Mesolithic cultures—Maglemosian. The Danish meaning of this word is "great bog." The swamp in question is located on the west coast of present-day Zealand near the town of Mullerup, but the settlement that has told us most about Maglemosian culture is on the east coast of England. A few miles south of Scarborough is the site called Star Carr. When it was excavated in 1949–51 the remains of a 9,600-year-old village were found. The settlement stood on the shore of a now-vanished lake in Yorkshire, and the peat that formed over it preserved the wood and bone artifacts.

Interpretation of what was recovered there indicates that only about 15 to 25 people lived in Star Carr and that they used the place as winter camp and went elsewhere during the warmer months. Nor was the site used very long—perhaps only 12 or 15 years.

The artifacts "include some 2,500 finished or utilized flints, dominated by scrapers, burins, and microliths—minute, carefully retouched bladelets employed as arrowheads or projectile barbs. A number of axes or adzes were also found. Considerable use of bone and antler was made, particularly for barbed antler points, mattock heads, batons (for working flint?), bodkins, fastening pins, and in one case, as a harpoon head. . . . [A fragment of a] wooden paddle was found. . . . Man's modification of or mastery over the environment was no more conspicuous than during the late Pleistocene" (Butzer, 1964, p. 415).

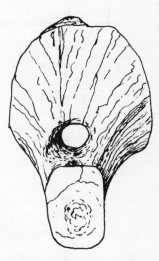

A mattock made from elk antler. Found at Star Carr

199

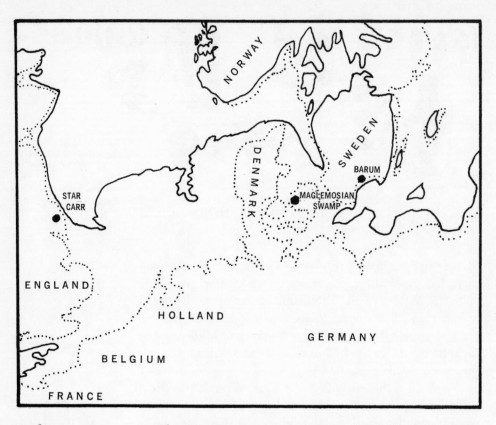

Northwestern Europe in Mesolithic times. Dotted line indicates present-day shores

The Star Carr excavations show that the people who lived there were great users of wood and birch bark. Some of the branches thrown down to fill in the ground and support dwellings have been recovered. Two felled trees still show the marks of the stone axe that chopped them down; they are believed to be the oldest such marks ever found.

THE MAGLEMOSIANS were not an artistic people, but they did engrave a few figures on bone and antler. Human forms appear on two that were discovered in Denmark (Lauring, 1957, pp. 22 and 23). As was true even during the great period of Paleolithic art in France and Spain, the portrayals are far from being realistic. The human figure was evidently still under some kind of taboo.

The Mesolithic Danish people who lived on the coast were largely dependent upon the sea for their subsistence. Over a long period of time they deposited vast quantities of oyster shells on the shore in huge mounds called kitchen

middens. These heaps of shells and fish bones are mined for the artifacts that were lost or discarded in them. Since the shells are alkaline they preserve the animal bones that are found in them. Teeth marks on some of the bones show that these people kept dogs, although the animals were probably more like the Eskimos' half-wild huskies than family pets.

The kitchen middens were not just places for feasting near the shore. People lived on or alongside them. Lauring (1957, p. 32) describes what these settlements were like; "Men, women, and children spent the day up against their vast rubbish heaps; their fire stones lie there still, buried by fresh layers of refuse. Flint-working was carried on there, as was cooking and anything else that had to be done. It is impossible to imagine a high cultural standard when the interesting details of the excavations are translated into everyday terms. What we get is an extensive mound made up entirely of slimy oyster shells, fish guts, offal from gutted game, cods' heads, intestines of birds, fur scrapings, and, mixed up in the general mess, various superfluities of the human body. The stench must have been appalling, and in summer the flies will have formed a compact, buzzing blue cloud above the heap. It is incomprehensible that anyone survived this astonishing filth."

Corpses were sometimes buried in the shell heaps, and a few have been recovered. So have wooden dugouts. More easily handled and swifter skin-over-a-frame boats may have been in use then, but they were so fragile that none have survived.

Kitchen middens, of course, are not peculiar to Denmark. They are found wherever men lived near a beach and discarded the shells of the seafood they ate. America has many of them. Excavations on Boston Common, for instance, occasionally bring up shells left there by Indians.

Above: the earliest human figures found in Denmark. They were scratched on a bone.

Below: a human figure of the Maglemosian period. Both are from Zealand [Danish National Museum]

PERHAPS the most important thing accomplished by Meso-lithic people was their pushing on to new frontiers. Since they lived at a time when the retreat of the glacier was making more land available, they settled northern Europe. The population of the British Isles, which had been so small, now began to increase, a process which has continued (except for Ireland) to this day. Scandinavia also began to be settled, although a few deer bones, broken open to get at the marrow, indicate that man may have entered Denmark at an earlier period. Some of the people of eastern Europe went farther north, perhaps to follow the reindeer.

Generally speaking, however, Mesolithic people continued to live very much as their Paleolithic ancestors had. But they did domesticate the dog, and for this we owe them a great debt of gratitude, for of all animals, the dog has become closest to man. Even now, when he seldom serves any useful economic purpose, he lives in our homes, protects them with dauntless courage, and lavishes so much affection —which is often undeserved—upon his adored master that he sometimes embarrasses him. Dog lovers appreciate the true worth of these goodhearted companions; others don't know what a wealth of affection and loyalty they are missing.

The dog, the hearth fire, fur clothing, leather, cooked meat, fruit, berries, nuts, and edible roots are about all we have left of the far-off days when man was a professional hunter and the whole world was his domain.

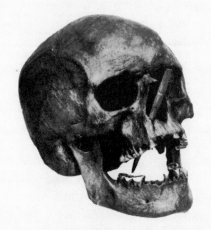

A bone arrowhead is piercing the roof of the mouth of this late Mesolithic skull from Porsmose, Denmark [Danish National Museum]

202

PHASE SIX

19. The Neolithic Revolution

THE MOST IMPORTANT STEPS in mankind's development were: coming down from the trees and learning to stand up and walk on two feet; acquiring a taste for meat and using random tools for slaying animals for food; learning how to make tools; finding out how to use fire for cooking, for warmth, and for defense; living in shelters, natural or man-made; burying the dead, an act which indicates a respect for fellow men and a realization that there is a future as well as a present; seeking to influence that future by magical means, a motivation which led to religion and art. By this time the human population of the world had grown in such numbers that man was no longer a minor and relatively scarce species that might easily have been exterminated.

Somewhere along the line (we don't know just where), man acquired the ability to speak and to symbol.

These were the first major steps that took this ingenious and ambitious biped out of a day-to-day animalian type of existence. With them went a steady increase in intelligence and manual dexterity. The creature that was beginning to think also developed a keener awareness of time, of the imminence of death, and of the importance that chance has on everyday affairs. Once man had gone this far, it was not hard for him to go farther. Several million years had been needed for his earlier advance; now his progress began to move with accelerating speed. At this stage he invented bows and arrows, boats, sledges, and skis.

About 10,000 or more years ago, the Neolithic Revolution began; it was a radically new phase when men learned how to polish stone implements, live in houses built in villages, raise crops, store food, domesticate animals, make pottery, and weave cloth. These innovations led to forging and casting metals and eventually to living in cities.

Meanwhile, the world's population kept growing. With metals, cities, and increasing numbers of people came wheeled vehicles, bigger ships, swords, armies, navies, officers, priests, and kings. Lists and inventories were needed to keep track of things, so writing began. It was improved by the alphabet and then disseminated widely by the invention of printing. Swords were replaced by guns, ballista by cannon. Political and religious warfare went on increasingly during this long period when man's lot was seemingly being improved. Finally exploration enlarged the known world and gave rise to the Industrial Revolution, of which our present Atomic Age is merely an extension.

DURING the earlier phases of his existence, man's primary task was simply to survive, not only as an individual but as a species.

It is impossible to make an exact determination of the world's population in remote ages because firm data cannot be established. Nevertheless, scientists have done their best. Here is a recent estimate, rough as it necessarily is (Deevey, 1960, p. 195–96):

A partly polished
Neolithic axe from France
[Author's collection]

PREHISTORIC WORLD POPULATION

Lower Paleolithic (1,000,000 years ago)	125,000
Middle Paleolithic (300,000 years ago)	1,000,000
Upper Paleolithic (25,000 years ago)	3,340,000
Mesolithic (before 10,000 years ago)	5,320,000

If these figures are even fairly correct, there were a little more than 5 million human beings when the hunting and food-gathering phase of mankind's existence reached its full development. The long, slow increase in population was brought about by improved weapons, better hunting techniques, and more capable methods of dealing with cold weather, predatory beasts, and other natural threats to existence. Getting more food made it possible for more people to stay alive and breed even more people. But the population still needed a plentiful supply of game. Women continued to search for nuts, berries, snails, shellfish, and other minor natural foods. It was not until some brighter-than-ordinary person noticed that seeds accidentally dropped near the home camp sprouted, grew, and produced more vegetable food of the same kind that man was ready to take his next great step forward. He did this when he learned that such seeds could be deliberately planted, harvested, and used or stored through the long winters.

This came about during the so-called Neolithic Period. Sir John Lubbock invented the term for his book entitled *Pre-historic Times* (1865). In distinction to the Paleolithic or Old Stone Age, when men had only rough-surfaced chipped implements, the Neolithic or New Stone Age saw the development of polished stone tools. They marked an advance in cutting efficiency over the earlier devices, but they were essentially the same in shape, size, and purpose.

The descriptive term Neolithic owes its origin to this new type of tool, but it covers much more than that. Partly polished axes, for one thing, had already been in use in Mesolithic and even in Late Paleolithic times. It took thousands of years to persuade men that the arduous work of rubbing axe-heads for countless hours on a rock surface to grind them down smoothly was worth the effort needed to produce a superior cutting edge. The new tools were much handsomer than the roughly chipped ones and were doubtless prized for their appearance as well as for their efficiency. After a while larger and more elaborate ones were made for purely ceremonial purposes. Some had holes bored through the centers so handles could be placed in them. Except for the use of steel instead of stone, modern axes and hammers follow the same pattern. So do the maces that are carried in front of public officials.

But the Neolithic Revolution affected far more than the polished surface of the stone implements that gave it its name. It was a transitional period of enormous importance, comparable in some ways to the Industrial Revolution, for it involved a basic change in the economy and mechanics of everyday life. Polished stone tools were only minor improvements. Far greater were agriculture, the utilization of domesticated animals for draft purposes as well as for a convenient source of food, permanent houses instead of cave dwellings, flint mining, pottery, and garments made of cloth. The coming of these mark the difference between modern and ancient man.

The word Neolithic has acquired so many meanings that it is hard to pin it down. It has been said that "in various contexts [Neolithic] has meant a self-sufficient food-produc-

Partly polished Neolithic axe from Denmark [Author's collection]

ing *economy*; an *assemblage* in which pottery is found; an *assemblage* in which polished tools are found; and a *culture* in which people are settled but have no polished stone or pottery" (Hole and Heizer, 1965, p. 241).

And then, to make matters even more complicated, the Neolithic Period has different dates in the Middle East, where it originated; in eastern Europe, to which it soon spread; and in northwestern Europe, where it was late in arriving. To simplify this confusing and much-misunderstood term, let us say that the Neolithic period was the time when men gradually abandoned hunting and became farmers and villagers. Polished stone tools, pottery, and cloth weaving are all subsidiary to this major change in a way of life.

New discoveries, new research, and more thorough thinking since the Second World War have taught us a great deal about Neolithic times that we did not know before. We had, in fact, acquired some distorted views about this important transitional period in man's social evolution. It was long believed, for instance, that agriculture came before village dwelling, that the earliest plantings were for food, that agriculture originated only in the Middle East, that it started there long before it did in the Americas, that it began fairly recently and in grassland areas, that it came into being because parts of the Middle East were drying up and making game scarce, that the dog was the first animal to be domesticated and that he was taken on as a companion in hunting. These and many other ideas have undergone revision. Some of them have proved to be almost surely wrong, others perhaps so, while still others are at least open to question. It must be pointed out, though, that scientists do not agree unanimously about them. And it is, of course, always possible that new discoveries in the field will alter present-day opinions.

THE AGRICULTURE that was to affect Europe began nine or ten millenia ago in the 2,500-mile-wide strip that runs from Asia Minor through Iraq to the Jordan Rift Valley and the Persian Gulf. It became warmer there when the great ice sheets covering northern Europe melted away. Warmer weather meant longer growing seasons, which made it possible to raise crops where they could not have been brought

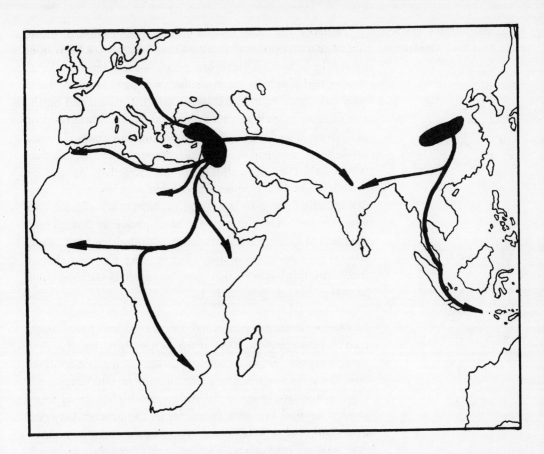

to full fruition before. And the region then had more rain than it has now. It was therefore no coincidence that the Old World Neolithic Revolution began where it did. Weather, plants, animals, and man's advanced development in the Middle East all made it possible for it to take place there at this time.

One would expect that men first began to plant crops, then domesticate animals, and finally settle down in villages. But it did not—in some places, at least—always work out that way. In 1965, Maurits van Loon, of the University of Chicago's Oriental Institute, excavated Tell Murebat, an ancient village mound near the Euphrates River in Syria. There he was able to establish the fact that the 9,500-year-old community had consisted of closely crowded-together houses built at a time when its inhabitants were still dependent upon game as their primary source of food. And the grains that supplemented their diet were wild varieties.

The beginnings and spread of agriculture throughout the Old World

207

Actually, the exact succession of living in villages, growing plants, and domesticating animals has not yet been fully established. Some Paleolithic people—even in Neandertal times—had dwelt in communities of a sort. Many of their sites have been found in Russia, eastern Europe, and northern Greece as well as in France and Spain. The group of early men who lived in Les Eyzies for thousands of years doubtless developed a sense of sodality as strong as that which held later agricultural villagers together. As will be seen later in this chapter, Paleolithic men may also have domesticated the reindeer—and perhaps other animals—to some degree. They may even have grown a few plants, although they may not have been intended for food. This, however, is only speculation. But it must be remembered that thoughtful speculation sometimes predicts things that later become accepted as facts.

So FAR AS planting is concerned, Braidwood and Reed (1957, p. 21) have proposed the word vegeculture for the first stage because "fields (*ager:* agriculture) are not implied until the level has reached a high degree of intensification." Vegeculture would cover the early period when seeds were planted around the cave entrance, in the ground between tree stumps after land had been cleared, or in any place that seemed convenient. Planted fields (true agriculture) came later when established communities grew populous enough to need large quantities of food.

It is also possible that the earliest plantings were not made by seed but by roots, tubers, and cuttings. This was likely in warm, moist countries—and especially in the New World. Nor were the first plantings necessarily for food. D. R. Harris (1967, p. 106) suggests others, such as "ornamental, protective, medicinal, dye, and fiber plants" as well as "plants used as utensils, stimulants, and poisons. . . . Perhaps they offer a crucial clue to an understanding of the transition from nonagricultural to agricultural ways of life." In line with this, Sauer (1952, p. 24) says that "the taking of fish by the use of plant extracts to stun or kill them . . . is apparently older than, and may be a forerunner of, agriculture."

It can also be seen that thorn bushes, uprooted and then put in the ground to serve as fences, may have been used to protect dwelling places long before plants were grown for food. Anyone who has ever stuck bits of cactus into the sand in tropical country and watched them quickly become re-established, knows how easy it is to make certain kinds of vegetation flourish in places where climate and soil favor them.

The bottle gourd, which has long been used as a utensil and a fishing float, is of special importance in searching for the non-food-plant beginnings of agriculture, because *Lagenaria siceraria*, which is believed to have originated in India or Africa, is so widely disseminated throughout the New World as well as the Old that it may have been brought there by early migrants. Harris (1967, p. 102) has said of it: "Detailed taxonomic, genetic, and ethno-botanical study of the varieties and uses of the bottle gourd in both hemispheres would make a fundamental contribution to the resolution of the question whether pre-Columbian contact with the Old World influenced the beginning of agriculture in the Americas."

It is also possible, though, that hollow bottle gourds, which float on water, may have been carried across the oceans by winds and currents.

VEGECULTURE had more than one place of origin. Sauer (1952, p. 24) believes that it began in southeastern Asia. We know now that its New World origins in Mexico are as ancient as they are in the Old World (MacNeish, 1965, p. 88). Both date back to 9,000—or more—years ago (Harris, 1967, p. 101).

Sauer, who has done outstanding work on the invention of agriculture, suggests that it began long before this date (1952, p. 19). He also says that "agriculture did not originate from a growing or chronic shortage of food. People living in the shadow of famine do not have the means or time to undertake the slow and leisurely experimental steps out of which a better and distant food supply is to develop in a somewhat distant future. . . . The improvement of plants by selection for better utility to man was accomplished only by a people who lived at a comfortable margin above the level of want." He goes on to say that there had to be a good assortment of plants and animals present and that "agriculture began in wooded lands. Primitive cultivations could readily

209

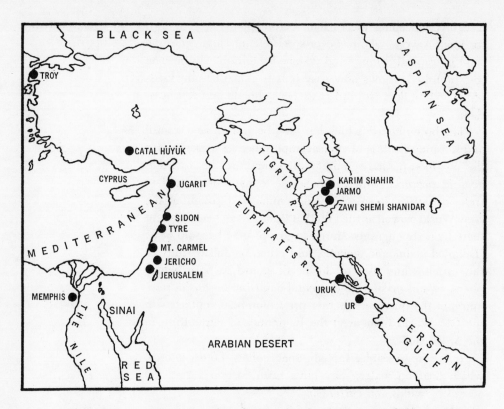

The ancient Middle East

open spaces for planting by deadening trees; they could not dig in sod or eradicate vigorous stoloniferous grasses." He gives due credit to N. I. Vavilov for this idea, an idea which has been confirmed by the fact that the villages in the Middle East where agriculture was first practiced "were all found within or at the peripheries of the woodland belt" (Butzer, 1964, p. 424) that runs from Greece across Asia Minor, Cyprus, and Palestine to Iraq and the Persian Gulf. The group that is farthest east—Jarmo, Zawi Chemi Shanidar, and Karim Shahir—have been of special interest for what was discovered in them. These villages are situated in the kind of terrain that Sauer (1952, p. 5) considers ideal for being "the cradle of our race," an area of "what would seem to us pleasant places, of mild weather with alternating rainy and dry seasons, of varied woodland, shrub and herbs, a land of hills and valleys, of streams and springs, with alluvial reaches and rock shelters in cliffs."

The early sites in Palestine, however, have poorer natural surroundings and climate. The very ancient town of Jericho is located in a hot, dry valley north of the Dead Sea.

210

An ever-flowing spring which guaranteed a plentiful supply of water drew people to this otherwise uninviting site. It is believed though that the climate was somewhat wetter then than it is now.

The fact that Middle Eastern agriculture began in hilly woodland country rather than in the drier and hotter lowlands and deserts disproves a theory originated during the first part of this century. It held that increasing desiccation of the land forced people to seek new sources of food and that men and beasts were crowded together around vanishing streams and oases so that they were thrown into close contact with each other there.

It was the Middle East that gave man some of his most important food crops such as wheat, barley, lentils, and peas. There, too, sheep, goats, and cattle were first domesticated. The use of metal also first began there.

Wheat has been called "the critical crop, the key to the origin of settled cultivation" that can "support civilization alone as no other grain crop can" (Darlington, 1963, p. 143).

Rice from southeast Asia and corn (maize) from the Americas are the other chief cereals that feed a hungry world, but wheat is identified with European civilization. Bread made from it has been eaten since Neolithic times, and its use has spread to post-Columbian America and other lands settled by emigrants from the Old World.

The original stocks from which all these essential food plants came were scrawny, poor in yield, and not very palatable. Thousands of years of cultivation by early man made them into much superior products; still further development by modern scientific methods has improved them even more.

And in the Middle East men not only improved their plant food but their meat supplies as well. In this part of the world not dogs but sheep were the first animals to be domesticated. Sheep bones nearly 11,000 years old have been found at Zawi Chemi Shanidar, one of the sites in Iraq which Sauer describes so idyllically. There is nothing odd about sheep being domesticated in the Middle East before dogs were. Wild sheep were more plentiful there and were easy to capture and tame.

There is some dispute among scientists as to whether

sheep or goats were domesticated first because it is difficult
even for experts to tell their bones apart. One thing they
agree on, however, is that sheep were soon preferred to
goats because they are more tractable (Reed, 1963, p. 213).
This, oddly enough, bears out a shrewd bit of speculation
made in the first century B.C. by Marcus Terentius Varro,
who said: "There is reason to believe that amongst animals
sheep were the first to be adopted, on account of their usefulness and gentle nature, because they are extremely gentle
and especially fitted for association with man's life, for
through them milk and cheese were added to his food;
while for his body they furnished clothing in the shape of
skins." Varro was astute when he mentioned sheep skins instead of wool for use as clothing because weaving was unknown when man first domesticated sheep.

The problem of identifying the bones of early domesticated animals is still further complicated by the fact that it
takes many generations of living under the protection of
man for the bones of a captive creature to be obviously affected. Then they tend to become smaller, whiter, and softer
than those of the same species that is still in a wild state.
But in the earlier stages it is hard to tell the difference, so
there is often a dispute as to whether newly found bones are
those of a creature hunted and killed in the field or of one
that was brought up and slaughtered for meat at home. As a
result, it is difficult to establish the exact chronological order
in which the different species of animals were first domesticated. In Europe, the dog seems to have priority; in the
Middle East, sheep—although a good claim could be made
for the goat.

An even earlier possibility, however, is the reindeer, although definite proof of this is lacking. But it will be remembered that this animal played an important part in the
life of Paleolithic man. Females, captured young, could be
brought up to serve as decoys and so enable their hunter-
owners to get close to wild reindeer for the kill.

Zeuner says, in A History of Domesticated Animals
(1963, pp. 124–25): "There is no intrinsic reason why reindeer should not have been domesticated early in prehistoric
times. In fact, it might have occurred prior to the introduction of agriculture, since nomadic tribes should be perfectly
capable of organizing the system of mobile control of the

212

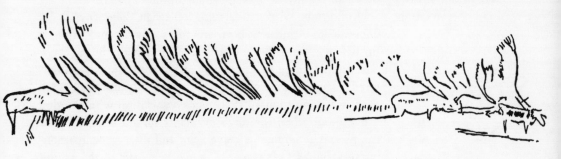

reindeer which is practiced even today. It is, therefore, not entirely futile to look for indications of incipient domestication of the reindeer in Mesolithic and Paleolithic times." The German scientist H. Polhausen also supports the idea. If firm evidence is ever discovered to substantiate it, Zawi Chemi Shanidar with its 11,000-year-old sheep bones, will lose the honor of being the oldest known site to have the remains of domesticated animals, and some European place where reindeer once lived closely with men will replace it.

Herd of reindeer depicted by a Paleolithic artist in Teyjat [After Breuil]

In connection with this, it should be noted that modern Laplanders have found a way to deal with the sometimes truculent reindeer males. They castrate them soon after they become mature and thus prevent the deadly rutting contests that would otherwise make trouble. Prehistoric men may have done this too.

By Neolithic times, however, the reindeer had long since vanished from Europe except in far northern areas. It is unlikely that any memory of man's relationship with them persisted to this date. If the domestication of animals had indeed begun with the reindeer, it now had to be started anew, and with different species—dogs, sheep, goats, pigs, and cattle.

It is generally agreed that the ancestor of the European dog was the wolf—with some possible interbreeding with the jackal. The wolf, like the gorilla, has been much maligned; he is not as ferocious as he was once thought to be, and he is far more considerate of his fellow wolves than many humans are of their fellow men. Since he is a pack hunter, he has developed a strong sense of loyalty to his leader, and it is easy for him to transfer that loyalty to a human owner. Experiments with modern wolves show that

213

they can readily be tamed when captured young.

Full-grown wild animals are too set in their ways to be domesticated, but new born creatures, caught and brought up by men, soon become used to living with them. Those that did not adapt to a new way of life were quickly slaughtered, so a process of selection of more docile animals began.

It was long thought that man's association with the dog came about when the dog's ancestors lurked around men's camps and acted first as scavengers and then as companion-hunters. Sauer (1952, p. 29), however, scoffs at the notion and says that "this attractive myth is a projection into the past from modern European romantic views," that "really primitive peoples do not hunt with dogs," and that "the great hunters of the Upper Paleolithic had no dogs. . . . [They] appear archeologically first with Mesolithic folk, who were not much engaged in hunting, at least not on the land."

Sauer believes that the dog may not have been derived directly from the wolf but from a common ancestor. He concludes by saying that "the dog is considered . . . as originating from a wild dog, native to Southeastern Asia, living in forested monsoon lands, perhaps resembling the fox in food and social habits." Wolf blood could have been introduced into the strain, especially in northern lands.

Others now think that the man-and-dog relationship not only did not begin as hunting companions, but that man was the hunter and the dog the prey that was slaughtered for food (Degerbøl, 1962, pp. 334–41). Dog flesh, of course, is still eaten today, especially in Asia and South America. And it was long a favorite with certain American Indian tribes.

Wolf engraved on the walls of Les Combarelles by a Paleolithic artist

But somewhere, at some time, cuddly little puppies won over the hearts of children and women, who then persuaded the unsentimental adult males to refrain from using the tiny animals as food. Since dogs are highly intelligent—perhaps the most intelligent of all carnivores—they quickly learned how to live with men and make themselves useful hunters that could scent game, run it down, and corner it for their owners. In this relationship they did not change the economy of their masters as farm animals did. But later on, when men owned herds that had to be guarded and rounded up, dogs developed new skills which made them even more essential to the agricultural community than they had been to

214

a hunting economy.

Dogs and cats are the only carnivores that have been widely domesticated, perhaps because the flesh of meat-eating animals is generally thought to be tougher and less desirable than that of herbivores. Yet dogs have been and are used for food while cat meat is not ordinarily eaten. The cat has been more fortunate than most other animals in his dealings with men. His association with humans is late; it probably did not begin until agriculture was developed sufficiently to need storage for large quantities of grain. Then the cat became useful because he was an ever-active guard against rodents.

Some scientists, however, do not think that animals were domesticated only for utilitarian purposes. Zeuner (1963, p. 39) puts the case for this: "There are men who feed the sparrows that have intruded into their domain, and there may well have been a stage of throwing morsels to wild dogs that invaded the camps of pre-Neolithic man, long prior to the use of dogs. Such acts are elementary manifestations of the solidarity of life, especially of related life. It is characteristic of most higher animals that have developed a social medium of some sort and which are not enemies. It finds a simple expression in animal friendships as they occur under conditions of domestication between cats and dogs, or, stranger still, between cats and tame birds. It finds a higher expression in man's desire to keep all sorts of pets, and its highest expression in the naturalist who finds supreme satisfaction in observing, understanding, and feeling as one with other living creatures."

It must be noted, however, that animals in their wild state do not become friendly with those of other species. They may live with them in a mutually beneficial symbiotic relationship, but ordinarily they only tolerate their presence.

Much work remains to be done on two areas of the man-and-animal relationship—the motivation for wanting and keeping pets, especially the desire to handle and fondle them; and, perhaps closely allied to this, sexual acts performed by humans with animals. The latter aspect has been kept so hush-hush that it still awaits serious investigation. Pictures illustrating sexual relationships between men and animals have long been known to prehistorians. Some only suggest such acts, but others depict it frankly.

215

The importance of these pictures is the very close physical relationship they show between men and "wild" animals. It seems unlikely that humans could have had such intimate sexual contact with feral beasts unless they had been fairly well tamed, for it would be dangerous to do so. But taming individual animals, which were probably captured when young, is only a foreshadowing of true domestication. It was not until Neolithic times that man domesticated them in sufficient numbers to alter his way of life and change the basic structure of his economy.

*A man having intercourse
with an animal.
Camonica Valley
[After Anati]*

That sexual intercourse between men and beasts continued openly throughout prehistoric times is indicated by some of the rock engravings made in northern Italy's Camonica Valley about 3,000 years ago. The Greeks and Romans also did not hesitate to depict such acts and display works of art based on this theme in their gardens and houses. Public acceptance of such erotica did not die out until the Judeo-Christian ethic replaced "pagan" attitudes toward sex.

Animals kept by man for many generations not only become tamer, they also change in others ways. Zeuner (1954, p. 340) explains this: "The sole interest of the Neolithic husbandman was to keep the animals subjugated. To give them good living conditions and to provide them with the most suitable provender were ideas that could not enter the minds of men whose own requirements of food and shelter were so elementary. Animals kept in captivity must inevitably have deteriorated. Their progeny would tend to be

216

smaller, weaker, and more docile than their wild ancestors, being selected, consciously or unconsciously, for precisely those qualities. . . . Once, however, the domestication of the species had been thoroughly effected, the idea of increasing the body size is likely to have been regarded as useful, in order to increase either the meat supply or the working strength of the animals. Under primitive conditions, interbreeding with wild specimens was an easy matter."

Tying up domesticated female animals in places where wild males can impregnate them while they are in heat is a practice that man followed as long as such wild stock was at large. He usually did so because such breeding methods cost him nothing, but he was also introducing new and perhaps more vigorous blood. Zeuner says that "with increasing experience in keeping domesticated stock, it would also have occurred to prehistoric man from time to time to restart the entire process from fresh wild stock."

Fairly successful attempts have been made in modern times to breed back in order to obtain supposedly extinct varieties that resemble the parent wild stock from which the domesticated presumably came. In this way, very large cattle that looked like aurochs were produced in Germany early in the 1930's, more than 300 years after the last original one had been killed in Poland.

Castration had showed men how to subdue the reindeer and make the otherwise fierce and enormously powerful bull into a placid but still strong ox. Later on, this technique was to be applied to intractable wild stallions, which then became manageable geldings.

The still extant Przewalski's horses show what the basic wild horse stock may have been like, but according to George Gaylord Simpson (1951 and 1961, p. 22), they are suspect. It is possible, he says, that "the supposed Przewalski's horses seen by modern explorers in Central Asia or exhibited in zoos have had an admixture of domestic horse blood and that a pure wild race has not existed for some time."

All the so-called wild horses in the Americas are feral animals descended from domestic stock brought from the Old World. European tarpans survived in eastern Russia as late as the twentieth century, but they are now extinct. No true wild horses now exist.

THE PART man has played in reshaping the animal world has been an ever-increasingly dominant one. He has exterminated many species or made them so scarce that they are allowed to continue only as specimens in zoos or parks, and he has favored others so much that their population, like his own, has grown enormously. Those he keeps in his own home may become spoiled house pets, but those he grows for their meat get little consideration. (Witness chickens and turkeys, which are raised in vast quantities in factory-like surroundings where they pass quickly from egg to marketable flesh without any but the most impersonal human contact.)

When Darwin wrote *Animals and Plants under Domestication* (1868) he showed how man decided the fate of the living creatures he had taken from the wilderness and made his own: "Unconscious selection is that which follows from men naturally preserving the most valued and destroying the less valued individuals without any thought of altering the breed; and undoubtedly this process slowly works great changes. Unconscious selection graduates into methodical, and only extreme cases can be distinctly separated; for he who preserves a useful or perfect animal will generally breed from it with the hope of getting offspring of the same character; but as long as he has not a predetermined purpose to improve the breed, he may be said to be selecting unconsciously."

It will thus be seen that stud books rank high in our modern civilization even though we make little attempt to apply to men what we do to improve the breed of the animals we control. Slavery, incidentally, deserves some consideration here, for it was a system of "domesticating" human beings in which conscious selection was sometimes practiced.

At one time or another, men seem to have domesticated or made pets of just about every kind of animal that could live in captivity. The Swiss lakeside dwellers had tame foxes, while the ancient Egyptians collected all sorts of strange beasts—hyenas, baboons, gazelles, antelopes, and hawks as well as more familiar cats, camels, asses, and greyhounds. Yet the number of species that man has kept and thought important is rather small. The farmer's natural conservatism and reluctance to try anything new undoubtedly contributed to this, but it is also true that some animals are difficult to tame. Many species can be induced to behave so long as someone to whom they have become accustomed is with them, but they cannot be trusted with strangers. Others, although not dangerous, are untrainable; still others are considered not worth keeping.

By trial and error over the centuries man has made the selection of animals he wants. He may have missed some highly useful species, but he has done very well in his exploitation of these living resources. Actually, he owes them a great debt which he will surely never repay.

IT HAS TAKEN man only 10,000 years or so to bring most of the animal world under his control. His progress in domination during the past few generations has been so astoundingly swift that he tends to take sweeping changes for granted. But he needed a long time for his first great economic advance, the transition from food gathering to food producing.

D. R. Harris (1967, p. 107) points out that "from the welter of new facts bearing on the problem of agricultural origins one general conclusion may be drawn. The transition from nonagricultural to agricultural ways of life can no longer be envisaged as a single 'revolutionary' step. It is now clear that plant domestication and the beginnings of cultivation were slow and complex processes involving varied and gradual adjustments between man and the land over long periods of time and in many different habitats. . . . In the present ferment of fresh facts and theories, old orthodoxies, which envisage man's cultural development as proceeding through ordered stages, are dissolving, and the problem has taken on greater but more realistic complexity. It remains far from a solution, but already these new approaches promise fundamental gains in our understanding of how, where, and when agriculture began."

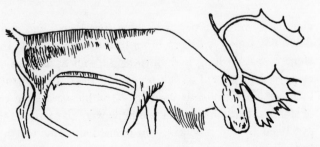

Grazing reindeer engraved on antler in Paleolithic times. Found in Kesserloch, Switzerland

219

20. How Neolithic People Lived

SINCE THE Neolithic Period lasted for nearly 6,000 years during its spread from the Middle East to northwestern Europe, it is obvious that in the beginning it differed very little from the hunting phase that preceded it. Later it became more complex. It always differed a great deal from place to place; the older areas were naturally more advanced than the newer ones, and climate was also an important factor.

In the Middle East, where a location near dependable source of water was sought after, some communities stayed rooted to the same site for thousands of years. New houses were built on the collapsed and leveled ruins of previous ones so that what now remains of these ancient villages is only a rounded mound or what the Arabs call a *tell*. In Europe, communities seldom occupied the same site for long. When soil in the surrounding fields became exhausted, the villagers moved on. In many cases the new area had to be cleared, and the sharper, more efficient polished axes expedited this work. Modern Danish experiments made with

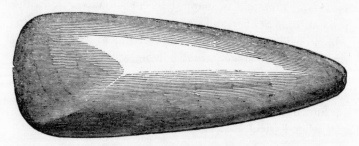

A fully polished stone axe from Ireland [Lubbock]

genuine Neolithic axe-heads show that three men can cut down 600 square yards of birch forest in four hours. In ancient times, girdling and burning as well as cutting were employed to get rid of the unwanted trees. Except for the fact that the axe heads used by Neolithic men were made of stone instead of steel, the methods were the same as those practiced by the pioneers who opened up America in historic times.

In the Middle East, where wood and stone were scarce or nonexistent, sun-dried mud was the chief building material. At first the walls were made only of rammed mud (*pisé*); later, large bricks of mud mixed with straw were used. In Europe wooden houses were almost universal except in places where there were no trees. In remote areas people still clung to the primitive habitations they had used in earlier times. Cave dwelling, of course, was never entirely given up. Families still live in underground shelters in certain parts of France and Italy. In the late Neolithic village of Skara Brae, on one of Scotland's treeless Orkney Islands, stone and whale bone served as building materials. Even furniture—beds, chairs, and storage units—were fashioned out of the native flat rock that could easily be split into smooth-surfaced slabs. The houses had round corners and were drained by stone-lined sewers. They may even have had indoor toilets. Because Skara Brae's buildings were made of stone, they have lasted far longer than others of the same period.

In the Middle East village houses were clustered close together inside defensive walls. What seems to have been the oldest and largest of them was Jericho, of Biblical fame. Located in Jordan, north of the Dead Sea, it had a prehistoric population of some 2,000 or 3,000 and has been inhabited—although not continuously—for 10,000 years. It was a strongly fortified place with stone walls, towers, and a ditch. An ever-flowing spring was the precious asset that induced people to settle there, originally in Mesolithic times.

Besides its valuable spring, Jericho's citizens evidently owned property that required protection. But it was certainly not agricultural wealth that had to be jealously guarded, for the surrounding countryside has never been very productive. Its prosperity may have come from trade. Many of the objects found in the excavations came from places hundreds of miles away. There were native materials in the neighborhood, salt, bitumen, and sulphur among them, that may have been primary sources for this early trading center's wealth.

Jericho is particularly interesting for the light it casts on Neolithic domestic habits. Its people buried the dead under the dirt floors of their houses, and they decorated the skulls of the deceased by covering them with clay smoothed out

20. HOW NEOLITHIC
PEOPLE LIVED

221

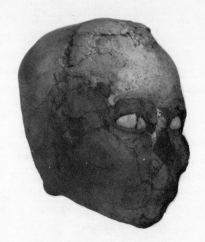

*Plastered skull from
Jericho with shells
for eyes
[British Museum]*

to look like flesh, while sea shells served as realistic-looking eyes. Three fairly large human figures were also found in what was evidently a shrine. They represent a man, a woman, and a child, and are early examples of the family trinity that was to recur countless times in the art of the world.

Several smaller Neolithic communities that are not quite as old as Jericho have been discovered in northern Iraq. Jarmo, which was excavated from 1948 to 1955, was inhabited by people who also buried their dead under the house floors. Little clay figures of animals have been dug up there, and Mother Goddess statuettes have been found in both Jarmo and Jericho.

Even more recently investigated than ancient Jarmo and Jericho is the Anatolian Neolithic town of Çatal Hüyük. This 30-acre double tell, which rises above the wheat fields on a high plateau, was a thriving community some 8,000 or more years ago. And it was an exceedingly interesting place. It was not only three or four times as large as Jericho; it was far advanced in the use of cold-hammered copper, lead casting, pottery making, and weaving. Yet its people were still dependent for protein upon such wild game as deer and aurochs.

*Hand decorations from
Çatal Hüyük*

The great wild aurochs—particularly the bull—was held in great esteem there. Some of the rooms in the many buildings were not only decorated with murals and plaster reliefs, but rows of aurochs horns and human skulls stood upon the

222

*One of the rooms in
Çatal Hüyük
[From Çatal Hüyük,
a Neolithic Town in
Anatolia by James
Mellaart. © 1967,
Thames & Hudson, Ltd.
Used with permission of
McGraw-Hill Book
Company]*

floors. And some of the paintings indicate that not only wild
bulls but leopards and vultures were ritual animals in this
strange culture. The pictures of people resemble those of
eastern Spain in their active stylized forms.

The masculine symbolism of the bull was important in
Çatal Hüyük, but the long-established Mother Goddess was
still supreme, as the many cult images of her show. Some of
them look like the fat ladies of Malta. James Mellaart, who
was in charge of the University of London expedition that
did the excavation, thinks that the local religion was dominated by women. Much more is still to be learned about this
fascinating community, however. More than a hundred
rooms have been uncovered, but a good part of the town
awaits further exploratory digging. What has already been
found is so rich that the future may reveal even more facts
about life in a Middle Eastern Neolithic community.

APPARENTLY there was less need for defense in Neolithic
Europe than in the more restless Middle East. Jacquetta
Hawkes (1963, p. 265) gives the probable reasons for this:
"The general absence of weapons of war among the grave
furniture of [European Neolithic] burials provides . . . convincing proof of the absence of martial ideals in the hearts
of the new peasantry. . . . Although it is rash to push economic explanations too far—many peoples have loved to
fight their neighbors without any need for *Lebensraum*—it
seems probable that the fact that good land was to be had

223

for the taking and that each generation could find a good living did partly account for the peacefulness of early Neolithic communities. And similarly that the more warlike ideals of the succeeding phase were due to mounting populations and the shortage of new land to feed them."

Archeologists have been able to trace the sites of many long-vanished European Neolithic wooden houses by locating holes in the ground in which upright supporting posts once stood. This gives us an accurate idea of the floor plan and size of the house but tells us nothing about the part that was above ground. Fortunately, clay models of some Neolithic dwellings exist to show us what the doors, windows, walls, and roofs were like. Because of Europe's wet climate, the roofs had to be slanted in order to shed rain and snow.

Unlike Middle Eastern villages, in which the houses were crowded closely together for protection within town walls, European communities apparently had no need for defense in those early days, so separate dwellings could be built. A new type of architecture soon appeared—the long house, a building that extended for 100 feet or more and in which a number of families could live under one roof. One such house in Denmark was 266 feet long. The Iroquois and some Indian tribes in British Columbia also used long houses made of upright posts covered by bark roofs.

Originally it was believed that the Neolithic Swiss lake villages were completely surrounded by water and that the houses were supported on piles driven into the bottom of the lake. Recent research, however, has shown that these settlements were located on shore near the water's edge. Their houses were built on piles only to protect them against a sudden flood.

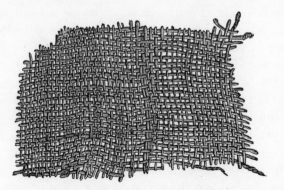

Opposite page: the underpinnings of Niederwyl, which show that most lacustrine villages were built on shore near the edge of the water [Keller] Left: cloth from Robenhausen [Lubbock]

225

Although one of these lacustrine villages had been found in 1829 near Ober Meilen on Lake Zurich, not much attention was paid to them until the winter of 1853–54, when the level of Swiss lakes fell so low that wooden pilings could be seen. Intensive recovery work brought up an enormous amount of material, for the water had preserved all sorts of

Bronze fishhooks
from Nidau-Steinberg,
Switzerland

things that ordinarily decay, such as basketry, fish nets, cloth, grain, nuts, and fruit seed. Later investigation showed that there were similar lakeside communities in the Alpine regions of France, Italy, and Germany. Most English and Irish lake villages are post-Neolithic, but it will be remembered that Mesolithic Star Carr was built on filled-in ground alongside a lake.

PERHAPS the most important thing that was taking place in Neolithic times was the drawing together of people into larger social units. The hunters had lived their more or less nomadic existence in small bands; now with a more settled economy, villages and towns became possible. Some means of communication between them was necessary. A few paths had been made by the hunters, and their successors simply took these over. But more people living in more and more communities needed more paths, so Neolithic Europe was eventually crisscrossed with an elaborate network of them. The more important ones were made into roads when wheeled vehicles came in; others were abandoned; a few remain and are still used by hikers.

This is especially true in England, where parts of the ancient Ridgeway and its lower parallel course, Iknield, are favorites with hardy people who like to take long journeys on foot. There is no way of telling just how old some of these paths are, but there is no doubt that they go far back in time. Earliest of all may be the Jurassic Zone, which is not a man-made path but a natural one that runs from East

226

Yorkshire to the Cotswolds. It is a long strip of open ground on which foot travelers could make their way without being impeded by woods or underbrush.

Wheeled vehicles did not come into general use until late Neolithic or early Bronze Age times. They were slow in coming because animals large enough to pull them had to be domesticated and then harness, yokes, shafts, traces, and other such equipment had to be devised. The plow may have led the way when some clever farmer realized that a forked stick drawn through the ground would be faster and more effective than any hand-chopping method. In the beginning the plow had to be drawn by a rope attached to a man—or a woman—while another person walked behind to manipulate the handle. When animals were attached to the plow stronger harness had to be invented.

Animal-drawn plows, travois, and sledges for use on snow or bare ground were early, but just how early is not known except that they obviously could not have come in before beasts of burden did. Carts and wagons evolved from these. Wheels for transportation are believed to have been inspired by the potter's wheel, although rotary motion had been utilized in far earlier times when the drill was employed for cutting neat round holes and eventually for making fire by friction.

Since the first transport wheels were made entirely of wood, practically all of them have perished. Surviving examples are rather late, and most of them were shaped by metal tools and may have some metal parts.

It is easy for a modern person to say that all you have to do is take a log, cut a section out of it, bore a hole in the center for an axle, and you have a wheel. True enough, but how would you cut a section out of a tree trunk without using a metal saw? Perhaps it can be done with stone tools. And perhaps it was done. Some ingenious fellow may have had the idea and actually did carry it out. But it took a lot of time and patience. His individually produced wheel may have caused a lot of talk, but no one went into the business of making them in quantity. That had to wait for the need for them—and for metal saws.

Opposite page and above: flint implements mounted in antler holders from Lake Bienne, Switzerland [Metropolitan Museum of Art; gift of Heber R. Bishop, 1902]

The very advanced peoples who lived in Central and South America never got around to making transport wheels, probably because they had no useful beasts to draw them.

227

But they knew about wheels and put them on some of their children's toys.

The unknown genius who invented the wheel may have gotten the idea from the roller, for sections of logs were used to move big stones across the land. But a broad leap of the imagination is needed to bridge the gap between a rolling log placed under a heavy load and a revolving circular disk mounted underneath a box of some kind.

The first wheels were made of solid wood, but they were eventually replaced by those constructed by fastening three thick circular planks together with the grain of the wood placed at right angles. This prevented pieces being split off along the grain. Such wheels, which took considerably more time and trouble to make, had the great advantage of lasting longer than the solid ones did. The spoke came in much later when fast-moving wheels were needed on chariots so kings and soldiers could overtake their enemies. Neolithic farmers and villagers had no occasion for such speed.

Norwegian rock engraving of a skin-covered boat. Below: a dugout from France

BOATS HAD steadily become larger, but no one knows just when they became large enough to be called ships. The distinction is a tenuous one even today. Perhaps the most useful working definition is that a ship is a vessel big enough to carry a boat. No one, however, has ever settled the question of how small the boat can be.

Neolithic watercraft must have been fairly large and were certainly seaworthy, for known migration routes show that they went far from shore. Islands in the Mediterranean and the Atlantic now became settled, and the fact that the

*A Norwegian rock
carving of a large boat
carrying a sun disk*

British Isles were now separated from the continent did
not stop people from going to them. The ever-rising sea
level had made them into islands during the seventh millen-
nium B.C.

By this time men had developed better means of transport and had learned the benefits of trading with distant
lands. Migrations still continued and would go on for thousands of years, but they were now more orderly, perhaps
because men possessed more worldly goods to take with
them. Ships, pack animals, and then wheeled vehicles made
this possible.

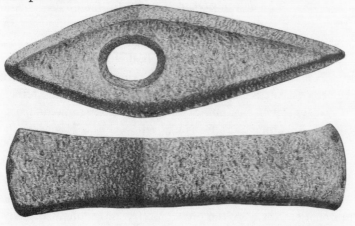

*Top and side views
of a battle axe from
northern England [Joly]*

Running counter to these slower and more peaceful
migrations, however, were the swift movements of the
battle-axe people who were spreading rapidly across Europe. They had been quick to realize the advantages of
polished stone axes and hammers, and, as so often happens
when new and more effective weapons are developed, were
putting their new killing tools to use.

Civilization has not unjustly been blamed for furthering
war, but the battle-axe people were going into action even
before cities were known in Europe. Where these fiercely 229

aggressive tribesmen came from is still a mystery. Some prehistorians think they that arrived—suddenly and in great numbers—from an eastern source in southern Russia or perhaps from some place even farther east. Others believe that they originated in northern Europe and went eastward from there. Still others say that they may have had their origin in the Danubian basin.

Wherever the battle-axe people came from, one thing about them is certain: they were introducing violence to a part of the world that had previously been relatively peaceful. And, along with ruthless invasions, undeclared warfare, and appropriation of women as their rightful spoils, they were developing a society in which masculinity was supreme. An insatiable desire for property and power, together with insensitivity to pain and suffering in themselves as well as in others, characterized everything they did. In Scandinavia, the medieval Vikings were to be their heirs. And even in more modern times, Germany was to adopt their belief that might makes right. In should be noted, however, that this predominance of the masculine strain was nothing new in human affairs. The struggle between the Mother Goddess and the horned bull still goes on.

Not the battle-axe warriors but other more peaceful and more constructive Neolithic people, followers of the Mother Goddess, were beginning to build imposing monuments. Before this time Europeans had left very few large objects to testify to their existence. Now they began to move, shape, and put into position many huge rocks. They seem to have done this for religious reasons, for their simple everyday needs certainly did not call for such enormous expenditures of energy. Nor were the big stone structures intended to be protective fortresses. Their builders, however, may have thought of them as spiritual strongholds that would guard them from powers unseen and forces beyond the ken of man.

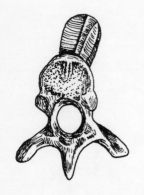

A javelin point still lodged in a human vertebra. From Montfort Cave

21. Neolithic Technology

THE POLISHED STONE IMPLEMENTS which inspired the term Neolithic were sharpened by being ground down on rocks that still show how they were used thousands of years ago. These boulders with V-shaped grooves worn into them by long-continued rubbing are aptly called *polissoirs* by the French.

A polissoir
from Grand-Pressigny
[Collection Musée
de l'Homme]

The nicely polished axe-head was not intended to be held in the hand; it was shafted on a stick to which it was fastened by tightly wound thongs, adhesives, or both. In some cases it was stuck into a hole cut into a wooden branch or a piece of antler. The haft made it far more efficient than the hand-axe because it served as a leverlike extension of the arm and thus gave more power to the striking head.

The many generations of people who had used flint had found out that the best material for making implements was that which was taken from deposits deep under the ground where it had been protected from air and weather. Surface nodules or those that came from shallow holes or trenches were inferior to these. But not until Neolithic times did man develop enough knowledge and skill to dig far down into the earth for the queerly shaped lumps of flint that were as

231

essential to prehistoric manufacturing as steel is to ours. Since sharp axes were needed for clearing forests, the demand for them increased so much that a new industry—mining—was created.

Neolithic food production was so successful that the burgeoning economy could afford to have specialized workmen who spent most of their time underground. It is possible, though, that flint mining was a seasonal occupation performed only in winter when men working below the surface would be warmer and drier than those above ground in Europe's cold, damp winter weather, which was even wetter then than it is now.

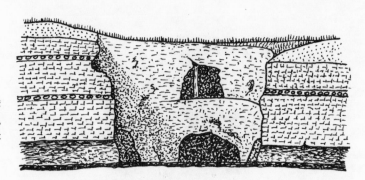

Flint mine at
Harrow Hill,
Worthing, Sussex

Miner's pick from
Grime's Graves

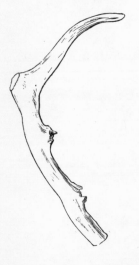

Some of these prehistoric mine shafts are 40 or more feet deep. From them galleries project into the chalk beds. The miners were so eager to get deep-level flint that they ignored the nodules near the surface. As was to be expected, the galleries sometimes collapsed on top of the men working in them. Perhaps most of the victims were quickly pulled out by their fellow workers, but others may still be buried under tons of chalk. At Obourg, in Belgium, the skeleton of a Neolithic flint miner was found crushed under a rock fall. Near him was the antler pick he had been using.

The chalk in which the flint nodules were imbedded was pried loose by hammering a pointed bone (or the tine of a deer horn) into a natural crack. The marks of these tools can still be seen in the walls of Grime's Graves near Cambridge, England.

Some of the unwanted chalk was pushed into worked-out galleries; the rest was hauled to the surface and thrown into abandoned mine shafts. Prehistoric men evidently had more respect for the countryside than most modern miners do, for they tried to fill up the dangerous open pits they had dug.

Their shovels were made of wood or the flat shoulder blades of cattle. Big nodules of flint were chipped down to useful sizes near the mine heads and were then sent for final finishing to the axe factories that dotted prehistoric Europe.

Flint was mined not only in England and Belgium but also in France, southern Sweden, Denmark, Portugal, and Sicily as well. Since there is no flint in Norway, stray pieces were sought on the shores of the North Sea where storms sometimes washed in fragments from chalk beds farther south.

Small chalk goddess found in Grime's Graves [British Museum]

The mining of flint and other good stone-working material led to trade with other places, some of them surprisingly far away. Flint itself is difficult to trace to its point of origin because most of it is pretty much the same, but other stones used for Neolithic implements can be identified by putting a thin sliver under a microscope. Petrological examination is a new tool for giving us more information about prehistoric migrations and trade routes.

Plenty of flint was still used in Neolithic times, but other kinds of stone were also sought. Kenneth Oakley (1961a, p. 21) says that the men who shaped implements "could make effective use of basalt and diorite which had relatively poor conchoidal fracture, and even chose them in preference to flint for making some classes of tool, such as celts (stone axes, adzes, or hoes wielded by a shaft), where toughness and a readily ground edge were important requirements. . . . Green rocks appear to have been favored. A greenish, close-grained lava . . . [from] North Wales was especially

A miner's chalk lamp from Cissbury

233

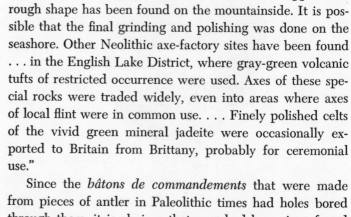

*Two small ceremonial
polished axes
[Author's collection]*

popular. The site where the axe-heads were chipped into
rough shape has been found on the mountainside. It is possible that the final grinding and polishing was done on the
seashore. Other Neolithic axe-factory sites have been found
. . . in the English Lake District, where gray-green volcanic
tufts of restricted occurrence were used. Axes of these special rocks were traded widely, even into areas where axes
of local flint were in common use. . . . Finely polished celts
of the vivid green mineral jadeite were occasionally exported to Britain from Brittany, probably for ceremonial
use."

Since the *bâtons de commandements* that were made
from pieces of antler in Paleolithic times had holes bored
through them, it is obvious that men had long since found
out how to drill through soft material. Neolithic people now
began to experiment with hard stone. Their earlier efforts,
made by drilling with pieces of flint from both sides of the
stone to meet in the middle, produced holes that were
shaped like two cones joined at their tips. These could be
reamed out to make a smoother opening, but the stoneworkers soon learned how to cut a perfect round hole by
drilling with hollow points made of reed or bone with sand
used as an abrasive to do the actual cutting.

*Bow drill for
boring holes in stone.
Found in Sweden*

Once the art of boring a smooth-walled hole through
hard material was mastered, stone heads no longer had to
be fastened clumsily and insecurely by thongs or adhesives
to a shaft. Axes, adzes, maces, and hammers were perfected

234

A finely made
flint arrowhead
[Danish National Museum]

in form until they became models for the metal tools that
were soon to be made.

With this newly developed mastery over stone and wood,
men who had been hunters could move out of their dark
cave dwellings to live in the houses they built on freshly
cleared land. The days of the free-roaming but always in-
secure nomad were passing. Men were learning how to plant
and grow their own vegetable food and have a supply of
fresh meat on hand in their animal herds.

ALTHOUGH archeology points to the Middle East as the area
where Old World agriculture began on a scale large enough
to affect mankind's social economy, some of the first experiments with raising plants may very well have been made
elsewhere. Since nothing remains of those primary attempts,
the matter may have to rest where it is as a tantalizing bit
of speculation.

Whenever and wherever men—or more likely women—
first began to grow plants, they probably just scratched the
surface of the ground with a stick, scattered the seeds or
planted tubers or cuttings, and then hoped for a good crop.
If the planted material, soil, and weather worked in their
favor—and if insects or disease did not destroy their efforts
—they were rewarded with a useful but scanty harvest.
There must have been many failures, so many that in the
more arid areas it is a wonder that these beginning farmers
kept on trying year after year. But eventually the basic
lessons about agriculture were learned, and the planters
realized that good seed, fertile soil, plenty of water, fertilizer, sunshine, and weed eradication were needed to insure
bountiful harvests.

During some years, of course, the weather was so bad
that little or nothing was produced, but farmers have always
had to gamble. So have hunters and fishermen. It is only in

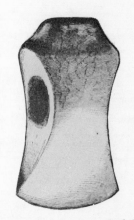

Diorite hammer axe [Joly]

235

modern times—and then only in a few favored places—that mankind's food supply has not been subject to risks that have to be encountered anew each season.

Before the plow was invented, soil was prepared for planting by loosening it with a pointed stick. Then it was found that a weighted stick dug deeper and required less muscular effort to push it into the ground. After men learned how to drill holes in stones, they made special weights for their digging sticks. Before that they had to make them heavier in any way they could, perhaps by tying stones on them. We don't know because nothing associated with the ancient digging sticks remains except the drilled weights.

This rudimentary tool was improved still further when one of its users discovered the fact that the projecting stub of a branch which stuck out low on the stick could serve as a footpiece that enabled him to push the point into the ground more easily. Then, when the rounded point of the stick was replaced by a flattened ending, the basic idea of the spade was born. Only metal was needed to perfect it.

Another important early agricultural tool was the hoe, which was needed to cut down weeds and break up the soil around the base of growing plants so water could permeate the ground near the roots. The first wooden hoe was probably made by taking a forked stick and cutting off one branch so the remaining section could serve as a blade. It wasn't a very good cutting or chopping tool, so stones, flat bones, or broad antler tines were attached to the handle to make a better hoe.

Prehistoric people probably did not devote enough attention to the cultivation of what they had planted, but somehow the hoped-for crop survived and became ready for harvesting. Larger vegetables were no problem, but tiny bits of grain were—and they were a major source of food. Fortunately, man had already had some experience with wild cereals before he planted his own. Since most ripe wild varieties drop off the stalk (or "shatter") when they are touched, the first harvesters probably knocked the grains into some kind of container made of hides or basketry. American Indians still gather wild rice by brushing it off overhanging stalks as they glide among them in their canoes.

The sickles with which ancient fieldworkers cut grain while it was still on the stalk have survived because they

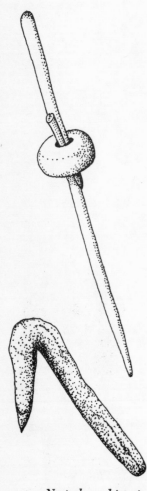

No truly prehistoric digging tools exist. The weighted digging stick is South African Bushman; the wooden hoe is Egyptian

236

*Flint sickles; the
second from the right
has a bronze blade
[Danish National Museum]*

were made of one or more pieces of flint mounted on a
wooden handle. Some handles were straight, but most were
curved like our modern sickles. In areas where there was no
stone that could be given a sharp cutting edge, sickle blades
were made of fired clay, but these came into use only after
pottery had been invented.

Some of the ancient sickles still have a glossy sheen on
their blades from the plants they cut, for grain straw is so
rich in silica that a thin coating of it was deposited on the
surface of the cutting tools. Flint or clay sickles were not
sharp enough to slice through hard, dry stalks as they stood
in the field, so the straw was bunched together in one hand
while the other sawed through the tight bundle with the
blade.

Since sickles were also used for cutting wild grain, their
presence on a site does not necessarily mean that the people
who lived there had learned how to raise their own crops.
Mortars and pestles, which were used for grinding the grain,
also preceded the cultivation of cereals, so they too may be
earlier than planted crops.

Baskets, which were needed for carrying the grain from
the field, were also made during the precultivation stage.
Our oldest examples of them are not the baskets or mats
themselves but impressions that woven reed left in Jarmo
about 7,000 years ago. The idea of weaving cloth presumably came from basket making.

Grain brought in while still on the stalk had to be

*Pictures from ancient
Egypt showing how
(1) grain stalks
were grasped by the left
hand before cutting;
(2) grain was ground
on a saddle quern*

237

threshed, but we do not know how this was done in Neolithic times. The flail may seem to be an obvious device for
separating grain from chaff, but this simple method was a
late invention—perhaps as late as Roman times.

PREHISTORIANS, who are always seeking new ideas to explain
vanished ways of unrecorded life, have raised an interesting
question: Did men use grain for making beer before they
found out how to grind it into flour for making bread? When
the arguments for and against beer were first presented in
a symposium in the *American Anthropologist* (October
1953; Vol. 55, No. 4, pp. 515–26; Robert J. Braidwood *et al*),
beer lost—but by a fairly narrow margin. No one doubted
that this popular beverage had very early origins, but the
more probable sequence of events, as outlined by Paul C.
Mangelsdorf, is: parched or popped cereals, gruel, un-
leavened bread, leavened bread, and then beer. He sums up
the case for the priority of beer with these solemn words:
"Did these Neolithic farmers forgo the extraordinary food
values of cereals in favor of alcohol, for which they had no
physiological need? Are we to believe that the foundations
of Western Civilization were laid by an ill-fed people living
in a perpetual state of partial intoxication?"

PARCHED OR popped cereals and even boiled gruel can be
used as food without having to pulverize the grain first.
This was an important advantage before people learned
how to make and use stone mortars, querns, and other simple
pounding or grinding devices. In America, for instance,
Indians ate popped corn before they found other ways to
prepare the cereal that was to be the staff of life in the
Western Hemisphere.

Making flour, however, soon became widely practiced
throughout the world. One undesirable product of the stone
mills was grit, the fine abrasive particles of stone that were
torn loose from the grinding surfaces and then were mixed
in with the food. Grit wore down the teeth. The new diet
brought other changes, too. Meat eating had required plenty
of strong chewing which developed powerful jaw muscles.
But cereals, domesticated fruits and vegetables, and tender
cooked meat from little-exercised farm animals began to
238 make subtle changes in man's facial features.

The jaws and its muscles were naturally affected; so were the teeth—notably so, in fact. In less than 10,000 years they diminished in size so much that today "the smallest teeth belong to those people whose forebears first enjoyed the benefits of the food-producing revolution. . . . A broad band [of such people] extends from central Europe through the Middle East, across northern India into the Far East and Southeast Asia corresponding with the areas where the food-producing revolution has exercised its effects for the longest period of time" (Brace and Montagu, 1965, p. 301). Americans and other colonials descended from stock that came from these areas naturally share their ancestors' small-tooth characteristics.

WHEN MAN first domesticated plants he did not try to improve them, but he did so inadvertently by replanting those that had turned out to be larger, better tasting, or more attractive than others. Darwin noted this in 1868 and called it the principle of unconscious selection.

After a while the difference between some highly cultivated plants and their parent stock became so great that they bore little or no resemblance to each other. Some varieties have been altered so much that the original state cannot be traced. Perhaps it no longer exists. The very act of growing vegetable food in a planted field has also affected its evolutionary development: "Variants arise [in the crop] from two sources: internal recombination and hybridization with wild populations in the neighborhood" (Darlington, 1963, p. 151). The crop is still further changed by cultivation in which seed selection, tilled soil, fertilization, and weeding improve the basic stock. Migration, which takes place when the human growers move to a new and very different area carrying viable planting material with them, may also have an effect upon the crop they attempt to grow in the new location.

For many thousands of years plants were altered (i.e., improved) by man only by unconscious selection. It was not until the seventeenth century that growers deliberately tried to produce new and better varieties by controlled breeding. The Dutch tulip specialists were pioneers in this when they took Oriental bulbs and developed new flower colors, shapes, and sizes from the original stock. They did

239

this largely by trial-and-error methods, for they did not understand the scientific principles involved in plant breeding, which were learned much later.

SINCE harvested crops had to supply food for a whole winter, dry, cool, and insect- and rodent-free storage places had to be provided for them. Baskets were used not only for gathering grain but for storing it. They were sometimes coated with clay to make them pestproof. Then when fire—probably by accident—baked one of these clay-smeared containers and hardened the covering into an impermeable substance, the basic idea for making pottery vessels was discovered. Paleolithic man had made figurines of fired clay, but it now became possible to produce large numbers of containers, utensils, and other useful objects from material that only had to be dug out of the ground. Until this time man had had nothing that could be placed over a fire for cooking. Boiling had been done by dropping hot stones into a container full of water.

A stone cup or ladle bowl from Mochlos, Crete [Metropolitan Museum of Art. Purchase, 1924; funds from various donors]

But even before men made pottery they fabricated bowls, dishes, jars, and similar objects out of solid stone. Since doing this required an enormous amount of highly skilled labor, such things were naturally highly cherished; one did not use such valuable containers for cooking.

The same craftsmen who worked patiently for long periods of time to produce a polished axe could turn their stone-shaping skill to making other things. And they had gained some previous experience when they carved roughly finished mortars, pestles, and querns out of rock.

Stone utensils were so durable that they could last for generations and may actually have held back the development of pottery in some places. It is believed that this happened at Jarmo and Jericho.

An object made of fired clay was much more breakable than one carved out of stone, but it could easily and cheaply be replaced. Before long, large quantities of pottery were being turned out wherever the right kind of clay was available. They were so plentiful that pottery products soon became important articles of trade. Since we have learned to trace pottery's origins, even when nothing but shards are left, we can determine ancient trade routes and date early settlements by analyzing the indestructible bits and fragments found on the sites.

The first pottery was presumably shaped by sticking the thumbs into a ball of soft clay to hollow out the center; then the side walls were pressed to make them thinner. Finally a crude watertight container was formed. Baking this in the fire would harden it sufficiently for limited use—limited because inadequate firing produced a vessel that could easily be broken.

Women are believed to have been the first potters. They soon found out that a round-bottomed support that could be turned made a good working surface for shaping the clay. A curved piece of large broken pottery served the purpose, and rotary motion enabled them to round out the clay. The device was, in fact, a primitive potter's wheel except that it would not keep turning for long because it was so light that the original spinning impetus given to it quickly died out.

Another early step in pottery making was to roll the clay into long snakelike coils that could be placed one above the other to build up a bowl or jar. Then a roundish hard object was held inside the finished clay piece so the potter could pound the outside surface against it with a flat paddle to smooth out the exterior. This method of making pottery was so similar to the way that baskets were built up by coiling a rope of twisted fiber into a desired shape (and then binding the coils together) that it was probably derived from it.

A further advance in pottery making was the turntable, which was simply an improvement of the earlier round-bottomed revolving support. The turntable was carefully fashioned for a particular purpose, and was better conceived and more efficient. It made the shaping of round clay vessels somewhat easier but it did not change the method or the end product.

The potter's wheel did. It was a heavy, flat, circular disk that turned on a pivot at an evenly maintained speed which was great enough to impart centrifugal force to a lump of soft clay placed at the center of the wheel. The clay tended to expand outward, and the hand of the potter could easily and quickly mold the pliable material into any wanted circular shape. The inside could then be hollowed out into amazingly thin walls.

The potter's wheel is one of mankind's first manufacturing mechanisms. As the demand for fired-clay vessels increased, what had been a woman's tribal art became big business and was naturally dominated by men. The wheel itself required no great amount of strength to keep it in motion; a push by the foot would do. But carrying the heavy clay vessels in quantity to the fire—and supplying kindling, stacking the pots, and tending the kiln—were considered to be work for men although women probably helped.

The earliest-known potter's wheel was found at Ur in 1930, but the device is believed to have come into use long before cities were built. Radiocarbon dating gives the Ur wheel an age of 5,250 ± 250 years. This is late, but pottery shaped on the wheel has easily identifiable striations around it, and shards with such marks have been found that are definitely Neolithic.

*Early potter's wheel
shown on an archaic
Greek plaque*

Prehistoric methods of firing clay did not produce temperatures high enough to give the baked objects the vitrified porcelain surface we are used to on our modern tableware, but the pots were serviceable enough to be used as common utensils. Most of what we know about prehistoric firing methods comes from the observation of primitive people living in modern times, although some early baking hearths have been found. The first pottery was heated to a temperature of slightly more than 450 degrees Centigrade in an open fire with dried-out pots filled with and surrounded by hot ashes. This method was used by peasants in Scotland as late as the mid-nineteenth century.

A temperature of somewhat more than 450 degrees Centigrade is required in order to drive chemically com-

242

bined water out of the clay and make a permanent structural change that keeps the baked pottery forever hard and resistant to crumbling. Later development enabled the Neolithic potters to produce higher temperatures when they learned how to use better heating methods. One still called for an open fire, but the pots were placed on a rack above the embers, and heat was conserved by piling incombustible materials on top of them. A far better method was the use of a closed kiln in which the heat could be controlled, directed, and replenished. With this, the making of pottery reached a state of perfection that has been little improved upon since.

Pottery is a form of sculpture; it is shaped by the hand, and the final product is three-dimensional in form. It appeals to the artistry in man, so it is only natural that it was decorated from earliest times. The easiest way to ornament the surface was to impress patterns in the surface of the clay while it was still soft. Fingernails, shells, sharp-pointed bits of wood and twisted cord are only some of the things that

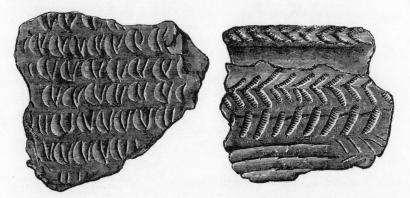

were used to mark the surface. When the potter's wheel came in, all kinds of decorative striations could be made on the clay as it revolved under the skilled hands of the ceramist.

Decorated pottery from the West Kennet Tumulus, England [Lubbock]

The surface could also be painted in color, which was then made permanent when it was baked on as a glaze. All these methods make the pottery identifiable even when it has been smashed to bits. Each fragment has a story to tell to expert eyes: it can be dated, classified according to probable use, and even traced back to its point of origin, sometimes to the very kiln in which it was baked.

When archeologists sort out enormous quantities of potsherds, their first task is to classify the individual pieces into groups according to the exact place in which they were found, their relative date as determined by their occurrence in stratified layers, the kind of clay from which they were made, and their more easily observable surface characteristics. In recent years science had come to the aid of archeology and made even more subtle distinctions possible.

The same kind of petrological examination that is used on stone axes can be applied to pottery. Spectrographic analysis reveals relative proportions of elements to determine the source of the clay from which the vessel was made. Nuclear bombardment has also been used for the same purpose, and it has the great advantage of not harming rare specimens. X-ray fluorescent spectrometry is still another technique that does not damage the material inspected.

A very new and promising method is thermoluminescent dating, which has been described by Dr. Froelich G. Rainey, director of the University of Pennsylvania Museum, as follows: "Radiation from the minute traces of radioactive elements [primarily thorium and uranium] in pottery clay bombards other substances in the clay and raises electrons to metastable [slightly unstable] levels. When the clay is fired in the kiln each electron falls back to its stable position and emits a photon of light. Then, when a fragment of ancient pottery is reheated in the laboratory, the amount of thermoluminescence observed is representative of the accumulated radiation damage and hence of the time elapsed since the original firing of the pottery" ("New Techniques in Archeology," Philadelphia, November 12, 1965). Dr. Rainey says that the technique has an average uncertainty of plus or minus 300 years.

Even more remarkable is thermoremanent magnetic dating which enables scientists to establish a date for the ancient kiln in which the pottery was fired.

POTTERY was one great Neolithic invention; another was the weaving of cloth. But pottery, even when broken, lasts indefinitely, whereas cloth quickly decays. Very little really old fabric has come down to us to tell us what Neolithic people wore, and the few examples we do have are relatively late.

When an agricultural way of life replaces a hunting economy, animal skins become scarce, so a new kind of material for making garments is needed. Some experience in weaving had been gained from making fishnets and baskets. Thread and cord had long been used for fishing lines, for sewing leather garments, and for tying axe-heads to shafts. In many cases sinews were used instead of thread, but the principle is the same. The way was ready for weaving cloth, and the making of it soon became a reality. Felt, which is made by pressing wet fibers together, was also produced, especially in eastern Europe.

The weaving of cloth began before looms were invented, and we have great numbers of enduring artifacts that tell us just where and when people did the weaving. These are the almost imperishable stone or baked-clay spindle whorls. More than 8,000 of them have been found in Troy alone. They, and not the cloth they helped to produce, are our best evidence about weaving in Neolithic times. Millions of them must have been made.

A few bits of very old cloth come from Egypt, where they were woven about 7,000 years ago. As has been mentioned, the oldest European cloth specimens were found in the Swiss lakeside villages where undisturbed submergence in water had preserved them. Ancient clothing was still on the permanently frozen bodies of Scythian chieftains who were buried in deep underground tombs, but they are of a more recent date, as are the well-preserved corpses dug out of peat bogs in Scandinavia and northern Germany (see chapter 27).

JUST AS agriculture and the domestication of animals originated independently in the Americas, so were pottery making and cloth weaving also invented there. There is some doubt as to just how "independent" these originations were because recent studies show that the New World was not quite as isolated from the Old as it was long thought to be.

But animals that would pull wheeled vehicles were lacking in both North and South America. Aside from dogs, the South American llama and alpaca were the only beasts of burden available, and they are inferior in size and strength to the horse or the ox. Of the two, only the llama is useful as a pack animal; the alpaca provides wool but does not

A sandstone spindle whorl from Holyhead, England [Joly]

do any work.

The horse originated in the New World but became extinct there and was not reintroduced until February 1519, when Hernán Cortés brought 17 of them from Cuba for use in his conquest of Mexico. The bison, which roamed the plains of North America in vast herds, was hunted for its meat and hides but was not domesticated.

PRACTICALLY ALL of the world's primary inventions had been made by Neolithic times. Only metal remained to be discovered as a better material than stone for making implements and tools.

Neolithic people built imposing monuments, some of which remain almost intact to remind us of the long-dead people who constructed them. With them, prehistory comes out of the museum and stands out in the open for everyone to see.

Three amulets made from bone removed by trepanning. Found in France

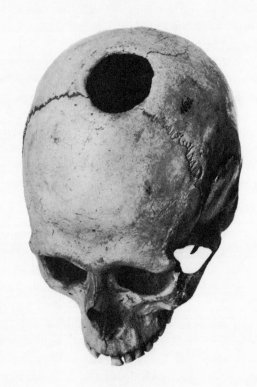

A trepanned skull. The rounded edges indicate that the patient recovered [Danish National Museum]

246

22. The Great Stone Monuments

OUT OF THE eastern Mediterranean, somewhat more than 5,000 years ago, came a new religion, complete with missionaries, priests, converts, and at least one ruling deity that we know of—the time-defying, all-pervasive Mother Goddess. This dimly perceived religion, however, went beyond her to embrace things that we do not know about. Its powerful force inspired the building of the great stone monuments. There are 40,000 or 50,000 of them scattered along the coastal areas of western Europe and on some of the sea islands. A few are located inland.

The cave murals were man's first large-sized, spiritually inspired productions that were evidently intended to last far beyond his own generation; these massive stone monuments were the second. Both testify to their creators' skill by having come down through the ages almost intact; both are still able to impress the beholder with an indefinable power that goes beyond the substance of which they are made.

Anyone who has ever seen the carefully placed big gray rocks of Stonehenge, Carnac, or numerous other major prehistoric sites knows how impressive they are. All kinds of legends have sprung up about the huge standing stones. To this day the people who live near them credit them with strange supernatural powers. These silent witnesses have stood there for so many centuries and have seen so many generations come and go that they seem to have taken on an anthropomorphic character from their long contact with people. All rocks are far older than mankind, but those that still remain in their original geological sites, unshaped by human hands, seem alien to us. The stones that make up the menhirs, the dolmens, the passage graves, the alignments, and the circles were put into position by people like ourselves. Something of that ancient bond with humanity still seems to cling to them. The rocks in the Grand Canyon and the high Alps may have grandeur, but they are remote, while the weatherbeaten stones of the megalithic monuments have long been associated with mankind.

The vast amount of energy expended in putting these heavy stones into place was the greatest output of concerted effort that men had yet made. All the work had to be done with human muscles unaided by animal power of any kind, and the builders had only primitive devices for moving the big stones and standing them upright.

The idea of hauling giant boulders to a chosen site and laboriously building monuments with them would never occur to people who were living in a sparse economy unless they were driven by extraordinary motives. Fear of the unknown, of higher powers, or of threats made by the priests may have sufficed, but there may have been more positive reasons. Strange but mighty beliefs were abroad in those days.

Whatever it was, we know that the impulse to build these great monuments moved westward along the Mediter-

A Carnac menhir

Opposite page: above, part of one of the Carnac alignments; below, the passage-grave chamber in King Asger's Barrow [Danish National Museum]

248

ranean and up the Atlantic coast leaving one example after another along the way. The passage grave at Île-Carn in western Brittany has a radiocarbon date of 3436 ± 75 B.C. This is older than the first pyramids of Egypt, for the Step Pyramid of Zoser is dated at 2686 B.C., while the Great Pyramid of Cheops is, of course, even later. And the pyramids were built by slave labor, by men who were driven to a hateful task, while work on the European megaliths was presumably done voluntarily. The Egyptian kings were erecting monuments to their own glory and to protect their own mummified bodies; the megalith builders had broader social reasons for what they did.

It should be noted here that at this time civilization was beginning in Sumer and that writing was soon to come into being. With writing, prehistory would become history, but it was to take thousands of years for the written word to penetrate the farthest parts of Europe.

GLYN DANIEL, who has specialized on the European megaliths, suggests that natural caves and the Minoan collective tombs called *tholoi* may be the origin of the European chamber graves (1963, p. 121).

Daniel believes that the idea of building collective rock tombs was probably brought to Europe by the Minoans, who made stops along the way in Malta, Spain, and southern France. In Sardinia and the Balearics they taught the native inhabitants how to build cyclopean architecture. From these five centers chamber tombs spread to "the rest of France, the British Isles, and Scandinavia" where it "manifested itself in many forms—the rock-cut tomb, the corbelled dry-walled vault, the megalithic chamber, the cyclopean tomb of *naveta*-Giants Grave type, or any intermediate form between these."

Cyclopean architecture differs from megalithic, for cyclopean structures are built by placing very large stones on top of one another very much as bricks are laid, whereas "the essentials of megalithic construction are either the single large slab or the large slab as walling stone with another large slab resting on two or more large walling stones as a capstone—a sort of house of cards architecture" (Daniel, 1963, p. 18).

The "Christianized" menhir at Saint-Duzec-en-Ploumeur, Brittany. It was decorated in medieval times to remove all pagan influences

In the enormous alignments of Brittany, where thousands of large rocks were placed in rows with "the individual stones often graduated in size, with the largest ones placed nearest to the culminating point of the alignment," a special problem arose. "How did the men who constructed the alignments solve the problem of supply for this complicated job? To arrange stones in graduated rows is far more difficult than to put them up in random order, because you need the right-sized one to put in place next. This requires having a great many stones of various sizes on hand to choose from" (Stern, 1967, p. 196).

Some of the many alignments at Carnac

In some cases, a need was felt for certain kinds of stone that could not be had anywhere near the site. The building material for the Moulins tomb near Châteauroux, for instance, was brought from a natural outcropping 30 miles away. An even more remarkable example of heavy rocks being moved for a great distance can be seen at Stonehenge, where the bluestones came from the Prescelly Mountains in Wales, which are 140 miles away. Details of the probable methods of transport are described in the next chapter.

MORE THAN A century ago (in 1864) W. C. Lukis made the first attempt to classify rock tombs by dividing them into those which had only a single chamber and those which are more complex. The simplest kind, which usually consist of a large capstone supported by walling rocks, is called a dolmen in France and a cromlech in Wales. The more elaborate

251

tombs are basically passage graves, although there are many variations. The finer points need not concern us here.

Some of the tombs had portholes cut into them. It is believed that these were made in order to let the spirits of the newly buried corpses depart from their enforced abode; that they were intended to permit food and drink be passed into the interior to satisfy the presumably importunate dead; or that they permitted more bones to be placed inside without having to move one of the heavy stones. Actually, we do not know why these holes were laboriously cut through solid rock.

Since the rock-chambered tombs were preceded in time (especially in England) by collective burials covered by mounds of earth, it is easy to see why many of the rock graves were also buried under huge heaps of soil. At some places the covering has been washed away or deliberately removed by local people, leaving only the basic rocks.

A bell-shaped round barrow [Dawkins]

The far simpler and earlier earthen mounds are called round barrows when they are circular in shape, long barrows when they are elongated. There are hundreds of both kinds on the treeless downs near Stonehenge. And some 20 miles north, near the great stone circle at Avebury, is Silbury Hill, the biggest artificial mound in Europe. It is about 125 feet high and covers more then five acres. Exploratory shafts and tunnels have been dug into it during the past two centuries, but nothing of significance was found. The impressive-looking hill is now being excavated again. Perhaps the new work will tell us something about the reason for its existence. There must have been a powerful motive for going to so much trouble, for more than 12,000,000 cubic feet of earth had to be carried up an ever-growing slope in small containers by numerous workers who had to be housed and fed for a long time.

*Silbury Hill as seen
from the air [British
Ministry of Public
Building and Works]*

Both barrows and rock-chambered tombs were used for
collective burials. Families and tribes understandably
wanted to be interred together, just as they do now. Oddly
enough, however, once the corpses were reduced to skeletons, their positions in the mass grave were no longer re-
spected, and the disjointed bones were often pushed aside
to make room for additional bodies.

Nearly all the megalithic monuments were funerary in
purpose, but a few had to do with life rather than death.
Simplest of all are the menhirs, which can be found in many
places in Europe although the greatest concentration of
them is in Brittany. They are usually long, slender stones
stood on end. A few have been roughly shaped and some
even have been carved, but most of them are natural rocks
that were brought to the site where they were given significance by their location, their spatial relationship to one another, and by their standing erect for centuries. But the
law of gravity must eventually prevail; many have fallen;
others have been pulled down by farmers who wanted to
get rid of them; still others have been deliberately broken
up by wall and road builders.

Some of the menhirs stand alone, put in place perhaps
either to commemorate some forgotten event that occurred
where they are now located or to mark a spot that was believed to have some magical or religious power.

The biggest of them all, the Breton giant of Locmariaquer, which was nearly 70 feet high when it was put up, fell

253

The great fallen menhir at Locmariaquer

centuries ago and was broken into five huge pieces when it hit the ground. Only a few feet away from it is the Table des Marchands, which is a fine example of a large dolmen with carved symbols on the inner faces of its rocks.

This part of Brittany has so many megaliths that one is hardly ever out of sight of the big gray standing stones. Carnac has the greatest concentration of them. There the alignments contain thousands of menhirs arranged in parallel rows that run for miles. Scattered among them are dolmens and other megalithic monuments. Carnac also has the Tumulus Saint Michel, which is 350 feet long and 40 feet high and was used as a burial place. Located on an island in the Gulf of Morbihan is the Tumulus de Gavr'inis, which has some interesting carved stones in its underground chamber.

This part of southern Brittany, like the area around Stonehenge, was a religious center just as Jerusalem and the Vatican are now. To it came large numbers of pilgrims to attend ceremonies that must forever remain unknown. One thing about them, however, is certain and that is that the priests who presided over them were not Druids (nor were there Druids at Stonehenge), for they did not come on the scene until many centuries later. The Druids were contemporary with Julius Caesar, who describes their rites in 53 B.C. in his *Commentaries*, Book VI.

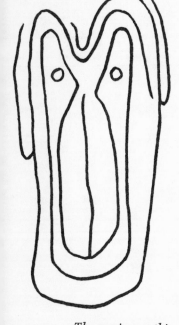

The carving on this menhir at Lufang, Brittany, may be a cephalopod—or perhaps a human face

CARVINGS on the megaliths are rather rare and in some areas do not exist. But there are a fair number of them in Malta, Corsica, southern France, Brittany, and Ireland, especially at New Grange. These rock carvings are all late, for the men who built the monuments became interested in decorating

254

them only after they had learned how to handle the heavy stones. It is also quite possible that in some instances the rocks were carved centuries after they had originally been put in place.

Since the earliest carvings were executed long before metal came into use in this part of Europe, they had to be done by chipping away the rock surface with hand-held stones. In some protected places pockmarked areas remain to show that this was the method employed. Sharp flints may have been used for putting in finer details.

It has been said that some ancient peoples—in Peru, for instance—knew how to soften rocks by applying certain strong liquid mixtures to them (Sanderson, 1967, Ch. 7). If this could have been done, the number of expert man-hours needed to carve elaborate bas-reliefs would have been considerably reduced. But even if it is true, the materials found in tropical jungles were not likely to have been available in prehistoric Europe.

As MORE AND MORE evidence about the migrations of the people who built the European megalithic monuments is uncovered, classified, compared, and interpreted, scientists are beginning to trace the connections between the various builders. Oríordáin and Daniel (1964, pp. 133*ff.*) say that some of them "crossed the sea from Brittany or Spain to Ireland and settled there. New Grange and the tombs in the Bend of the Boyne are, then, the tombs of these settlers, who spread up from Ireland and Wales to Scotland and the Orkneys. The great tomb of Maes Howe in Orkney . . . is particularly interesting in that its side chambers are not placed at ground level as at New Grange but up in the sides of the walls—a feature exactly paralleled at Alcalá in south Portugal."

Carved chalk drums from Folkton Wold, Yorkshire, c. 1800–1500 B.C. [British Museum]

255

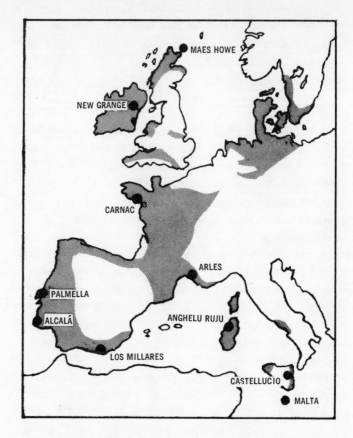

*Some of the more
important megalithic
sites in western Europe
[After Daniel]*

Óríordáin and Daniel believe that contacts between the
various colonies was kept up over the centuries and that it
was for this reason that the carved stones of New Grange
and Gavr'inis (in Brittany) are so similar. They also point
out other resemblances. Decorations on the pots from passage graves in the Copenhagen National Museum, for instance, are very much like "the ancient oculi patterns . . . on
the *symbolkeramik* of southern Iberia." And, they say, one
can "look at the scribings on the tomb of the Holm of Papa
Westray in Orkney or the slab from Eday now in the National Museum of Antiquities of Scotland and see the ghostly
end of Mediterranean megalithic art in Ultima Thule." Nor
is this all, for the megalithic stone carvers evidently got to
the Canary Islands, where examples of their work can be
seen on rock surfaces rather than on tombs.

Any metal which the later megalithic builders may have
256 brought with them from the more advanced lands of the

*Kit's Coty in Kent—
all that remains of
what was once a
chambered long barrow
covered over with earth
[Lubbock]*

eastern Mediterranean must have been a wonder to the
primitive people they encountered in Europe. But the natives there did not take readily to the new material. They
were glad enough to get a few finished implements made
of it, but they were slow to learn how to mine, smelt, and
work it. And it is possible that knowledge of such skilled arts
was deliberately withheld from them by the newcomers. As
a result, metal is seldom found in excavations of megalithic
monuments. It may, however, have been removed by people who came later and who would not hesitate to rob the
tombs for it.

The large and very prominent megalithic monuments
have been around for so many centuries that they have been
pretty well picked over. Scientific excavation still uncovers
some important artifacts, but amateur or semiamateur dig-
gers have long ago taken away most of the major objects.
Fortunately, a good bit of the material that was discovered
earlier has been safely deposited in European museums.

WHEN THE spreaders of megalithic culture arrived in Scandinavia, they found that some small rock-chambered tombs
were already in existence there, having—apparently—been
developed independently. All archeologists, however, do not
agree about this. Glyn Daniel, who believes in the independent origin, says (1963, pp. 56ff.): "The most probable
view at present, as well as the most widely held, is that
while the *dös/dysse* type of monument originated in south
Denmark . . . the Passage Grave builders . . . came by sea
from western Europe. . . . The precise area is difficult to

257

define; I would myself think in terms of direct contact with Brittany and Portugal, and that the route taken was via the English Channel. Others have argued for the spread to have taken place round the north of Scotland, claiming a likeness between some of the north Scottish tomb plans and the T-shaped Passage Graves of northern Europe. . . . Now that it seems likely that the *dös/dysse* type of monument was independently developed in northern Europe, we can perhaps see the Passage Grave builders, instead, as the Atlantic voyagers who effected the conversion to a new religion, or at least to new mortuary cults; and see this conversion as all the more easily effected in an area where already small megalithic tombs, the *dös/dysse* type, were being constructed."

Since the megalithic monuments were built after men had learned how to make utensils out of baked clay, shards and even some unbroken vessels have helped to date and trace the origins, affiliations, and trade routes of the men who brought foreign-made pottery into Europe. And since the monuments continued to be built well into the period when copper and bronze implements came into use, the megaliths bridge the long span of time between the New Stone Age and the Age of Metals.

During these many thousands of years cities were rising in the Middle East, in Egypt, and on some of the Mediterranean islands. Unlike our modern cities, which are subordinated to the nations in which they are located, these early large communities were city-states that completely dominated the territory around them. The culture of cities, which we call civilization, was well under way. But in the more remote areas of Europe where Rome, Madrid, Paris, Brussels, Amsterdam, London, Copenhagen, Bergen, Stockholm, and Moscow are now situated, prehistoric ways of living still continued. In places that were even more remote, Mesolithic and even Paleolithic conditions continued almost unchanged. This uneven rate of development must always be kept in mind. Since we live in a world where there are still primitive tribes in certain areas, it should not be hard to understand this.

23. Prehistoric Religious Centers

WHEN ENGLAND was cut off from the mainland by the rising level of the sea, the art of building boats and ships was so well advanced that people continued to settle there. While the land bridge was still in existence, settlers tended to remain in the south near the place where they had first arrived. But once they came by sea, all the coasts were available to them, and communities sprang up in remote areas. Yet from that day to this, the south of England has been the favored region, probably because the climate is better there.

The British Neolithic settlement about which we have most knowledge is Windmill Hill, which is located on the northern edge of a section of southern England that soon became the most populated region in the British Isles. Within a walk of it are the vast stone circles of Avebury; 20 miles to the south is Stonehenge. All around are barrows, passage graves, and ceremonial avenues that testify to the religious activities that were practiced there in ancient times.

Since these times extended from the Neolithic period to the Bronze Age in England, the monuments span both eras. For the sake of convenience they are being discussed together here.

The best-known prehistoric monument in Europe is undoubtedly Stonehenge. Its fame is well founded, for it is easy to visit and stands in a prominent place where it can be seen for miles. And despite a certain amount of damage, Stonehenge is still an imposing sight. As a result, the literature on it goes further back in time than the writings on any other European prehistoric stone monument do.

The Stonehenge one sees today consists of a circular earthen bank and an outer ditch more than 380 feet in diameter, within which are the remains of a circle of large standing stones. These sarsen stones enclose a ring of smaller bluestones and five big trilithons arranged in horseshoe form. Inside this horseshoe is a smaller one made of bluestones. 259

Originally all five of the trilithons were capped by lintels that were firmly fixed in place by mortises and tenons chiseled out of the rock. Countless storms and deliberate destruction have brought down many of the stones, and some have been broken to pieces and carted away. At one time hammers could be rented by visitors who wanted to chip off a piece of rock to take home as a souvenir. Now the British Ministry of Public Works carefully guards the celebrated monument and makes sure it is not damaged.

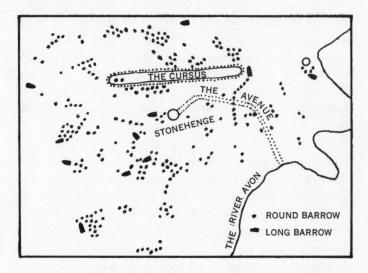

The area around Stonehenge shows how many burial mounds were located near it

North of Stonehenge is the Cursus, a narrow strip of land nearly two miles long with ditches and banks marking its sides. And the Avenue, which has almost been obliterated by centuries of plowing, connects Stonehenge with the Salisbury Avon River. Both presumably were used as processional ways.

It is evident from the great number of prehistoric earthworks and purposely positioned stones in this region that it was once sacred territory, a holy place where people wanted to be buried and to which they came regularly to attend religious ceremonies.

Stonehenge I was built nearly 4,000 years ago in Neolithic times. This first phase of the monument consisted only of a large circular bank and ditch, three standing stones, some wooden posts, and a 274-foot-diameter inner ring of 56 small round holes that may have been filled in shortly after they were dug. Cremated human bones were put in

some of them. They are called the Aubrey Holes after John Aubrey, the antiquary who first brought them to public attention in 1666.

Stonehenge II had a double circle of 80 or more bluestones. This phase lasted for only about half a century, but during that time the first Bronze Age settlers arrived in England. There could not have been many of them, nor did the metal tools they brought seem to have any noticeable effect upon the technique of building Stonehenge III.

For this final and most ambitious construction the double ring of bluestones was removed, and the tall sarsen stones

Stonehenge. Note the tenon on top of the upright stone. Below: a view of the Heelstone from the center of the circle

261

and their massive lintels were put up in a closed circle within which the bluestones were reset in their present arrangement. Several alterations were made, but the last positioning of the stones was completed about 400 years after the first work on Stonehenge I had begun. Like the great medieval cathedrals, this prehistoric temple took time to build and rebuild. And like them it was built to defy time.

The engineering required to move the heavy stones, roughly cut them into shape, and put them into place has been the subject of much inquiry in modern times. The big sarsen stones, some of which weigh nearly 50 tons, were dragged 20 miles overland from the Marlborough Downs northeast of Avebury, while the bluestones were brought from the Prescelly Mountains in southern Wales, the only place where rocks of this kind can be found. These mountains are about 140 miles west of Stonehenge, but any practicable route would have had to be much longer than that. It is believed that the big stones were put on rafts and then ferried across the Bristol Channel to the mouth of the Bristol Avon River. From there they were taken upstream while still on the rafts. (The rafts may have been canoes lashed together.)

At some point along the river nearest to Stonehenge, the big rocks were taken ashore to be moved on rollers. Large numbers of men hauling on twisted or braided rawhide cables supplied the motive power. It is possible that some smaller streams may have been used with portages in between them.

The sarsen stones, which were much larger and heavier, could be moved across land in the same way. It has been suggested that the overland work may have been done during the winter when snow and ice would have made it possible to slide the stones across the ground, and there would have been no problem with mud in cold weather. But the climate in England was rather warm then, so there may not have been enough snow or ice to make the work easier.

One way or another, the enormous task of building Stonehenge was finally completed, and the monument, which was far more advanced in concept and construction than anything in western Europe, stood in all its glory on the cloud-swept downs. It has been estimated that the 400-hundred-year-long concerted effort to build Stonehenge I, II,

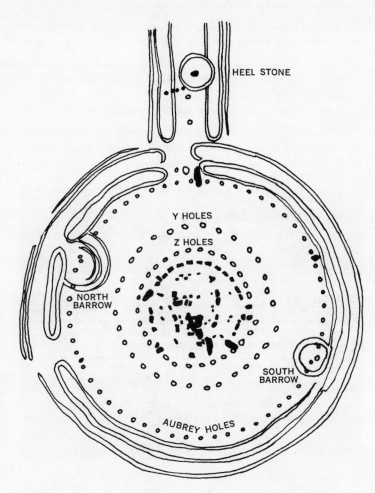

HEEL STONE

Y HOLES

Z HOLES

NORTH
BARROW

SOUTH
BARROW

AUBREY HOLES

*A plan of Stonehenge
showing its circular
ditches and salient
features*

and III required 1.5 million man-days of exceedingly hard labor. How were the sparsely fed, poorly housed, ignorant, and completely illiterate people of southern England persuaded to work so strenuously for so many generations? They were evidently inspired by the same kind of religious fervor that built the great cathedrals of Europe many centuries later. But who, in so backward and uneducated a land, could plan such an enormous undertaking, figure out the engineering methods needed, have a knowledge of the logistics required, and also design the elaborate architecture of the structure itself? Nor is this all, for Stonehenge apparently was intended to serve as an astronomical observatory as well.

263

It has been said that such masterly work could have been the product only of a single mind, the mind of a nameless genius fit to rank with Leonardo da Vinci. Since no one man can live for 400 years, there must have been others. Where did they come from and how did they acquire the necessary background for the task?

Some light was cast on these questions in June 1953 when R. J. C. Atkinson, the noted specialist on Stonehenge, found several axe-heads and a hilted dagger carved on one of the stones. Since then more than 30 other such symbols

The daggers and axe heads on one of the upright stones; photo has been slightly retouched to make them visible

have been discovered. Their design points to a Mycenaen or Minoan origin. Did some experienced designer come to England from the eastern Mediterranean to plan Stonehenge? And did he bring some skilled workmen with him? It is not impossible, for Aegean seafarers had reached the Atlantic by then.

Whoever planned Stonehenge was a master architect who knew as much about building as anyone in Europe did at that time. And it has recently been suggested that Stonehenge was intended to be more than a temple, that its primary purpose was to observe the sun and the moon and predict their eclipses. Anyone who could do that in prehistoric England would of course, be in a position of extraordinary power.

264   As far back as the seventeenth century it had been noted

that Stonehenge's main axis was oriented so that a man standing in the center of the monument could look through the opening between stones Number 1 and 30 and see the sun rise over the Heelstone at dawn on the day of the summer solstice (about June 21). But there the matter was allowed to rest for many years. In 1872 James Ferguson, in his pioneering book, *Rude Stone Monuments* (p. 7), scoffed at the idea that Stonehenge had ever had any astronomical functions. It is true that the sun does not rise exactly over the Heelstone at that crucial moment nowadays, but the big rock has shifted a bit during the last 4,000 years.

In 1963 Gerald S. Hawkins, an English-born astronomer working at the Smithsonian Astrophysical Observatory in Cambridge, Massachusetts, sent an article entitled "Stonehenge Decoded" to *Nature*, which published it on October 26. It presents the findings he had made by using a computer to determine some of the possible alignments of the stones in relation to sky positions of the sun and the moon. In this, and in an elaboration of the original article which appeared as a book of the same title in 1965, Hawkins came up with several new ideas about Stonehenge. Despite the fact that some stones had fallen, had moved out of position, or were missing entirely, he showed that as Stonehenge was originally built, its "sun-moon alignments were created . . . [to make] a calendar, particularly useful to tell the time for planting crops; they [also] helped to create and maintain priestly power by enabling the priest to call out the multitude to see the spectacular risings and settings of the sun and the moon, most especially the midsummer sunrise over the heelstone through the great trilithon" (Hawkins, 1965, p. 117). Even more remarkable, Hawkins also found out that the 56 Aubrey Holes, which encircle the monument, could serve as a device to predict eclipses of the sun and the moon. All one had to do was move marking stones in a certain order around the hitherto mysterious circle of small holes. This obviously called for mathematical insight of a high order.

Hawkins' book immediately aroused a controversy that still goes on. One of the leaders of the opposition was R. J. C. Atkinson, the acknowledged expert on Stonehenge. He said that he doubted whether "a barbarous and illiterate community . . . which has left us no other evidence of numeracy" could have designed Stonehenge to be an elaborate astronomical instrument. But according to Oxford's Alexander Thom, who has made a specialty of studying British megaliths and the arrangement of their stones, the men who built them knew something about geometry and trigonometry long before the Greeks did.

But the most unexpected defense of Hawkins came from Fred Hoyle, the noted Cambridge astronomer (*Nature*, July 1966). He not only supported the general thesis but showed how the Aubrey Hole prediction method could be improved by the use of six indicator stones, two of which would represent lunar nodes, which are the points at which the moon's orbit intersects the plane of the earth's equator. Unlike the sun (S) and the moon (M), which can be seen, the nodes are conceptual, not visible. With this in mind, Hoyle goes on to an interesting bit of speculation about certain widespread religious ideas. "Suppose this [Stonehenge] system was invented by a society with cultural beliefs associated with the sun and the moon. If the sun and the moon are given godlike qualities, what shall we say of N [node]? Observation shows that whenever M and S are closely associated with N [in the sky], eclipses occur. Our [visible] gods are then eliminated. Evidently then, N must be a still more powerful God. But N is unseen. Could this be the origin of an invisible all-powerful God, the God of Isaiah? . . . Could M, N, and S be the origin of the Trinity, the three in one, the one in three?"

It must be pointed out here that the possibility that Stonehenge could be used as an astronomical observatory does not necessarily mean that it was so used. Conceivably the stones could have been placed as they are purely by accident. But the odds against this, when calculated by Hawkins for the sun-moon alignments alone, are one in a million. Combined with all the other factors, especially the Aubrey Holes, the odds against an unplanned astronomical arrangement become fantastic.

Mental powers of the highest order were needed to conceive of, plan, and construct so advanced a project as Stonehenge. Hoyle (*Antiquity*, December 1966, p. 274) says of this: "It seems to me that the three essential requirements for high intellectual achievement are availability of food, leisure and social stability, and good communication. It must be possible for people in one district to know what is being done in other districts. Outstanding individuals must be able to get together. The young must be taught. Preferably the brightest youngsters should be brought into a 'university.' There seems to be no reason why the society in southern England around 2000 B.C. did not meet all these requirements."

Hoyle went even farther than this when he said that in 2000 B.C. the human gene pool may not have been as well mixed as it is now and then added: "In which case it is likely that the intellectual norm of some groups was higher, and perhaps considerably higher, than the present-day norm."

Hawkins refused to go along with Hoyle's idea of the superior intellect of the men who planned and built Stonehenge, however, and he also said (1967, p. 92): "It may be, I feel, that no astronomer—not even one as gifted and versatile as Hoyle—is equipped to go as a guide so far into the regions of archeology and anthropology, and the mazes of the spirit."

Shortly after this Jacquetta Hawkes summarized the Hawkins-Hoyle theories about Stonehenge in an article in *Antiquity* entitled "God in the Machine" (1967, pp. 174–80) and was quite skeptical about them. She began by saying that "every age has the Stonehenge it desires—and deserves" and concluded by stating her belief that "nothing of any great moment has been established by the astronomical *nouveau vague* flowing over Stonehenge."

The controversy, however, still goes on. It is just as well that it should because sharply contrasting views by experts keeps a subject alive and the Stonehenge problem may benefit from the added thought and field investigation that should result from this lively tilt at arms.

THE UNITED STATES has a Stonehenge, too. It is a modern one located near Maryhill, Washington, a town on the Columbia River about 100 miles east of Portland, Oregon. There a full-sized replica of Stonehenge III was built of concrete during the 1920's to serve as a war memorial. Since it is five degrees farther south than the original Stonehenge, its sun-moon alignments are different.

THE MEN—and the religious ideas—that were responsible   267 for Stonehenge also built the great circular earthwork and stone circles of Avebury. There once were about a hundred big sarsen stones in the circle just inside the encompassing mound and ditch. There are basically two kinds of them, pillars and lozenges, but they are rough because no attempt was made to trim them into shape. The surrounding bank is so large—about 1,300 feet in diameter—that it covers 28 acres. Within it are two smaller stone circles and traces of a third one. Avebury is so vast that each inner circle is larger than the similar one at Stonehenge. In fact, they are larger than Stonehenge's surrounding bank and ditch.

Much of Avebury was systematically destroyed from the fourteenth to the eighteenth centuries when local people tried to get rid of the stones by burying them. Actually, this was fortunate, for modern archeologists have been able to dig them up and put them back in place. What was done during the decades around 1700 was worse because many of the stones were burned or broken up then. The houses and garden walls in the little town of Avebury, which is located inside the big monument, were constructed from pieces of these once-sacred stones.

An avenue leads south from the village, and this cere-monial way was lined with standing stones. Rome, the great road builder of ancient times, was an unoccupied hilly bit of land when the British processional ways were in use.

A mile south of Avebury is the huge mound called Sil-

The area around
Avebury

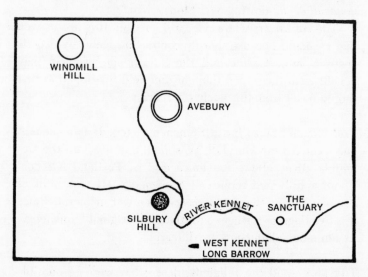

bury Hill, which was described in the previous chapter. Farther south is West Kennet Long Barrow, the largest rock-chambered tomb in England. A mile east of this is the Sanctuary, a double circle of standing stones that replaced an earlier one made of logs. These wooden circles, like Woodhenge near Stonehenge, represent an earlier phase. It is believed that they were roofed over. Nothing remains of them now except the filled-in post holes.

Nor does much remain visible of the famous type site, Windmill Hill. Archeological excavation shows that this now-isolated place was once a thriving Neolithic settlement (2570 ± 150 B.C.), although it may not have been an all-year one. Three concentric rings of eight-foot-deep ditches had been dug there to make a 20-acre cattle enclosure. It is believed that scattered tribes brought their herds to this in the autumn and lived off their meat during the winter.

These very early Britons dwelled on the outskirts of the huge cattle corral in rude timber huts, dressed in animal skins which they prepared by using flint scrapers, and made excellent polished stone implements. They dug their far-flung ditches with antler tools, raised meager crops of wheat and barley in soil that was prepared by digging-sticks, and stored grain for the winter months.

They had come from northern France, as is shown by their pottery and burial customs, for they interred their dead collectively in long barrows.

Ceremonial stones and relatively modern houses are all mixed together at Avebury

The bottom stone in the kerb circle at New Grange

The region around Avebury and Stonehenge is rich with prehistoric monuments of various kinds, but the British Isles have many others. An outstanding one is on the east coast of Ireland on the northern shore of the Bend of Boyne. This is New Grange, which is celebrated for its finely carved stones, some of which resemble those found in Malta and Crete.

A standing stone in the Orkney Islands with multiple arcs, concentric circles, and spirals

New Grange is a round barrow 280 feet in diameter, 40 feet high, and about an acre in extent. Inside the earthen mound is a well-built cruciform stone burial chamber with a long rock-lined passage leading to it. Originally the mound was entirely covered with white pebbles and was surrounded by a circle of some 30 standing stones. On the top stood a single megalith. Little remains of what once was outside, but the corbel-vaulted interior passages are in excellent shape. The monument probably dates to about 2500 B.C.

New Grange's chief feature is the wealth of carved decoration on its big stones. Spirals, circles, cupules, zigzags, triangles, lozenges, and other abstract symbols cover many of them. The motifs are like those found on the carved rocks of Brittany, Portugal, and Spain. Since they are closely connected with the Mother Goddess, they will be dealt with in the next chapter.

Except for Stonehenge, which seems far in advance of its time, Europe's most remarkable megaliths are located in Brittany. There are thousands of big stones there, many of them arranged in long parallel lines. We do not know why they were put in place, but the most likely explanation is that they mark ceremonial procession ways.

In some cases the coastal areas where they were erected have changed. In the Gulf of Morbihan, two tangential circles of stones on the island of Er Lannic are partly submerged at high tide, although they originally stood on dry land.

CARVED STONES are scarce in England, more plentiful in Ireland, fairly common in France, and present in still larger

A Sardinian nuragh

numbers on some of the Mediterranean islands. Corsica has more than 70 carved menhirs, although they are rather late (1400 to 1200 B.C.). Many have human faces; some also have swords and daggers; others are clearly phallic in shape. At Filitosa a fortified hill shows how invaders who took the island away from the menhir carvers smashed up the stones and used fragments of them for building material.

Other Mediterranean islands—Sardinia and Sicily especially—have megalithic monuments, but Malta has the greatest collection of them. It was an important religious center in ancient times, and its massive stone temples, many of them richly ornamented with carvings, testify to the activity that once went on there.

Since the Maltese Islands, Malta and Gozo, can be seen from southern Sicily in clear weather, it is easy to understand why the first settlers came from there. The impressed pottery they brought along with them proves their origin. The Neolithic newcomers apparently arrived more than 5,000 years ago and ferried their domesticated animals to the islands. They had no metal but managed to get along quite well with stone tools.

One of the carved menhirs at Filitosa, Corsica. This is late, for long swords could only be made of metal

271

The Maltese Islands are so small (122 square miles) that they are hardly much larger than the County of London (117 square miles), and they would be lost in Greater London with its 692 square miles. They are only four times larger than Manhattan Island and just a trifle smaller than the Borough of Queens. Yet these tiny islands witnessed the growth of an extraordinary Neolithic culture that reached its height about 1500 B.C., by which time a number of highly individual rock temples and a large underground funerary structure had been completed. Since Malta is covered with soft, easily worked limestone, its architects, masons, and sculptors had plenty of good material at hand. From it they wrought miracles of art and architecture. Since Malta is out of the mainstream of European art, its ancient works are not as well known as they should be. One reason for this is that most of them were not discovered until fairly modern times. The ruins that were aboveground, of course, have long been known, but the rich treasures that lay below the surface were brought to light in this century.

The time schedule of Maltese prehistoric culture is very much in dispute. One recently determined radiocarbon date places the building of Gozo's early temple, Ġgantija, at 3290 B.C., which is nearly 600 years before any previously calculated date. Ġgantija—or Gigantia as the British spell it—is built of roughly hewn rocks stood on end and surmounted by others that are piled one on top of the other in the cyclopean manner.

Supposedly even earlier than Ġgantija is Mġarr's Ta Hagrat, which consists of two joined buildings. Although straight lines are not unknown in prehistoric Maltese architecture, curvilinear forms for the walls of the temples were very popular, so much so that it has been seriously suggested that the ground plans of these buildings follow the outlines of the grossly fat Mother Goddess figures that dominated the islands' art.

Hagar Qim, Mnajdra, and Hal Tarxien on the southern end of Malta largely follow the curvilinear pattern, although Hal Tarxien has many straight walls. At first the stones were decorated by painstakingly pockmarking their surfaces with regular blows from a hand-held rock. Then a bow drill was used to make numerous close-together holes to create an over-all ornamental pattern. In later times, fine relief-carv-

*The curved lines of Hagar
Kim, below [Efesco Photo],
may reflect the similar
lines of Malta's fat
Mother Goddesses, left
[British Museum]*

ings of scrolls, abstract figures, and realistic domestic animals were cut on the walls.

The heavy building blocks were put into position by moving them on limestone rollers, some of which can still be seen. Spherical stones were also used. J. D. Evans (1959, p. 108) says of the construction techniques: "The rough dressing was probably done by much the same means as were used to excavate the soft rock when making the tomb-chambers . . . at the Hypogeum, where evidence of the method used remains in some parts; namely, stone mauls or mallets and picks of horn or antler tines. The final finish was probably laboriously obtained with small flint blades."

Pieces of chert rather than flint may have served as scraping tools because it occurs on the island whereas flint does not and would have to be imported.

For a long while Malta remained rather isolated and was therefore able to develop its own ideas. Toward the end, Minoan and Mycenaen cultures had a profound effect upon Maltese art, although the actual contact was slight. It was at this time that spirals and floral decorations like those found in Crete and Mycenae began to appear on Maltese temples.

Similar ornamentation can be seen in the rock carvings of Brittany and Ireland, as has already been mentioned.

Since writing had reached Crete and Mycenae, it is more than likely that it was also known in Malta. One bit of evidence we have is a recurrent symbol that appears on personal ornaments. It may be, however, that these small objects were imported rather than made locally.

The curvilinear ground plans of the Maltese temples may have had some influence on the great stone *nuraghi* of Sardinia, although they came later. Later also were the distinctive bronze statuettes of human figures that show how advanced the Sardinians were in metallurgy and art.

In Malta the megalithic temples tell only part of the story. The Hypogeum of Hal Saflieni, a large underground tomb that once contained the remains of 7,000 people, is hollowed out of solid rock and has a number of carefully shaped embrasures in the walls. Here too are stone trilithons like the ones in Stonehenge, but those in the Hypogeum have no architectural function and are built into the walls. This tripartite device evidently had some kind of special significance in late Neolithic times.

A pebble pendant with a trilithon incised on it

Some of the chambers are painted with large red spirals and were equipped with devices that enabled the unseen priests to speak to their followers in sepulchral, deep-sounding voices. The Mnajdra temple has a speaking tube which may have served a double purpose, for a priest could not only address a communicant through it but could also let a

The underground Hypogeum of Hal Saflieni [Bromofoto]

275

small token slide down it to fall mysteriously at his feet. Everything about these buildings shows that Malta was an important cult center. Priests rather than kings ruled Malta, and they were evidently a highly sophisticated class.

Sacrifices were performed on the altars, as is shown at Mnajdra where a sharp flint blade was found in a secret orifice plugged up by carefully fitted removable stone. The bones discovered in a nearby compartment were all those of animals, so human sacrifice presumably was not practiced there.

The tiny
Sleeping Lady
of Malta's Hypogeum
[Efesco Photo]

But the most interesting and unique things found on Malta are the statues of enormously fat women which represent the Mother Goddess or the priestesses who served her. They vary from very small to large. One which stood in the Hal Tarxien was eight or nine feet high. Only the lower half of her grotesquely stout seated figure remains. Most of the sculptured pieces, however, are quite small. The terracotta statuette of the Sleeping Lady found in the Hypogeum is less than five inches long. It portrays her lying on her side in what may be a dream state.

Many artifacts have been recovered from the various sites on Malta, but a great deal remains unknown about the lives of the prehistoric people who lived there. No metal has been found, no houses or villages, and, amazingly, no weapons. Apparently the people of this period were neither

276

hunters nor warriors. They had domestic animals, but there are no traces of dogs. Evans says of the Maltese (1959, p. 158): "So far as we can judge from the evidence, no more peaceable society seems ever to have existed. It is easy, of course, to delude oneself with pictures of a primitive Mediterranean paradise; nevertheless, the earth seems to have yielded the primitive Maltese a living on fairly easy terms, for otherwise they would scarcely have had time or energy to spare to elaborate their strange cults or build or adorn their temples."

The Maltese were blessed with a good climate, the warmest in Europe, with an average winter temperature of 58 degrees and plenty of sunshine the year around.

Both Gozo and Malta have long, parallel furrows in the surface rock about 55 inches apart. It was once believed that these were made by the wheels of carts that carried the heavy stones to the temple sites. Recent research, however, has shown that they are more likely to be marks left by the two trailing wooden shafts that supported a slide-car as it was dragged over the rocks. The tracks are old, older than the Punic graves they cross, but it has yet to be proved that they were made by the people who built the temples.

THE CULTURE of these industrious megalithic temple builders came to a sudden end during the middle of the second millenium B.C. It is not known just what happened, but the artifacts overlaying those of the vanished stoneworkers were left by metal-using armed invaders who probably took the islands by force.

This period in history, when metal was coming into common use and leaders were struggling for power, was a violent one. Again and again inoffensive peoples were overwhelmed by ruthless outsiders to whom nothing but loot and lust meant anything. Gods and goddesses, priests and temples, art and culture went down before their mad onslaught. The pastoral, devoutly religious, and apparently gentle Maltese were some of the many meek who did not inherit the earth.

277

24. The Mother Goddess

THE LONGEST continuing spiritual idea which man has put
into tangible form is his concept of the Mother Goddess, the
tutelary deity who gives birth, shelter, protection, food, and
training to the race of man and then finally returns each individual to the grave, the eternal earth-womb. She is not
always beneficent, however, and in some places and some
ages she embodied terror, pain, and violent death, e.g.,
Lilith, Circe, Hecate, Medusa, and Kali. But in all her guises
she possessed enormous power and was the strongest of all
divinities until the male god of the Hebrews, the Greeks, the
Christians, and the northern Europeans gained greater influence in historic times. Even then she maintained her
powers in her special provinces of the home, the church, and
the invisible councils behind the state.

As a result of her exceedingly long reign—more than
30,000 years—she has been represented in art more than any
other religious figure. From the Venus of Willendorf to
Kwan Yin and the Virgin Mary, her images have covered
the entire world. Tiny cult statues of her adorned the
hearths of Paleolithic people; portrayals of her by great artists can be seen in our museums; and it may well be that a
bomb-shattered statue of her will someday look down com-
passionately at the ruins of a civilization which she graced
but could not save.

The Mother Goddess concept is so basic, so inborn, so
universal that it is only natural that men should have turned
toward the warm, protective creature who was the one human being nearest to them from the moment of birth—and
who then, through the cycle of mating and reproduction,
dominated their deepest emotions for the rest of their lives.
"Her ancestry . . . goes back to the Paleolithic period. . . .
Though no direct connection can be traced between . . .
Magdalenian women and the fertility goddess of the Neolithic and later periods, there can be little doubt that there
278   *was* a connection" (O. G. S. Crawford, 1956, p. 24).

In Neolithic times this goddess of many names was to take on many new forms, some of them highly abstract. But even the most schematic preserved the salient sexual features of the human female as she is sensed by the infant and thought of by the adult male. These are the breasts, the soft, warm, smooth, rounded, milk-giving, life-nurturing mammary glands that are the newborn child's first worldly contact with the human race. In some instances, the pubic triangle is omitted from prehistoric statuettes, but the breasts are almost always present in order to identify the figure as female. Actually, the variations of this theme are so numerous that some idols never had breasts; other ways were used to indicate their femininity. The fifth-century B.C. terracotta Baubo statuettes from Priene in Asia Minor have women's heads mounted directly above the vulva with no intervening area left for breasts. The portrayal of breasts reached its culmination in Diana of Ephesus, she of the many breasts. Most of the figures of her are very late, but one has been dated as early as the fifth century B.C. Neither the Diana figures nor the Baubo statuettes are prehistoric, but they serve as a link between the preliterate and literate periods.

The Mother Goddess was portrayed by many people over many centuries in whatever form seemed best suited to express their concepts of her. In the Cycladic Islands she appears as featureless violin-shaped idol that is usually made of smoothly finished white marble. This basic, starkly simple abstraction apparently appealed to many other people, for somewhat similar figures have been found in Persia, Malta, Sardinia, and Bulgaria. Some may have been imported from the Cyclades, but others seem to be native products. And the Cycladic statues are, of course, greatly sought

A torsoless Baubo figure from Priene

Cycyadic variations on a theme for violins as yet unmade

279

after by collectors of modern art because they are so much like twentieth-century abstract sculpture.

The megalith builders almost never portrayed the Mother Goddess realistically but only in schematic form. The carved passage-grave stones in Brittany and Ireland show her only as a symbol, sometimes as so abstract a symbol that it has little or no resemblance to the human figure.

Cycladic statuette in marble of a woman, c. 2500 B.C. [Metropolitan Museum of Art; Fletcher Fund, 1934] Above right: Cypriote terracotta figures, 2000–1200 B.C. [Metropolitan Museum of Art; Cesnola Collection, purchased 1874–76]

Nor is she always represented as a person; often a significant part of her body will do. We have seen how Paleolithic man carved isolated vulvas on the rock walls of his caves. He also made cupules, concave holes that are obviously breast-shaped. These are so ancient that they go back to the Neandertals.

Neolithic men occasionally took the trouble to chip away enough stone to leave a pair of breasts projecting from a rock, but this required enormous labor; the cupule is an easier and faster way of creating the same symbol. As a result there are thousands of them all over Europe. Many have never been noticed, for passers-by took it for granted that they were natural depressions in the rock rather than anything man-made.

Far more difficult to make are other basically rotary forms like concentric circles, spirals, and incomplete sections of roundness called multiple arcs. All these have one thing in common: they represent the female just as the rod,

280

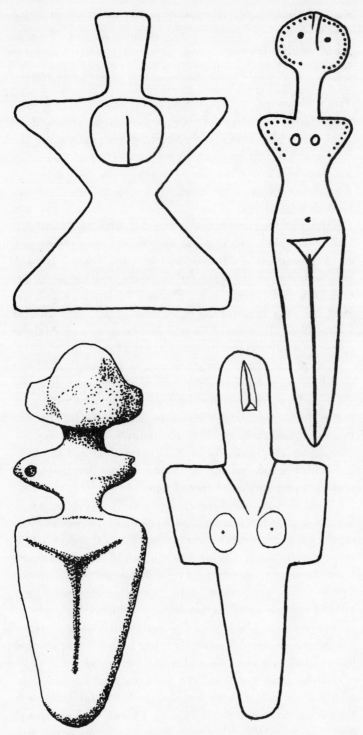

*Abstract figures from
various places. Clockwise
from upper left:
Tehran, white marble;
Vykhvatintsi cemetery,
U.S.S.R., clay;
Karanovo, Bulgaria, marble;
Senorbi, Sardinia, marble*

281

the club, the menhir, the sword, and other straight-line figures represent the male. Their roundness may be meant to portray either breasts or eyes; or, perhaps, interchangeably both, as O. G. S. Crawford has indicated (1956, p. 98).

THE EYE-GODDESS, a strange and attention-demanding form of the Great Mother, is of very ancient origin. Hundreds of 5,000-year-old figurines of her were discovered during the excavation of Tell Brak in eastern Syria. They all have staring eyes and few other distinctive features. No breasts or genitalia mark them as female, but they are obviously intended to be so.

The Eye-Goddess concept traveled from Syria—if that was its true place of origin—to Troy I and across the Aegean Sea to Europe, where it appeared in Spain, France, Ireland, and Scandinavia. As it moved westward it sloughed off literal form and become more abstract. In Brittany and Ireland the eyes are spirals, concentric circles, and arcs. It seems likely that the Minoan, Mycenaean, and Maltese spirals were also meant to symbolize the Goddess.

She of the staring eyes was not a rival of the Mother Goddess; she was that deity herself. Along with her, the male god, represented by the bull and symbolized by its horns, developed and became ever more powerful. Yet the two do not seem in any way competitive, for they are the complementary aspects of humanity, the seed and the sowing field, the rod and the circle, the conjunction that is required to perpetuate the race of man.

What we see now of the ancient gods is only what is left. We have only the images that were made of material enduring enough to survive destruction—and the destruction was often deliberate. Countless millions of them have perished. Some of these vanished representations of the Mother Goddess may have showed her in different aspects and marked her travels to lands where no evidence of her presence now exists. The bits and pieces we have surely cannot tell the whole story. A more complete record might compel us to change our ideas about her and her world.

But from what we do have, we know that she was protean in form. In Egypt she was slim; in Malta, fat. In Cyprus she had enormous pierced ears; in Phoenicia, huge round eyes. Crete portrayed her with snakes and imprisoned her

Alabaster figures
of Malta's fat Goddess
[Efesco Photo]

in pottery vessels with her breasts serving as pouring spouts. In the Cyclades she had the shape of what seems to us to be a musical instrument; in Brittany and Ireland she appeared on the rocks in abstract rounded patterns. In other lands she took on still other forms.

Men made of her what they wanted her to be. To the shepherd she was the guardian of the lambs; to the nomad in the wilderness, the watcher by the fireside; to the ill, the blessed healer; to the war-weary, the bearer of tidings of peace. She guided the ships at sea and brought the lost and the homeless home. She was the goddess of the brothel as well as of the marriage bed. In that guise she can be Astarte, Venus, Freya, and even so modern a creature as Lily Marlene. Time or place does not matter, for she is timeless and ubiquitous. She has always been with us and still is.

When Apuleius saw her in the second century A.D., he described her in *The Golden Ass* as she rose from the sea to tell him her many names:

She had a great abundance of hair, flowing and curling, dispersed and scattered about her divine neck; on the crown of her head she bare many garlands interlaced with flowers, and in the middle of her forehead was a plain circlet in fashion of a mirror, or rather resembling the moon by the light it gave forth; and this was borne up on either side by serpents that seemed to rise from the furrows of the earth, and above it were blades of corn set out. Her vestment was of finest linen yielding diverse colours, somewhere white and

Above: an Eye-Goddess
incised on a bone,
from Los Millares, Spain

283

shining, somewhere yellow like the crocus flower somewhere rosy red, somewhere flaming; and . . . her cloak was utterly dark and obscure covered with shining black and being wrapped round her from under her left arm to her right shoulder in manner of a shield, part of it fell down, pleated in most subtle fashion, to the skirts of her garment so that the welts appeared comely. Here and there upon the edge thereof and throughout its surface the stars glimpsed, and in the middle of them was placed the moon in midmonth, which shone like a flame of fire and round about the whole length of the border of that goodly robe was a crown or garland wreathing unbroken, made with all flowers and all fruits. Things quite diverse did she bear: for in her right hand she had a timbrel of brass, a flat piece of metal carved in manner of a girdle, wherein passed not many rods through the periphery of it; and when with her arm she moved these triple chords, they gave forth a shrill and clear sound. In her left hand she bare a cup of gold like unto a boat, upon the handle whereof, in the upper part which is best seen, an asp lifted up his head with a wide-swelling throat. Her odiferous feet were covered with shoes interlaced and wrought with victorious palm. . . . [Translation by William Adlington, 1566.]

When she spoke, she said: "My name, my divinity is adored throughout the world, in divers manners, in variable customs, and by many names. For the Phrygians, that are the first of all men, call me The Mother of the Gods at Pessinus; the Athenians, which are sprung from their own soil, Cecropian Minerva; the Cyprians, which are girt about by the sea, Paphian Venus; the Cretans which bear arrows, Dictynnian Diana; the Sicilians, which speak three tongues, Infernal Proserpine; the Eleusinians, their ancient goddess Ceres; some Juno, other Bellona, other Hecate, other Rhamnusia, and principally both sort of the Ethiopians which dwell in the Orient and are enlightened by the morning rays of the sun, and the Egyptians, which are excellent in all kind of ancient doctrine and by their proper ceremonies accustom to worship me, do call me by my true name, Queen Isis."

Early in the nineteenth century De Quincey celebrated her and her tripartite selves. First there was Levana, the Roman goddess whose duty it was to raise the newborn infant upright to present his head to the stars. Then there were her three sister-selves, *Mater Lachrymarum*, Our Lady of Tears, who mourns for the vanished faces of the dead; *Mater Suspiriorum*, Our Lady of Sighs, who is the patroness

284

Statue of a Snake Goddess in ivory and gold. Minoan, sixteenth century B.C. [Courtesy of Museum of Fine Arts, Boston; Mrs. W. Scott Fitz Fund]

of the meek, the humble, the downtrodden, and the oppressed; and lastly, *Mater Tenebrarum,* Our Lady of Darkness, she who haunts the shadows to be "the mother of lunacies and the suggestress of suicides, and who moves with incalculable motions, bounding, and with tiger's leaps."

Robert Graves described her in the twentieth century (1948, p. 10): "The Goddess is a lovely, slender woman with a hooked nose, deathly pale face, lips red as rowan-berries, startlingly blue eyes and long fair hair; she will suddenly transform herself into sow, mare, bitch, vixen, she-ass, weasel, serpent, owl, she-wolf, tigress, mermaid or loathsome hag. Her names and titles are innumerable. In ghost stories she often figures as 'The White Lady,' and in ancient re-

285

ligions, from the British Isles to the Caucasus, as the 'White Goddess.' . . . The test of a poet's vision, one might say, is the accuracy of his portrayal of the White Goddess. . . . The reason why the hairs stand on end, the skin crawls, and a shiver runs down the spine when one writes or reads a true poem is that a true poem is necessarily an invocation of the White Goddess, or Muse, the Mother of All Living, the ancient power of fright and lust—the female spider or the queen-bee whose embrace is death."

This multifaceted, undying Goddess defies Time and Death because she is one with them. Nothing can destroy her, for she has no substantial existence. She is only an idea, a projection of man's dearest wishes and longed-for desires. But that does not make her less real. In an unreal world, she transcends reality and is always there, smiling and forever indomitable. If her name is blessed it is because she blesses, comforts, and forgives.

Of all the intangible things that have come down to us from prehistoric times, the Mother Goddess is the most unchanged. She has walked untouched by the centuries that devour all things tangible and intangible. From rude tent to the finest palace she rules over the hearth and the home. She is the keeper of little children, the protectress of animals, the pagan love goddess who is also the most revered of all saints.

She is the Eternal Mother, the devoted mate, the loving mistress, the dream that men have of women when they see them as they want them to be. In her multiplicity of names and forms she is a single entity that is ever the same no matter how different her outer guises, symbols, and manifestations may be.

Her many images should be regarded with respect, for she is one of mankind's better aspects made real to remind beholders of all that she stands for. Each person will form his own concept of her, and this will be shaped by what she means to him. The simulacrum he sees is a poor depiction of the real Mother. She herself is within each one of us, cherished deep in our innermost hearts.

25. How Neolithic Ideas Spread

THE NEW IDEAS that took form during Neolithic times—and
that were going to transform the social structure of most of
mankind—spread very slowly across the world. Even in the
Middle East, where the ideas had originated and were
therefore longest in practice, not everyone accepted them.
Some nomadic hunters preferred to continue their way of
life; other people adopted a few of the ideas and rejected
those that did not appeal to them. In places farther away,
men had not even heard about what was happening. Cultural diffusion was slow in ancient times; in those preliterate
days, when communication was only from person to person,
it was even slower.

The mere announcement of new and useful ideas is
ordinarily not enough to make people want to adopt them.
They have to see for themselves that planted seeds will
grow, that wild animals can be domesticated, that cloth can
be woven. Traders who were trying to sell fabric were not
likely to want to educate their ignorant customers about its
manufacture. And even if they had been, it was unlikely
that they could teach them how to construct the necessary
looms. Migrating peoples, who took their baskets of seeds,
pottery, cloth and looms, and farm animals with them would
be far more convincing than occasional travelers bearing
news about the miracles that were being wrought in distant
places.

Such ideas therefore did not spread evenly or with any
regularity, yet they were constantly on the move, although
many delays and dying-out periods impeded their progress.
A vast educational process was under way. Men were beginning to learn that they did not have to take Nature as
they found her. They were discovering that they could improve conditions in the world around them.

The Neolithic Revolution took longer to get to China
and the Far East than it did to Europe. (It did not reach
China until nearly 5,000 years ago.) But it quickly crossed

the narrow straits of the Bosporus and the Dardanelles and moved into what is now Greece more than 8,000 years ago. The earliest settlements had no pottery; that came in some centuries later. The preceramic stage took place in Bulgaria, Rumania, Hungary, and Yugoslavia at about the same time. From these areas Neolithic cultural ideas spread north and west along the Danube River basin until they eventually reached the Low Countries about 6,500 years ago. The Neolithic wave kept going; in another thousand years or so it had gone beyond the British Isles to southern Scandinavia.

Another extension of Neolithic ideas went by waterborne craft along the shores of the Mediterranean to reach Spain 7,000 years ago. From there it took about 2,000 years to cross France to Switzerland and the Italian Lakes. It was not all straight going; there were undoubtedly many cross movements and mixtures.

It will thus be seen that Neolithic cultures were fairly well established in Europe 5,000 years ago. Remote areas remained primitive, but certain parts of the continent were rapidly reaching the metal-using stage.

The first Neolithic idea-bearing people arrived in regions that were already inhabited. Since there are no written records we cannot be certain how the old hunting and new farming cultures mixed, but the physical remains of the time seem to indicate that the newcomers did not meet much resistance. There was plenty of room, so the indigenous hunters may have retired to the hills and left the more fertile lowlands to the farmers. Contact between the two must have taught the earlier settlers a great deal. Eventually, they too became converted to agriculture as a way of life.

From now on there was a great deal of movement in Europe. Various culture groups went from place to place, sometimes to settle there, sometimes to stay only a few generations and then go on. The list of names given to these people grows, and the archeological terms multiply. Sir Leonard Woolley, who had to use the specialized language of his profession throughout his long and distinguished career, once said (1963, p. 828): "We talk of the 'Beaker' people, the 'Bell-barrow' people, the 'Terramare' people, and of the 'Aunjetitz' culture, the 'Adlerberg,' the 'Lausitz,' the 'El Argar,' and the 'Apennine' cultures, thus identifying a people by some peculiar product or feature, a culture by its habitat or, more often, by the name of the place in which the relics of it were first found. The fact is that we do not know who any of these people were; we know scarcely anything about them, only about the things they made and used." This could be further qualified by saying "a few of the things they made and used," for most of their artifacts have perished, and we may be misinterpreting the use of some of those that remain.

The erudite terminology can be left to specialists in the field. It is useful to know that the Beaker people were named after the characteristically shaped clay pots they made, but that is only a beginning, for there are B_1 or bell-shaped beakers, B_2 or barrel-shaped beakers, A or long-necked beakers, and C or short-necked beakers. Nor is this all; surface decoration classifies them still further. Some are marked with impressions of cords, fingernails, shells, hollow-bone or reed ends, and other devices. The kind of clay from which they were made, their contents (if any), and the sites at which they were found are also important. People, especially when they are illiterate and uneducated, tend to cling to their traditions. When they move, they continue to manufacture their pottery just as they did in the place they came from. In this way we can trace the origins of the bell-beaker people to Spain, the C or short-necked beaker people to Holland—and it may be that both C- and A-beaker people had a common Rhenish origin.

Artifacts like pottery, faience, amber ornaments, and certain kinds of stone implements, all of which can be traced to their point of origin, give us some knowledge of prehistoric migrations and trade routes. The subject has also been explored theoretically. Munro S. Edmonson had an article in the April 1961 issue of *Current Anthropology* entitled "Neolithic Diffusion Rates." In this he attempted to construct a hypothetical space-time model that would show how fast the ideas for new inventions like pottery and metallurgy travel from their point of origin throughout cultural space. He takes it for granted that the people involved would be "a homogeneous field of persons" and that in such a field "an invention at the center [of a given circle] might be expected to travel in all directions to the circumference at a uniform rate of speed."

By the use of many radiocarbon dates, some of which he

Early Bronze Age beakers. From top to bottom: long-necked, short-necked, bell (B1), barrel (B2)

289

admits may be questionable, he builds a framework which indicates that pottery originated in Outer Mongolia about 8200 B.C.; that it spread from there to the Middle East, Africa, Europe, India, China, Japan, southeast Asia, and the Americas over a determinable period of years. He then does the same thing for copper and bronze, starting at Meshed, Iran, as the point of origin in 4700 B.C. He also takes the diffusion of the use of maize in the New World to obtain still more data. Finally he comes up with an averaged-out figure of 1.15 miles per year as the diffusion rate for the spread of new ideas in Neolithic times.

After Edmonson himself had pointed out many possible errors in his data (especially in the radiocarbon dates) his article was submitted to a number of qualified scholars for comment. He was, he said, "rather surprised that eight colleagues were already prepared to give some measure of credence to my hypothesis." But they were not willing to follow him all the way, and several had serious reservations. Much of the doubt came from the validity of the dates used. Some came from the probability that diffusion by water routes would be faster than those on land. Other objections varied.

One, by Robert Heine-Geldern (*ibid*, p. 90*) showed how inconstant the diffusion rate could be for short periods of time. "A trait spreading from Jericho to Vladivostok might have taken 500 years to cover the first 1,000 miles, then, carried by migrations or under other particularly favorable circumstances, 50 years for the next 1,000 miles, and, slowing down again, 1,500 for all the rest of the way. Therefore, no useful purpose can be served by dividing the full number of miles by that of years (necessarily uncertain), thus computing a completely meaningless average."

Other objections were directed at the author's choice of purely theoretical reference points, such as placing the origin of pottery at Ulan Bator in Outer Mongolia: "By plotting the dates for the supposed earliest appearance of pottery on a map and by linking them together with lines he comes to the conclusion that pottery must have been invented where all his lines converge, i.e., at Ulan Bator" (*ibid*, p. 89). Yet Edmonson admits that the nearest radio-

* All *ibid's* in this section refer to *Current Anthropology*, April 1961.

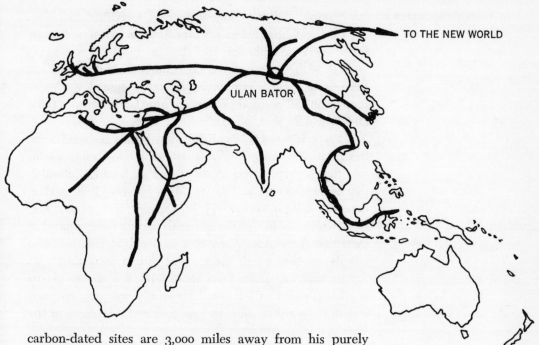

TO THE NEW WORLD

ULAN BATOR

carbon-dated sites are 3,000 miles away from his purely artificial point of origin in Outer Mongolia.

Some of the commentators saw genuine merit in Edmonson's attempt to construct a hypothetical model that would at least approximate reality in its over-all projections. A. L. Kroeber, for instance, said that "his 1,150 miles in 1,000 years as of 1960 is an achievement, a fine base from which to take off for further exploration" (*ibid*, p. 91). Merrick Posnansky wrote that "Edmonson's approach is original, if somewhat hypothetical. Its tremendous value, which cannot be underestimated, lies in its well-considered collation of the data bearing on the diffusion of the cultural traits of pottery and copper.... His world-wide approach is refreshing, as is his suggestion of a pottery origin in the Ulan Bator vicinity. Hitherto, perhaps too much attention has been focused on Middle Eastern origins" (*ibid*, pp. 95–96).

Sometimes the article provoked questions as interesting as those it raised. Irving Rouse said: "In my opinion, the process is complicated by a third dimension, that of a culture or society, and Edmonson's model should be revised to include that dimension. In its present form the model does not satisfactorily explain why some cultures have adopted traits more rapidly and more completely than others. Why,

The distribution of pottery from a theoretical point at Ulan Bator [After Edmonson]

291

for example, did the Chinese develop a civilization before the time of Christ, when our ancestors in Western Europe failed to do so although they had as much, if not more, contact with the center of civilization in the Near East, lived in a similar environment, and occupied a similar topographical position relative to the land masses of the Old World?" (*ibid*, p. 96).

It is evident that the Edmonson article inspired some fresh thinking and some self-questioning. One commentator said that perhaps it was ahead of its time because "chronology everywhere is still in its infancy today. Radiocarbon dates are still far too few" (J. M. Curxent, *ibid*, p. 96). And A. L. Kroeber said, "In the last analysis, it is fuller control of facts that determines what view is the right one, not who has the subtlest mind, the greatest gift of theorizing. . . . Let us have facts, new facts, more facts, relevant to almost anything, and I at least will cheerfully wait for the new superior theorist to show us new uses and relevances of the facts" (*ibid*, p. 91).

Whether or not Edmonson was entirely right in the way he marshaled the facts and drew conclusions from them is not important. What he did do was build a new model and conceive a new way of trying to solve an old problem; for that he deserves great credit. He himself said forthrightly: "What if I am wrong? . . . And what if I am right?" It is by taking such bold steps that the sum of human knowledge is increased.

ESTIMATED figures for world population from Lower Paleolithic through Mesolithic times were given on page 204. Now, with the superior methods of obtaining food that prevailed during the Neolithic period, the number of human beings began to increase enormously. The Mesolithic population was estimated to be 5.32 million; the Neolithic population expanded to 86.5 million about 6,000 years ago. By the beginning of the Christian Era, world population was 133 million. It has been growing ever since. By A.D. 1900 it was 1.61 billion and is now about 3.5 billion. It may be double that—or more—by the year 2000. The human race, from being a species desperately clinging to life half a million years ago—which is a short time in the evolutionary scale—is now so seriously threatened by overpopulation that the problem has become a matter of international concern.

The figures for ancient populations just quoted were compiled by Edward S. Deevey, Jr., and were published in an article entitled "The Distribution of Man," which appeared in *Scientific American* for September 1960. In this article Deevey also spoke about the number of people who have lived since the beginning of time. According to his calculations, there were 36 billion Paleolithic hunters and food-gatherers; 30 billion before agriculture was invented; and a cumulative total of 110 billion people altogether. Now our twentieth-century runaway increase makes all previous population figures look small. When Deevey says "that the patch of ground allotted to every person now alive may have been the lifetime habitat of 40 predecessors," it seems as though the one thing certain about this planet is that its soil will someday be well fertilized by the organic remains of those who returned to the dust from which they came. *Requiescant in pace.*

By NEOLITHIC TIMES man's trial period was over; 6,000 years ago the human race had established itself on a worldwide scale. The only other animal that was to populate the earth from pole to pole, in all climates and under all conditions, was one that man had taken under his protection, the dog. And he, poor creature, is not entirely at home in the vast cities that are rapidly covering the earth. He would much prefer to have things as they were and often sniffs longingly at the heady scent of the wilderness, the once-great green world that is being obliterated by asphalt and cement.

Now that man had mastered the art of making fine polished stone tools he was also learning about the superiority of metal implements. But a price had to be paid for this superiority. The keen cutting edges of metal were very effective for killing. Sharp swords were replacing stone axes, and arrows tipped with metallic barbed points were proving to be more lethal than stone-headed ones. Man was well on his way to the constantly improved weapons that were to make him the undisputed master of his world.

The major question about the new state of being that mankind was rapidly approaching some 6,000 years ago is: in ultimate values was it worth the cost? Is all that has resulted from it—our advanced culture, our scientific achievements, our amazingly complex technology, our enormously increased body of knowledge, our good health, our comfort, our luxury—worth the turmoil, anguish, bloodshed, cruelty, and wholesale murder that are part of the price we have had to pay—and are still paying—for these supposed gains?

The question must be asked in any discussion of man's presumed progress from animalian existence to what we call civilization. And it must be asked here, for man was now about to go from what seems to have been a fairly simple outdoor food-gathering and food-growing life to a new kind of existence in crowded communities that have always been at war with each other. That the human race moved forward is certain, but whether or not it went on to a condition that was better than what it had been is a matter that each person must answer for himself. Perhaps there are no definite answers, perhaps there never were and never will be, but this eternal question is the key to all inquiries into the greatness, the glory, and the incredible nastiness of man's career upon the earth he has ravaged.

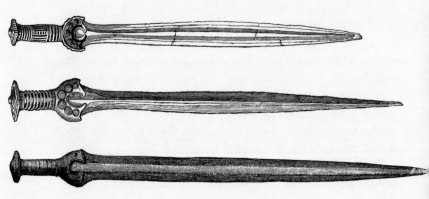

*Bronze swords
from Denmark
[Lubbock]*

PHASE SEVEN

26. Man Discovers Metal

THE FIRST PERSON who picked up a lump of one of the few metals that occur in fairly pure form in their native state— gold, copper, and meteoric iron—probably thought that the strange-looking material was some kind of stone. It took mankind a long time to find out that these odd "stones" had special uses and that they were particularly good for making implements. They could be shaped by pounding; they did not break as stone might; and they were heavier than ordinary bits of rock.

At first only copper seemed to be really useful. Gold was too soft to serve any practical purpose, and meteoric iron was too hard. It was also so rare that it was almost unknown in prehistoric times. Perhaps a few pieces were cherished as sacred objects, but that was all. Gold, too, was quite scarce; it might do for ornaments, but otherwise it was pretty but useless stuff. Paleolithic men must have come across countless gold nuggets in virgin stream beds and ignored them as worthless. But copper was soft enough to be hammered into useful shapes and yet hard enough to take a fair cutting edge. It was soon found out that some kinds of "copper"— especially those with a pale yellowish tinge—made better tools than the pure red-colored metal did. Early man did not know that these were natural bronzes, but he eventually found out that he could make such alloys by adding tin, zinc, antimony, or other metals to copper.

The so-called copper-using stage or Chalcolithic Period was rather short in the Middle East and Europe. There is no evidence of a copper-using time in the Orient; bronze was introduced there as a fully developed material. And in North America, where native copper occurred in large, easily worked quantities, Indians continued to hammer out objects made of it for thousands of years without ever finding out how to melt, cast, or alloy it.

Two recent discoveries show that man began to use metal far earlier than was previously thought. Both were in or near the Shanidar Valley, where Old World agriculture began. One find is an oval copper pendant about an inch long. It was taken from a human burial which its discoverer, Ralph S. Solecki of Columbia University, describes as having a radiocarbon date of 10,500 ± 300 years ago. The other discovery consists of several small pins made by hammering out native copper. They were found in 1964 by Robert J. Braidwood of the University of Chicago in the Diyarbakir region of southeastern Turkey and are believed to be about 9,000 years old.

The two communities in which these early metal objects were discovered were preceramic. It is interesting to note that the invaders who founded the city-states in Akkad and Sumer many thousands of years later passed through this remarkable area and may have stayed there long enough to interbreed with its inhabitants. The invaders' record before they reached Mesopotamia was in no way remarkable; perhaps the new blood from their stay near Shanidar was responsible for the astounding accomplishments of the Sumerians, the people who started civilization on its way and ended prehistory by inventing writing.

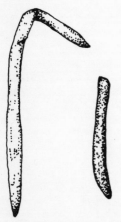

Very early copper pins from the Diyarbakir region of Turkey

A copper axe head from Ireland [Lubbock]

THE EARLIEST copper artifacts are small because the native metal is difficult to work unless it is heated. After men found out that the copper was more malleable when it was placed in a fire, they noted that when a strong wind was blowing to make the flames roar they sometimes got more metal than they had originally started with. This happened because the lumps of native copper often had bits of copper ore clinging to them, and these were smelted by the intense heat. A temperature of 700 to 800 degrees Centigrade is needed to reduce the ore to molten metal, but a wind-blown open fire can produce such heat. Pottery kilns were even better for the purpose, for they can build up a temperature as high at 1,200 degrees Centigrade. Smelting in closed kilns began, and copper became more plentiful.

The discovery of smelting was almost surely accidental; so was the making of bronze, in which the copper was alloyed with 5 to 15 per cent of tin in prehistoric times. When the copper ore contained some tin, a natural bronze was produced. It took a long time for the early smiths to find out that it was the tin that was responsible for a metal that was yellower, harder, and better to cast than the original copper. With bronze at hand, one could make sharp-pointed daggers and axe blades with good cutting edges. And bronze saws cut more easily and cleanly than copper or flint ones do.

Native copper and rich copper ore occur in many places in the Middle East, Egypt, and Europe, but tin was scarcer. In some places, however, both copper and tin could be found. This was especially true in Cornwall and Egypt. Bronze rapidly came into use, but not into common use; it was too rare for that. Stone implements therefore continued to be made for a long while. In some instances, flint daggers and finely fashioned stone axe and hammer heads were copied from the much-admired bronze ones.

Bronze remained scarce because the materials needed to make it were scarce. And the number of artisans who knew how to produce bronze were few; so were those who could work it. But since stone and even nodules of good flint were common, the men who could shape and polish stone far outnumbered those who could cast bronze. Metal implements were highly prized, so much so that they are seldom found in graves. It is believed that stone copies were sometimes made to be interred with a corpse while the bronze originals were kept for the benefit of the living.

IT TAKES far more skill and higher temperatures to produce iron than it does copper. And iron ore, when smelted with a necessary flux like limestone, does not yield recognizable metal but a spongy gray mass called bloom. It is likely that the first men who saw bloom emerge from their fire looked at it with disgust and threw the seemingly worthless stuff away. They had yet to learn that iron could be made out of it by hammering it repeatedly while it was still red hot.

The new metal hardly seemed worth so much trouble because the cutting edge of iron produced in this way is poor, and the surface eventually oxidizes and becomes covered with scaly brown rust. Early use of the metal was confined to making small ornaments.

A flint dagger copied from a bronze one [Danish National Museum]

No one, of course, suspected that the iron produced by man is the same as that which falls from the heavens. Meteoric iron is hard because it contains nickel. Terrestial iron can be made even harder when it is alloyed with the right metals.

Over the course of time, the smiths learned that long-repeated hammerings and numerous reheatings made a superior type of iron. They did not know why, but what was happening was that bits of charcoal (carbon) picked up from the fire were transforming the surface when they were pounded into the hot metal. The smiths also found out that cooling the iron very slowly resulted in a soft and malleable product, whereas plunging red-hot iron into cold water made it hard and enabled it to take a keen, durable cutting edge.

Copper and its alloys had many uses, but carburized iron and its final perfection—steel—were to change the world. Iron's value for weapons was obvious, but it also had many peaceful functions. It made the carpenter's tool kit into a fine assembly of hammers, hatchets, chisels, saws, files, scrapers, drills, awls, and holding devices which were so good that they have remained almost unaltered in form today. It replaced stone and wood implements for digging and was ideal for cutting down all kinds of standing vegetation from grain stalks to big trees. Shod with iron, the plow became an efficient agricultural instrument that could turn over the soil in large plots of land, while iron rakes and forks made it easier to handle straw and hay. When wheeled vehicles came in, iron protected the horses' hooves and served as long-wearing tires on the wooden wheels. With iron trowels for spreading mortar and with iron cutting tools for shaping stone, masons and sculptors were given a better command over their materials. Finally, iron led to the invention of machines, those mechanical extensions of hand tools that can do so much more than hand-held tools can. For the machines to function at their best, power had to be added. But that was a long way off. We are still dealing with prehistoric times.

A hut-urn (late Bronze or early Iron Age) from Albano, Italy [Lubbock]

IRON has been called the democratic metal because it could be used by the common man, while bronze was for heroes and kings and the statues erected to celebrate their fame.

298

Yet iron, too, continued to be scarce, and stone weapons and tools were used along with it for centuries to come.

Some of the early bronze has disappeared, not only because of oxidation, but because long-used implements were melted down with fresh batches of metal. It may be that certain weapons were thought to have a special power that could be transmitted to others if the old bronze was mixed with the new. In this way bronze could be reborn—an attribute that made it seem superior to stone.

A gold torque from Ireland [Lubbock]

Gold has long been called a noble metal, a substance so fine and so untarnishable that its use was set aside for the nobility, who were the only ones who could afford it. Since gold is not only valuable but easily worked, fine craftsmanship has been devoted to it from earliest times. But its high value is also its curse. Many beautiful ancient pieces have been destroyed by robbers who wanted the readily salable gold and who did not hesitate to melt down great works of art made of the all-too-precious metal.

Except for the bullion that has been lost or buried, we still have all the gold that was ever mined. The imperishable stuff is passed on from generation to generation, so milady's wedding ring may have in it molecules of gold from

299

Bronze razors with ship ornaments from Denmark [Lubbock]

A bronze spear head from northern England [Lubbock]

Egyptian temples, Greek ornaments, Inca idols, Spanish galleons, or a hundred other prehistoric and historic sources all over the world.

FAR MORE IMPORTANT than the use of any one metal was the idea of using metal at all. Man had gotten along without it for hundreds of thousands of years; it plays a part only in the later stages of his career. With its discovery and extended use he emerged from the Stone Age. A small body of skilled men took over its management and were responsible for everything that concerned metal, from its mining to its final shaping. These were the smiths, an elite class of artisans who were divided into groups according to the metals they specialized in: coppersmith, bronzesmith, tinsmith, goldsmith, ironsmith, and—from the dark color of the metal he worked in—blacksmith. "Smith" is obviously akin to the word "smite" and preserves the image of a powerfully muscled man pounding away at a piece of hot metal on his anvil.

Some of the early metalworkers wandered from place to place, confident that they could earn a good living anywhere they went. Some of them evidently carried quantities of roughly finished products, for hoards of these have been found. Such hoards are especially valuable to archeologists, for they contain objects which were all made at about the same time.

Regions where native metal, easily worked ore, and essential supplies of wood could be obtained were fortunate,

300

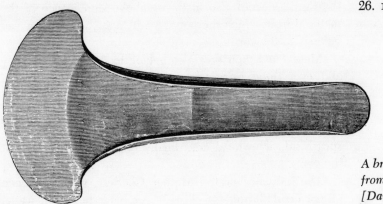

*A bronze axe head
from the Isle of Wight
[Dawkins]*

but some less fortunate areas quickly learned how to get the much-desired metals by trade. Mesopotamia had no metal or fuel, but it had no trouble obtaining copper alloys and gold. Egypt was blessed by having both. Neither region had much to do with the development of iron. Perhaps it was too plebian a metal to interest the royal kingdoms there. Yet some of the earliest iron objects have been found in both places. Their people—or their rulers—apparently did not appreciate the black metal's enormous potentialities.

Europe welcomed metal and quickly surpassed the lands that had first discovered the new material. Gordon Childe says (1957, p. 343): "In the Near East many metal types persisted unchanged for 2,000 years; in Temperate Europe an extraordinarily brisk evolution of tools and weapons and multiplication of types occupied a quarter of that time."

With metal—and especially with iron—man broke away from his limited past and entered a completely new phase. The Industrial Revolution, and with it our modern world, began on the day when some unknown smith took the first metal and began to beat it into a useful shape. The resounding blows that rang through the woods on that unrecorded but forever memorable occasion have been echoing ever since in the shops and foundries that now encircle the globe.

*A socketed celt found in
the Thames River [Dawkins]*

IN HIS BOOK *The Mothers* (1927, I, p. 466), Robert Briffault called pottery a feminine invention. Erich Neumann confirmed this by saying (1955, p. 134): "The sacral relation of woman to the pot originates in the symbolic significance of

301

the form . . . and also in the symbolic significance of the material from which the pot is made, namely, clay, for clay belongs to the earth."

Metals and their ores also belong to the earth, yet they and everything associated with them—mining, smelting, forging, casting, and finishing—are men's work. The sexual symbolism, however, still holds, for just as the round pot represents the womb so do the pointed dagger, sword, spearhead, arrowhead, and finally even the gun represent the penis.

The influence of the Mother Goddess, who had been all-powerful during the Stone Ages, now began to wane. Male deities, gods of war and conquest, were in the ascendant. Metal was the source of their might, and death-dealing armies equipped with bronze, iron, and steel weapons were carrying their mandates on the tips of their swords.

The Trundholm sun chariot; bronze and gold leaf [Danish National Museum]

27. . . . And Metal Helps to

Open Up the World

NEOLITHIC PEOPLE had carried on a trade in flint and other stones suitable for implements; with the coming of metal, more and longer trade routes were established. It was not so much the desire to sell manufactured goods as it was the need for raw materials, especially copper and tin, that caused ships to sail to far-off lands. Large copper ingots, sometimes shaped like ox hides, have been found in the depths of the Mediterranean where cargo vessels sank in ancient times. The metal-trade routes roughly followed those already taken by pottery, amber, and faience. And some of them followed those already taken by the megalith builders. This was only natural, for the best ways to get through coastal waters safely were determined by the geological forces that shaped the surface of the earth long before man appeared on it.

In some places the native people were backward enough to allow traders to take away their native copper or its ore in exchange for products made of the same metal. In other areas they learned how to mine and smelt their own copper, and new metal-producing centers sprang up there.

It was the essential tin, however, that caused a shortage of bronze-making in the ancient world, particularly in the Middle East. Joseph Alsop (1964, p. 87) points out that "local tin deposits began to be exhausted . . . as early as the third millenium B.C., and in the era of Sargon the Great [ca. 2371–16] unalloyed copper weapons actually came into use again in Mesopotamia, where first-class bronze weapons had been the rule before."

The urgent need for tin, of which only a small quantity was required for making bronze, sent navigators and traders to the western Mediterranean and the lands beyond it. In exchange for the precious tin, man-made products from the Aegean and Egypt were exported to far-away places. Colorful glass and faience beads of Middle Eastern origin have been found in burials in the British Isles, Brittany, southern France, Spain, Sicily, and many other countries, some of them in eastern Europe. Amber came down from the Baltic along established routes, while metal implements went north in exchange.

Gold-colored transparent or translucent amber is the fossilized resin of pine trees that grew from 45 to 60 million years ago in forests that stood on land now covered by the Baltic Sea. Storms and waves washed rounded bits of the highly prized resin ashore where amber hunters gathered it. Bronze implements taken in exchange for it show where their settlements and trading posts were located. And in the lands that got the amber, countless specimens have been recovered from tombs and building sites.

Amber has a peculiar hold on people, not only for its beauty and smoothness, but for its resemblance to sunlight. In fact, some of the earliest amber artifacts are sun disks. And, although of organic origin, amber is long-enduring, so it is ideal for tracing ancient trade routes. And now that spectroscopic analysis makes it possible to determine the source from which each piece came, it will be even more useful for that purpose.

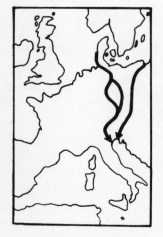

The principal amber routes in Europe

FAR MORE IMPORTANT than the baubles and trinkets, the pottery, or even the metal implements that were being distributed by this far-flung prehistoric trade were the ideas that went with it. The long isolation of small groups of separate people was ending. Men who were still living in swamps and forests were beginning to learn that others dwelt in places far beyond the horizon's rim. They may have thought that the strangers were probably unfriendly and perhaps hostile, but at least they knew that there were other people in the world. Even so late a traveler as Herodotus reported in the fifth century B.C. that mountain men had feet like goats, that people in the far north slept for half the year, and that living even farther north were one-eyed men who pilfered gold from the mighty griffins that were guarding it. He may not have believed these fanciful tales, but the men who told them to him evidently did. At any rate, the stories show that people knew that they were not alone, and if far-off strangers were odd creatures they at least had the semblance of human form. The world was growing smaller and more knowledgeable. It was also advancing toward cities, civilization, and writing. Only a few steps remained to be taken, and they had only to be refinements of things and ideas that already existed. The basic groundwork was complete.

ONE OF the important improvements in metallurgy was the art of casting. For this several pieces of apparatus were needed: a fireproof container for the metal that was to be melted, a mold into which to pour the liquified metal, and a well-maintained high temperature to provide the necessary heat.

The container was no problem; a crucible that would withstand intense heat without cracking or breaking could easily be made from clay or from clay mixed with sand. Nor was a mold difficult to invent. Hollowed-out pieces of wood or stone, in one piece for open casting and in two for closed, were good enough for the crude work of the early smiths. Refinements such as baked-clay cores and sand casting came later; so did the *cire-perdue*, or lost-wax, method. The oldest known *cire-perdue* casting is a copper model of a chariot drawn by four onagers, the Asiatic wild asses (*Equus hemionus*) that were domesticated before horses were. The casting was found while excavating Mesopotamia's Tell Agrab and is dated in the earlier part of the third millenium B.C.

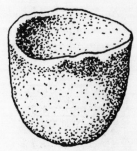

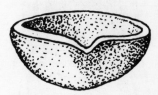

Prehistoric crucibles

Cire-perdue casting calls for making a wax model which is surrounded by a covering of refractory material; then, when the molten metal is poured into the space filled by the wax, that easily melted substance runs out and is replaced by the metal, which soon solidifies in the shape of the vanished wax. This method was commonly used throughout antiquity, and the sculptors and artisans who did such work developed great skill.

Cire-perdue casting made front-page news in December 1967 when New York's Metropolitan Museum announced that its world-famous "Greek" horse was apparently the work of a modern forger who had not studied art history and therefore had not learned that the sand-mold method was unknown 2,400 years ago when the horse was supposed to have been cast. It seemed to have mold marks which do

305

not occur in *cire-perdue castings*. But the matter was not allowed to rest there. A few months later, experts from Berlin and Boston defended the horse's authenticity. One of them said that it had been cast in two pieces which were then soldered together, which would explain the so-called mold marks. Until a method for determining the true age of bronze castings is found, the antiquity of the Greek horse may have to remain a subject for controversy among experts.

The early smiths solved the crucible and mold problems without trouble, but getting a forced draft to supply enough oxygen to make the fire hot was more difficult. At first they used animal skins filled with air which was pressed out through a narrow opening. Then they added a long pipe to this primitive bellows so the operator could stand away from the heat of the fire. Bellows of one kind or another continued to be used until modern times, when power-driven rotary air pumps replaced them.

An English mold made of bronze in which bronze celts were cast [Dawkins]

MOST OF the things that were made of metal in ancient times were weapons of some kind—cutting, piercing, or hammering instruments that mutilated and killed vast numbers of human beings. Fortunately, metal was also put to many other uses. Personal ornaments made of it became popular. Jewelry, even more than weapons, shows how advanced were the skills attained by the early metalworkers. Figurines, which previously had to be carved separately, could now be turned out in quantity as bronze castings. Before long, bronze statues increased in size until they became as large—or even larger—than life. The big ones were cast in sections with hollow cores and were then skillfully put together. The Greeks were so good at such work that their bronze statues have never been surpassed, even in modern times.

Belt buckles, pins, and other fastening devices, tools of all kinds, and agricultural implements were made of metal. Relatively few things for the kitchen were. Except for knives, ancient kitchenware was made largely of wood or pottery because metal was too expensive and hard to come by for such humble use. Kings might drink out of gold cups, but the common man had to use clay pots.

Metal continued to be fairly scarce for a long while. The one use for which expense was never spared—then or

*An early Bronze Age
chariot engraved on a
rock tomb at Kivik
in southern Sweden*

now—was the military. In ancient times a simple country boy might be allowed to have something made of metal for the first time in his life when he became a soldier.

In the army, good wheels with spokes, hubs, and axles made the fast-moving chariot possible. Onagers and other slow-moving beasts gave way to horses about 2000 B.C. Metal bits with bridles and reins made those swift, powerful animals manageable, but stirrups, oddly enough, were unknown until classical times, as early equestrian statues show.

When smiths learned how to hammer out and shape flat sheets of metal they could make helmets and armor. And metal-covered shields offered better protection than wood or wood-and-hide ones. Defense tried to keep up with offense, but, as always, it remained somewhat behind.

Since war materiel was favored, invention in that field advanced more rapidly than it did for civilian things. Swords have always been considered more important than plowshares because the need for them is more urgent. When an attack is threatened, swords are needed for defense; when someone wants to attack, plowshares can be melted down for metal from which swords can be made. Our modern world was shaping up according to predictable form.

Much that was learned from making weapons, however, could be applied to articles for everyday domestic use. The men who made wheels for chariots could also make wheels for wagons; the blacksmiths who hammered out spearheads

307

could reshape them for use as hoes; and the carpenters who built machines of war could turn their skills to the building of houses. When iron gradually supplanted bronze, even more peacetime uses for metal were found.

Somewhere in eastern Turkey the trick of making genuine steel was discovered. It was obviously superior to the carburized iron which had been produced before that, so superior that the Spartans are believed to have owed their success in war to the steel swords they introduced to the field of combat about 650 B.C.

WELL TO the north of Greece, two iron-using cultures are known by their type sites as Hallstatt and La Tène. The word Hallstatt comes from a small town in Austria where salt mines had been worked long before iron came into use. Here, in the mid-nineteenth century, a large graveyard was found. When excavated, it yielded great numbers of implements and weapons which traced clearly the evolution of metal using from bronze to iron. The Hallstatt culture dominated the northern part of central Europe from some time before 1000 B.C. to about 500 B.C., when it was succeeded by a not-too-dissimilar culture known as La Tène.

The name La Tène comes from a Swiss lake-dwelling site on the shore of Lake Neuchâtel, which was discovered about the same time as the Hallstatt cemetery. La Tène is late Iron Age, so late that it goes well into Roman times. It was the Romans who overwhelmed the great Iron Age British hill fort, Maiden Castle in Dorset, and massacred most of its inhabitants at some time between A.D. 43 and 47. This, of course, is long after prehistory had ended, even in

Part of the vast earthworks of Maiden Castle

England. But Maiden Castle had been a well-established community for several thousand years before this.

The Hallstatt people, who antedated the Romans, may have left them a warlike legacy, for their heavy iron swords, with certain modifications, were copied by later people. The Hallstatt warriors, however, usually fought on horseback, whereas the might of the Roman legions was based on solid ranks of foot soldiers. In some ways the Hallstatt cavalrymen seem to be precursors of the heavily armed mounted knights who dominated Europe during the Middle Ages.

The art of these Iron Age central European cultures—Hallstatt and La Tène both—shows an interchange with what was being done by the Scythians in central Russia, the early Etruscans in northern Italy, and the Scandinavians. The work of all these people at this time is ornate and somewhat stylized. Curlicues and tendrils characterize its ornament; its subjects are usually savage animals depicted in twisted curves and distorted attitudes. When human figures appear they are far more likely to represent men than women.

Most of the existing art was executed in metal, and the artisans who did it showed great skill, particularly in the pieces they made for the personal adornment of the leaders.

One thing binds all these European cultures together: they were strongly masculine and warlike. By this time and in this part of the world, the bull had triumphed over the Mother Goddess.

THE PEAT BOGS of Denmark and Schleswig-Holstein preserve organic material so well that corpse after corpse has been

Bronze head-circlet found in the village of Stitchel, Scotland [Dawkins]

309

taken from them in such good condition that it seems hard to believe that these are the remains of people who lived in prehistoric times. But they are, for civilization and writing had hardly reached northern Europe when they were alive. Most of the bodies date from the Iron Age. Pollen analysis has enabled scientists to say that the bog corpses are about 2,000 years old.

These tannic-acid-stained bodies have been turning up for two centuries, and nearly a hundred of them, in various states of preservation, have been found. Some of the earlier discovered ones were given Christian burials in local churchyards.

These people did not die natural deaths. It is believed that the women were scalped and slain because they had been unfaithful to their husbands, and that the men were killed because they had transgressed some law or perhaps were human sacrifices to an unknown god. Some were hanged, some had their throats cut or were bludgeoned to death; others were buried alive or drowned.

Opposite page, above: the Tollund Man with a strangling rope still hanging around his neck; below: a woman buried in an oak casket [Both: Danish National Museum]

The best known is Tollund Man, whose body was found in 1950 under more than six feet of peat. He was naked except for a leather belt, a leather cap, and a braided leather thong twisted tightly around his neck. The body was colored leather-brown by the tannic acid in the peat. The face, however, was smiling and was apparently undisturbed by its long-ago encounter with death.

Similarly preserved bodies of an even earlier date have been recovered in Denmark, where they had been buried in coffins made of the hollowed-out trunks of big oak trees. Again tannic acid, this time from the oak wood, kept the remains from decaying. Even the clothing was preserved.

The bog people's bodies tell us what northern European men and women looked like 2,000 years ago. (They looked very much as they do now.) Unlike far older Egyptian mummies, which had had their brains and inner organs removed when they were embalmed, the peat corpses undisturbed remains tell us much more than the mutilated mummies do. We know, for instance, that Tollund Man's last meal consisted of a vegetable gruel made of barley, linseed, sorrel, camelia, and seeds of lesser-known plants. Such food indicates that he probably met his death in the late fall or winter. In addition to his stomach contents,

sections of his brain and portions of his liver and heart have told pathologists a good deal about this truly ancient man. His enigmatic smile has lasted through the ages, and his eyes are still intact although they last looked out at a world that was just emerging from its prehistoric past.

A bronze palstave from Lincolnshire [Dawkins]

THE WORLD that Tollund Man last glimpsed had already undergone some radical changes in its more advanced areas. And nothing was more advanced than the art of war. Sharp-edged metal weapons were being used by soldiers who were learning new tactics which their superior armament made possible.

Not only weapons but armies and leaders are needed for waging war effectively. There had been neither kings nor soldiers in the Stone Ages, but the prototypes of future society were already in existence even then. The hunter-chieftain was a ruler, and his followers in the chase were the first noblemen. The shamans became priests. When agriculture replaced the hunt, the humble fieldworkers were serfs in what was becoming a feudal system. Traders and merchants—and their social allies—were the founders of what was much later to be the middle class.

The hunter-chieftain became a king; his leading followers acted as officers in his army; and the simple huntsmen, who were used to pursuit and slaughter, were easily transformed into soldiers. Since the most direct way to get property was to take it by force, wealth and power were obtained by killing off rivals.

Thus far the human race had been chiefly concerned with staying alive in a world in which nature was hostile. Now, with the ability to grow and store food, people had more time on their hands. With more time available and with ever-increasing populations and no pressing needs, the drive for privilege, property, and power began. We are still living in a culture in which the three "P's" are the dominating forces.

At this point man is about to move into a more advanced phase—urban culture. With it he can at last be called civilized, although just what civilization means, beyond the simple act of dwelling in a city, is open to dispute.

The creature who is now on his way to supreme power over the entire world was characterized in the seventeenth century by Blaise Pascal (*Pensées*, VII, p. 434): "What a chimera, then, is man! What a novelty! What a monster, what a chaos, what a contradiction, what a prodigy! Judge of all things, feeble worm of the earth, depositary of truth, a sink of uncertainty and error, the glory and the shame of the universe."

Shakespeare was more direct; in *Measure for Measure* he called man "an angry ape."

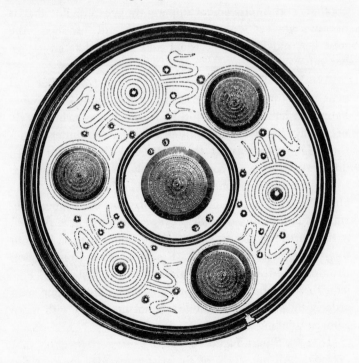

A bronze shield from Denmark decorated in repoussé *[Dawkins]*

313

PHASE EIGHT

28. The Beginnings of Cities
and Civilizations

WHEN WE LOOK BACK at mankind's long existence it seems
to be progressive in its development. One thing leads to
another, and improvement apparently goes on. But that is
because we see only the successful end products; the
mistakes and failures perished and seldom left any trace
behind.

We know that such and such resulted from what had
gone on before and therefore take it for granted that what
happened had to happen just as it did. But possibilities do
not always become probabilities and then certainties; sometimes fate goes against the odds, and things take place
differently from what could reasonably be expected of them.

Practically everyone who has ever bothered to think
about the matter assumes that civilization came about because it had to, because all previous circumstances pointed
in that direction and only in that direction. Emerson fell into
this trap when he said that "Egypt, Greece, Rome, Gaul,
Britain, America, lie folded already in the first man." Perhaps they did, but they do not necessarily unfold along such
orderly lines. Such inevitability is not in accord with more
modern thinking.

In 1965 Stuart Piggott refuted Emerson when he said
(p. 20): "All my study of the past persuades me that the
emergence of what we call civilisation is a most abnormal
and unpredictable event, perhaps in all its Old World manifestations ultimately due to a single set of unique circumstances in a restricted area of western Asia some 5,000 years
ago. . . . It is, I would rather suggest, the non-civilised
314   societies of antiquity that were the norm."

Civilization, as the Latin word "civitas" indicates, is city culture, the product of multiple contacts, good and bad, the result of many people being in close touch with each other for long periods of time.

It is unfortunate that the commonly used expression "civilization" implies that an advanced way of life is possible only in large communities. The narrowness of the definition forbids us to call the men who painted the great Lascaux murals "civilized" while it practically compels us to say that vicious criminals who happen to live in metropolitan centers are. A new word is needed, for "city" no longer means that citizens are necessarily civil or that they are—in the true sense—civilized.

The essential character of a city has been defined by Gordon Childe (1957, p. 36) as "a community that comprises a substantial proportion of professional rulers, officials, artisans, and merchants who do not catch or grow their own food but live on the surplus produced by farmers or fishermen who may dwell within the city or in villages outside its walls. These professional and full-time specialists represent a new class of persons, an absolute addition to the population that could be included in, or supported by, any barbarian community." He also says that writing "not only represents a new instrument for the transmission of human experience and the accumulation of knowledge, but is also symptomatic of a quite novel socio-economic structure—the city." It is for these reasons that Childe speaks of the transition from hunting, agriculture, and village cultures to city culture as the Urban Revolution.

How big did a community have to be in ancient times before it could justly be called a city? The answer seems to be: not very big. Sir Leonard Woolley (1963, p. 428) said that the Mesopotamian city of Ur may have had a population of 300,000 but most early cities would be called towns today. Homer's Troy, for instance, was only about five acres in extent. Excavations show that even with outlying buildings the average ancient city seldom covered more than a dozen acres or so. Çatal Hüyük was unusually large, for it was 30 or 35 acres in extent.

But what counted was not these ancient cities' size but their accomplishment. Early "cities" no larger than Rutland, Vermont; Keokuk, Iowa; Laramie, Wyoming; Banbury,

England; or Arcachon, France, made fine pottery, produced sculpture of museum quality, and turned out exquisitely wrought metalwork. In fact, the artistic output in ancient times was probably higher than it ever has been since. Art, religion, and daily life were closely connected then, and the result was an integrated product of man's best creative activities. The figures of ancient gods and men have an intangible quality that is seldom found in more recent work. Perhaps that quality is somehow associated with belief.

THE CIVILIZATION which Piggott considers an abnormal incident nevertheless did emerge. This new and vitally important phase of man's cultural evolution began in Mesopotamia, the land of two rivers. There the Tigris and the Euphrates flow between broad stretches of swampy ground; beyond the swamps is the desert. Unlike the Nile, which is a dependable source of water, the Mesopotamian rivers are not, so there is a constant threat of flood or drought.

In the southern part is a region known in ancient times as Sumer. It is smaller than Belgium, smaller than the state of Maryland, and except for some fertile soil near the rivers it has little to offer. Its winters are cold; its summers hot, so hot that the temperature can rise to 120 degrees in the shade.

People have lived in Mesopotamia since Paleolithic times, and for more than 100,000 years they showed no signs of being any different from other Middle Eastern hunters, nomads, and farmers. But Mesopotamia is in that magic area which saw so many of our modern world's origins. Jarmo and Shanidar, where agriculture began, are only a few hundred miles to the north; Jericho is not much farther than that to the west; and northwest of Shanidar is the region where metal was first used.

Something happened in Sumer during the fifth millenium B.C., when all the rest of the world was still so primitive that the Sumerians had to make their own way. The initial stages proceeded slowly for a thousand years or more, and then, during the five centuries between 3300 and 2800 B.C., culture accelerated so rapidly that in this brief time villages became cities and cities grew into city-states. Temples and palaces soon covered land that had never been

316

built on before. Swamps were drained by irrigation canals, and the fertile reclaimed soil made it possible to raise enough food to supply an expanding population. The simplicities of village life developed into the complexities of city culture, something the world had never seen before.

In Mesopotamia, according to Georges Roux (1964, p. 67), "the passage from village to city . . . coincides . . . with the appearance of new pottery forms, the invention of the potter's wheel, the replacement of the stamp-seal by the cylinder seal, and several other developments culminating in the invention of writing shortly before 3000 B.C. These changes are so important that, in the opinion of several scholars, they can have resulted only from a foreign invasion. Yet, if invaders are postulated, it is surprising how little we know of them. Their country of origin, their numerical importance, the road they followed, and the form taken by their intrusion are questions either unanswerable or open to much controversy."

And if these questions ever are answered it would simply mean that some other people preceded the Sumerians, and the time scale for the beginnings of civilization would move back another notch. And from what invaders could the Sumerians have possibly learned anything? So far as we know, no people were more advanced than they. No one but beings from outer space could have taught them anything they did not already know. Perhaps some of these out-of-this-world mentors also showed the Franco-Cantabrian cave people how to paint. Perhaps they gave lessons in higher astronomy to the British savages who were thinking about building Stonehenge.

Roux merely says of this extraordinarily rapid cultural development in Sumer that "a close examination reveals no drastic changes in social organization, no real break in architectural or in religious traditions. We are confronted here, not with sudden revolution, but with the final term of an evolution which had started in Mesopotamia itself several centuries before." Perhaps. But perhaps he is applying our modern time scale to an age when centuries were equivalent to our decades. For a village to become a city in a few hundred years when there had never been a city anywhere before, is, to put it mildly, something more than ordinary evolution.

317

THE BIBLE often mentions places in Mesopotamia, beginning with Ur of the Chaldees from which Abraham is supposed to have come. Actually, his Ur may have been another city, and there is some dispute as to whether he was a historical figure. If he was, he is believed to have lived from about 1920 to 1800 B.C. Most other Biblical references are to the more recent Babylonian and Assyrian civilizations that were contemporary with the Hebrew authors of the Bible.

Sumer was unknown to them. Even its name had been forgotten by their time, and the existence of the city remained obliterated from the minds of men until the second half of the nineteenth century, when some exploratory digging brought the ruins to light.

That such an important civilization should have vanished so completely is amazing, particularly so because writing began there some 5,000 years ago. But the writing was on clay tablets that remained buried until recently, when they were dug up and deciphered. (See Chapter 29.)

Once Sumer was discovered, facts came out of the ground in such vast quantities that we now know a great deal about its civilization. In the 1920's, excavation of the huge mounds, which are all that remain of the massive ziggurats and walled cities, showed how luxurious life was for the nobility. Sir Leonard Woolley, who found the graves of the kings of Ur, describes the treasure that had been buried with Mes-Kalam-Dug, a prince of the royal house (1929, p. 75): "The body lay in normal fashion on its right side; round the waist was a broad belt of silver . . . from which hung a gold dagger and a whetstone of lapis lazuli and gold beads, hundreds in all; between the hands was placed a bowl of heavy gold. A larger oval gold bowl lay close by, and near the elbow a gold lamp in the form of a shell, while yet another gold bowl stood behind the head. Against the right shoulder was a double axe-head of electrum, and an electrum axe-head of normal type was by the left shoulder; behind the body there were jumbled together in a heap a gold head-dress, bracelets, beads, and amulets, lunate ear-rings, and spiral rings of gold wire. . . . The prevailing note was struck . . . by the gold, clean as when it was put into the grave; and most of all . . . by the helmet which still covered the rotten fragments of the skull. It was

The restored statue of a ram found in the royal graves of Ur

318

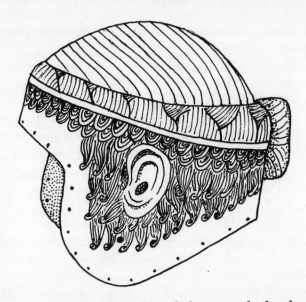

a helmet of beaten gold made to fit low over the head with
cheek-pieces to protect the face, and it was in the form of a
wig, the locks of hair hammered up in relief, the individual
hairs shown by delicate engraved lines. . . . As an example
of goldsmith's work this is the most beautiful thing we have
found in the cemetery . . . and if there were nothing else by
which the art of these ancient Sumerians could be judged
we should still, on the strength of it alone, accord them high
rank in the roll of civilised races."

And with the remains of a queen Woolley found "the
golden head-dress of one of high rank, a long curved golden
pin . . . a fluted and engraved tumbler of gold, and . . . a
golden cylinder seal" (1929, p. 71).

But with this evidence of a luxurious existence for the
royal court something else was discovered which showed
that life even on that level was not all pleasure. What was
dug up made it clear that when a ruler died, his queen and
some of his courtiers, servants, and soldiers entered the big
grave pit, took poison, and were immured with their king.

Despite this mass sacrifice, Woolley believes that "the
contents of the tombs illustrate a very highly developed
state of society of an urban type" (1929, p. 87), which had
highly skilled architects, artists, metalworkers, merchants,
and a well-organized and well-equipped army. This was
civilization in every sense of the word, and if it seems to

*The golden helmet of
Mes-Kalam-Dug, Ur*

*Black diorite statue of
Gudea of Lagash, a late
Sumerian ruler*

319

have had its shortcomings, so have all others, including our own.

As a place to live, cities have certain social attractions, and in those early times they had few of the disadvantages they have now. Sewage disposal was unknown—but so was air pollution. And it was safer then in the city streets than in the open countryside where predatory bandits were at large to rob, rape, burn, and kill. Walled towns and cities were places of refuge into which people from the surrounding villages customarily took shelter from attack.

WHAT was taking place in Sumer was closely paralleled in Egypt. And we know that there was communication between the two countries because "four seals of undoubted Mesopotamian origin, dated the Uruk-Jemdat Nasr period [*ca.* 3500–2900 B.C.], were found there. Egyptian artifacts associated with them dated to the Late Predynastic period . . . immediately prior to the First Dynasty" [*ca.* 3100 B.C.] (Emery, 1961, p. 30).

Egyptian writing may have owed its origin to Sumer, but its characters took on an entirely different form. So did Egyptian art, architecture, and religion. Temples were important to both countries, but Egypt housed its kings in even finer palaces than the Sumerians did. The common man did badly in all early civilizations; slaves, who were originally taken as prisoners of war, did even worse. Educated, privileged slaves came later.

Since the Egyptians had plenty of good stone, their buildings have lasted far better than the mud-brick structures of the Mesopotamians. And the hot, exceedingly dry air of the Sahara Desert which surrounds the Kingdom of the Nile acted so well as a preservative that artifacts made of wood, cloth, and other organic substances have come down to us in amazingly fine condition.

Today one can see the impressive stone ruins of Egypt while the tells of Mesopotamia look like nothing but large rounded mounds of earth. But Mesopotamia once had more big cities than Egypt did, for there were only two of any consequence, Thebes and Memphis, in all that mighty land. In fact, the entire population of ancient Egypt probably "did not greatly exceed a million" (Aldred, 1961, p. 60).

Thebes and Memphis were royal residences where lesser

people were allowed to stay only because some of them were needed to serve the all-powerful pharoahs. Yet the kings of Egypt had had modest beginnings. In early times they were shown "in the habit of a pastoral citizen, carrying the crook and the flail-like *ladanesterion,* wearing an animal tail at their backs, and the beard of their goat-flocks on their chins. . . . Like all such divine kings, in prehistoric times they were ritually killed when their powers began to wane, and their corpses were probably dismembered and buried, or burnt and the ashes scattered for the greater fertility of the land" (Aldred, 1961, p. 157).

Although boastful and absurdly exaggerated claims were made for the astuteness, ability, personal bravery, and tremendous power of the rulers of all these early kingdoms, it was not they but their priests and courtiers who were responsible for the building of their cities and the development of their cultures. Architects, artists, artisans, stewards, overseers, and scribes, shipwrights, sailors, and soldiers, as well as humble food growers, miners, stonemasons, and laborers all helped to make Egypt great. Inscriptions on the monuments commemorate the pharoahs, but the monuments themselves commemorate the nameless men who did the actual construction work. It was the same in Mesopotamia and everywhere else.

An early Egyptian king. From the Narmer palette

WE KNOW the names of many Mesopotamian and Egyptian rulers because the most widely read book in the Western World, the Bible, has made them familiar to us. The 24 books of the Old Testament, particularly the first five, the Pentateuch, which includes Genesis, Exodus, Leviticus, Numbers, and Deuteronomy, describe the early experiences of the Jews.

Since much of the Bible is nonhistorical, it is difficult to separate fact from fancy. As a result it is hard to trace the origins of the nomadic tribes who called themselves God's chosen people. Their prehistoric beginnings cannot be differentiated from those of other tribes living in the same area. And the fairly dependable knowledge we have of them belongs to historic rather than prehistoric times. Yet the Jews are important in any consideration of the development of mankind because their records tell us a great deal about early customs, ways of thinking, morals, and human rela-

321

tionships. And their encounters with the Egyptians, Mesopotamians, and other nearby people give us some much-
needed information about the inhabitants of those countries.
Their chief city, Jerusalem, however, was so late in its
founding (tenth century B.C.) that the original city of Ur
had been sacked and burned a thousand years before that.

More is known about the Jews than about any other
ancient people, for their Bible is read by millions today,
while the Mesopotamian, Egyptian, and Minoan texts are
studied by only a handful of scholars. The Jews were among
the initiators of written history because they went from
legend and epic to the recording of facts about actual events
and real persons.

Cyrus Gordon (1953–65, p. 167) says that with the
founding of Jerusalem "Hebrew historiography comes into
its own, for the sense of national greatness evoked a pride
in the story of the nation. The composition of real history
is the greatest achievement of that period. It antedates
Greek historiography by over five hundred years. Prior to
the Ugaritic discoveries, the origin of Hebrew historiography was a mystery. But now that we know it was created
through the application of epic values to current events, it
still remains a miracle that not the large nations (such as
Babylonia, Assyria or Egypt) but tiny Israel made that
momentous contribution to civilization. National, like individual, genius cannot be explained by analysis in a test tube.
Every nation in the Bible World had epic traditions and
experienced current events. It took the genius of Israel to
create historiography by combining them."

The city of Ugarit, to which Gordon refers, was a seaport
in northern Syria. It has been known only since its discovery
in 1929, but its cuneiform tablets have "so many striking literary parallels to the Hebrew Bible that it is universally recognized that the two literatures are variants of one Ca-
naanite tradition. . . . That Ugarit is the greatest literary
discovery from antiquity since the decipherment of the
Egyptian hieroglyphs is generally recognized. That it lies
closer than any other literature to the Hebrew Bible is also
well known" (Gordon, 1954–65, pp. 94 and 99). Some scholars may not agree with Professor Gordon, but there is no
doubt about the importance of Ugaritic cuneiform, for it is

322 an alphabetic script. And it casts new light on the Bible.

Ugarit was one of several cities that flourished on the eastern coast of the Mediterranean. This well-populated section was bitterly contested for, and its ownership changed hands several times over the centuries. It is the Biblical land of Canaan, the lower part of which was eventually taken over by the Philistines while the northern half was occupied by the Phoenicians whose port cities, Sidon and Tyre, were bases for their trading ships.

Trade, conquest, and migration were the main forces that helped to spread civilization just as they had spread Paleolithic and Neolithic ideas thousands of years before.

The Phoenicians were good traders but mediocre artists. Most of the wares they carried from port to port came from countries other than their own. The few they did manufacture are largely derivative, with decorative motifs obviously taken from Egypt or Mesopotamia. But one exceedingly important thing they originated—the alphabet—did more to further civilization than all their ships or widespread trade. The Ugaritic cuneiform script was alphabetic, but its wedge-shaped characters were complicated, and they had to be impressed in clay. The Phoenician alphabet was much better; it can be written with a pen, a pencil, or a brush, and its characters can be chiseled in stone. It is so flexible that it can be used to record any language. It made writing and reading easier, clearer, and faster. For that we can thank the Phoenicians. The monument to their ingenuity is written in indelible letters in books and periodicals throughout the Western World.

The great ziggurat of Ur and the ruins around it [University Museum, Philadelphia]

29. Writing

ANYONE READING THIS BOOK must find it hard to realize that the entire world was completely illiterate less than 6,000 years ago. Writing and reading are now part of our daily lives, but men got along without them for hundreds of thousands of years and undoubtedly could do so again.

The written word is the binder that keeps our civilized world from coming apart, but if civilization itself was "a most abnormal and unpredictable event," so was writing. Cities and property were needed before there was a call for records of any detailed kind. There were records and tallies in earlier times, but they were far simpler.

And then, when writing was invented, it came into use so slowly that the few specimens we have of that early period do not cast much light on what happened during the next several thousand years. Furthermore, it took time for the written word to travel from its place of origin in the Middle East. While it made its way across the world, many lands remained in their preliterate stage for millenia. It did not come into really wide use until Gutenberg invented printing from movable type about A.D. 1450. It will thus be seen that writing has played a part in mankind's activities for only a few thousand years; a fairly important part for only the last 2,500 years; and a major part for less than 500 years.

Next to language itself, however, writing is the major intellectual invention made by man. Only with it—or with its very modern extensions like film, sound recordings, and data for computers—are people able to have large banks of reasonably exact information readily available. And the art of literature, which had to be uncertainly conveyed orally in ancient times, entered a new phase when an author's words could be put down just as he wanted them to be. Once they were so recorded they could transcend distance and time.

Before writing made the transmission of information easy, men had to use clumsy and often undependable de-

vices. When you tie a bit of cord around your finger to remind you to do something, you are reviving one of mankind's oldest mnemonic tricks. Herodotus (IV, 98) tells how
Darius used knots to give instructions to some men who
were to guard a bridge for 60 days while he marched on
toward Scythia. After showing them a leather thong with 60
knots tied in it, he said: "Untie one knot each day. If I do
not return before the last knot is untied, you may then go
home."

The ancient Peruvians used the quipus, a mnemonic instrument consisting of cords of varying lengths and colors
suspended from a cross-piece. Knots tied in the cords served
as reminders for numerical and other kinds of information.
Only well-trained and skilled interpreters could use such a
complicated and difficult device.

Picture writing was another early form of transmitting
information. Boy Scouts who study Indian lore know that
days can be indicated by suns or moons, peace by clasped
hands, war by arrows, and so forth. Pictographic writing
preceded most other kinds, but it is limited to simple messages, and is liable to be misinterpreted by the reader.

It is a long cry from mnemonic devices and pictographs
to true writing. Most histories of the subject begin with
Mesopotamian and Egyptian scripts and ignore the fact that
the abstract symbols engraved or painted by the Paleolithic
artists were almost surely intended to convey information.
Since no enduring system of keeping records emerged from
them, they have not been given much attention as the precursors of writing.

*A Paleolithic bone
with "alphabetiform"
symbols inscribed on it,
found in Le Placard Cave*

We do know, however, that early Stone Age men used
tallies. In an article in *Science* for November 6, 1964, Alexander Marshack said that marks made on ivory, bone, and
stone for tens of thousands of years were attempts to record
the phases of the moon. By inference, it also seems more
than likely that the highly intelligent men who designed
and built Stonehenge as an astronomical observatory must
have been able to keep fairly accurate records. No trace of

them has been found, but that does not mean that they did not exist. Writing had been in use for a long while in other parts of the world when Stonehenge was built. If experts from the eastern Mediterranean helped to build it, they could have brought a knowledge of writing with them.

ACTUAL WRITING seems to have been invented in Sumer somewhat more than 5,000 years ago. The Sumerian specialist, Samuel Noah Kramer (1956–59, p. xix), points out that the "first attempts were crude and pictographic," but that after a while the writing "completely lost its pictographic character and became a purely phonetic system." By the second half of the third millenium B.C., Sumerian writing had become sufficiently developed to enable its scribes to put down "complicated historical and literary compositions." Most of the clay tablets bearing cuneiform characters, however, do not deal with literature but have economic, administrative, and votive inscriptions.

Although the Sumerians are usually credited with the invention of writing, some authorities at least question their priority. David Diringer (1962, p. 36), for instance, says that writing's "ultimate source may have been earlier Semitic inhabitants of the land, or it may have been brought into Mesopotamia from some other place. The problem of its origin is complicated by the fact that the early Sumerian script bears resemblances of undetermined significance to the early linear script of the Elamites [who lived east of the lower Tigris River], to Egyptian hieroglyphic writing, and to the Indus Valley script."

The recent excavation of a grave pit in Rumania brought to light three baked tablets made of local clay with what seem to be written characters incised on them (*New York Times*, March 26, 1967). They are supposed to be more than 6,000 years old, although the dating is not yet firm. They were made by migrants from some unknown place in the Middle East who may have learned the art of writing before they came to Europe.

THE CUNEIFORM SCRIPT of the Sumerians came into being because the people of the Mesopotamian alluvial plains had plenty of clay and very little else to use as writing material. Conceivably they may also have used some organic substance made from the many swamp plants that grew there, but if they did it was too perishable to survive in that damp climate. Egyptian papyrus was preserved by the very dry air of the Sahara Desert.

Cuneiform script was shaped by wedge-ended styluses that were impressed into the soft clay. The marks thus made could be grouped into meaningful symbols which became more and more abstract as their pictographic origins were left behind. The written-upon clay tablet was then baked or hardened in the sun until it became quite permanent, although it can easily be broken.

The fully developed cuneiform script was exceedingly complicated. Its characters sometimes stood for more than one thing and had to be differentiated by determinatives placed before or after each questionable one. Cuneiform writing underwent modification and simplification when it was adopted by the Babylonians, Assyrians, and Persians, but it remained difficult to use. It continued without basic changes for thousands of years and did not die out until A.D. 75. One wonders why its writers and readers put up with it for so long, for it stayed in use for centuries after the much simpler alphabetic system was invented. It, too, eventually became alphabetic, but the slow-to-make and hard-to interpret cuneiform characters remained very much the same.

WRITING also began at a very early date in Egypt, perhaps only a few centuries after it started in Sumer. Since communication existed between the two countries, the basic idea may have come from Sumer, but the Egyptians devised a new system of their own. The wedge-shaped cuneiform characters seem to have had no influence on the Egyptian hieroglyphs. But pictorial as Egyptian writing is, it is not pictographic; it is far more complex than that.

The Egyptian scribes began by using characters that stood for a whole word. Barbara Mertz (1964, p. 270) explains how these evolved into the hieroglyphs: "The word for brother had the same consonants as the word for arrowhead—'s' and 'n.' The Egyptians could then use an arrowhead to write the word 'brother.' But there was an ambiguity in writing which did not occur in speech. The two words may have been pronounced differently, but since the vowels were not written (as in Hebrew), they looked exactly alike

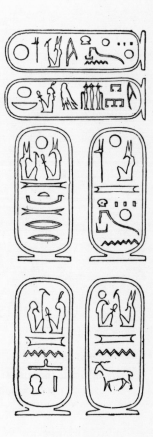

Hieroglyphs

327

in script. The Egyptian solution to this problem was typically ingenious—and typically complex. When they wanted to write the word 'brother,' they added a second sign to the arrowhead—a seated man, which designated the class 'human.'"

Egyptian hieroglyphs, however, went far beyond this in complexity, although the basic idea for an alphabet was inherent in the modified system. But for some strange reason the conservative scribes never abandoned their cumbersome methods and left the much more easily written alphabet to be invented by other people.

Meanwhile, it should be noted that the materials at hand shaped the forms of the written characters. In Mesopotamia, clay and wedge-ended styluses resulted in cuneiforms. In Egypt, where the situation was somewhat more complicated, three kinds of characters developed. The true hieroglyphs, which dealt with gods and kings, were cut in stone and were quite formal in shape. So were the painted ones. But papyrus plants grew in the Nile Valley, and the world's first writing paper was made from thin slices of pith taken from

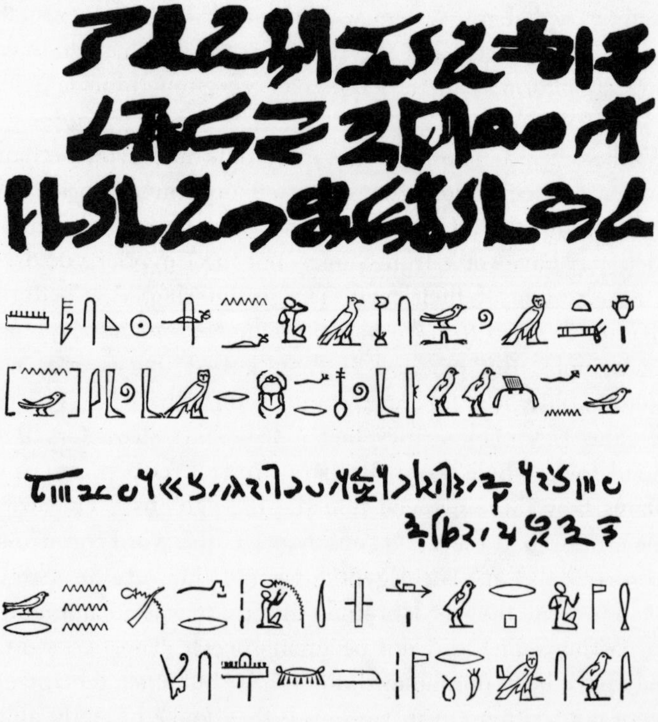

Hieratic

Hieroglyphic transcript of the hieratic

Demotic

Hieroglyphic transcript of the demotic

328

them. Characters brushed or penned on papyrus became more cursive. The higher order of these were called hieratic, while an even more rapid script that developed later for everyday affairs was called demotic. All the characters were derived from the basic hieroglyphs, but hasty writing changed their shapes into more easily made forms.

PREALPHABETIC writing had many characters, determinatives, and other complicated devices to differentiate words that looked alike but which had separate meanings. The few learned people who could write tended to make their already elaborate structures of written language even more complex. One of the more awkward methods they developed was the syllabary. In this, separate characters stood for separate syllables. It was an awkward system, but it was a step toward the phonetic recording of speech, which is the basic principle of the alphabet.

Some time after 1800 B.C., and somewhere in Palestine or Syria, the idea of simplifying writing in a new and radical way was born. Diringer (1962, pp. 120–21) says of this momentous discovery: "The inventor or inventors of the Alphabet were certainly influenced by Egyptian hieroglyphic writing. . . . Since the Alphabet was an invention requiring great intelligence (indeed genius), there is little doubt that the man or men who invented it were acquainted with, or aware of, most of the scripts current in the eastern Mediterranean at the time. . . . Nor should we exclude the possibility that a single man was in fact responsible for the conceptual leap involved in the creation of this unique form of writing: the leap from what had previously been achieved— imperfectly phonetic writings of various kinds—to the idea of representing each single sound by a single unvarying symbol. It is the kind of sudden intuitive perception which single men like Newton have more than once accomplished, even when others did the elaborating and perfecting."

There are few very early alphabets, and their texts are so brief that little can be learned from them. But it is obvious that the idea was afoot. In fact, it was borrowed for use in cuneiform characters. Sometime about 1400 B.C. an alphabet of that kind came into being in Ugarit, as was mentioned in Chapter 28. Diringer thinks that the people there had learned about the basic usefulness of the alphabet and had made it over into one with cuneiform characters because they were accustomed to writing on clay tablets with a stylus. Cyrus Gordon (1966, p. 15) points out that the Ugaritic cuneiform alphabet had 30 characters arranged very much as they are now: a b g ḫ d h w z ḥ ṭ y k š l m d n z s ᶜ p ṣ q r ṯ ǵ t i u s̀.

Ugaritic cuneiform

The alphabet, however, came down to us not from cuneiform characters but from those devised by the Phoenicians. These were taken over by the Greeks and then by the Etruscans and the Romans. The letter forms perfected in Rome and seen at their best on Trajan's column (A.D. 114) are the capitals we use now. Our small letters or minuscules were derived from the capitals when medieval writers, who needed a more quickly written script, reduced them to cursive form.

THE ALPHABET has been called "the most important and useful invention of civilized man" (Gordon, 1966, p. 15). Alphabetic characters, which are ordinarily open to only one interpretation, have made it possible for those who use them to transmit vast quantities of information, give form and permanence to literature, and enable millions of people to read and write who would otherwise have had to remain illiterate. And the alphabet has the further advantage of being adaptable to many languages, even to those that have no writing system of their own. Yet it was not the alphabet but writing itself that was the primary invention. Important as the alphabet is, it is only an improvement of the basic concept. Once writing came into use, someone, somewhere, was sure to see that a limited number of phonetic symbols could record anything that was said. Words were thus picked out of the air and put down on more durable surfaces.

But man could have gone on forever as a viable species without knowing how to write or read. He did for nearly all of his existence, and some primitive people—as well as some not so primitive—still do. The invention of writing can be compared to the invention of agriculture; the invention of the alphabet then becomes comparable to the invention of the plow.

In the beginning, writing had to go through certain evolutionary phases, and these took time because the number of people who could read or write was very limited. These small coteries were conservative, so much so that they often jealously guarded their special knowledge and prevented others from acquiring it. Such an attitude prevented improvement and discouraged progressive experimentation. But over the centuries writing did slough off its retarding forms and gradually become simpler, more exact, and easier to understand.

The first phase was economic. N. K. Sandars says of it (1960, p. 12): "The majority of ancient texts are commercial and administrative documents, business archives, lists, and inventories which, though profoundly interesting to the historian, are not for general reading. The recent decipherment of the so-called 'linear B' script of Bronze-Age Mycenae and Crete has revealed no literature. A huge library discovered at Kültepe in Central Anatolia is entirely made up of records of business transactions; and apart from a solitary text, and that a curse, there is not one of a literary kind. The importance of the excavations at Nippur, Nineveh, and other great centres of early civilization in Mesopotamia is that they have restored a literature of high quality and of unique character."

The Sumerians, who invented writing, seem to have been the first to use it for literature. The Gilgamesh Cycle is not the earliest of their epics, but it is the longest, the most interesting, and the most human, for "it is Gilgamesh as a man who dominates the action of the poem. The gods and their activities serve only as a background and setting for the dramatic episodes in the hero's life" (Kramer, 1959, p. 184). Gilgamesh was two-thirds god and one-third human, but as a man, fallible and mortal, he becomes the first major character in literature and is the prototype of such central figures in later heroic ages as Hercules, Odysseus, Hector, Ajax, Achilles, Samson, David, Siegfried, Beowulf, Saint George, Galahad, and Roland.

The most complete version of the Epic of Gilgamesh is a late seventh-century B.C. Babylonian text. But recent investigations show that it goes back to Sumer and that Gilgamesh was probably a real person who ruled over Uruk in the third millenium B.C. Tales about his strength and his fabulous exploits were told orally; when they were set down in cuneiform characters writing departed from its humble beginnings as mere records and became a fine art. History, too, is foreshadowed in the Gilgamesh Cycle, even though much of it is obviously legend. As fact, Gilgamesh is undependable, but so are the early books of the Bible, and that great book derives many of its most memorable episodes, such as the Flood, the Ark, the Garden of Paradise, and the rib-created Eve, from Sumerian sources.

Gilgamesh is important in the evolution of culture, for it shows how much more revealing writing can be in comparison with the best possible assemblage of archeological evidence. For the first time we are told the names of gods, people, places, and things. And we also learn how the men of those days felt about human emotions, ambitions, and relationships. Even dreams are recorded; so are reflections about the inevitability of death.

Archeological evidence consists of things lost, abandoned, or buried with the dead. No matter whether they are crude bits of stone or finished works of art, they are always material objects, static, divorced from temporal references, and uninformative about what was going on inside their creators' minds. They tell a great deal; but compared with the written word, they do not tell enough.

Artifacts can seldom represent complex ideas, although exceedingly complex thinking may lay behind them. The ideas associated with the Mother Goddess are complex ones, but their complexity is only hinted at in the many images made of her. Statues and pictures are a notable advance in man's desire to communicate his thoughts, but they are limited because they express single instants in time and have little or nothing to say about what went on before or may happen afterward. But writing can express the most complex ideas that man can conceive. It has no limitations. Time, space, reality, the unreal, people, animals—anything and everything fall within its province.

And writing has still another great advantage: the reader can return to it again and again to reinterpret, ponder over, analyze, and study what it says. Like music, literature has far more in it than appears on the surface. It has the magic of association, of the recall of half-remembered images, of

332 thoughts that ordinarily are buried deep in the unconscious

*Shell plaques
with scenes believed
to illustrate the
Epic of Gilgamesh
[University Museum,
Philadelphia]*

mind. The man who invented writing was a greater magi-
cian than all the shamans who came before him, for he
enabled poets and writers to summon up magic in glorious
phrases that are repeated down the ages and in far-distant
lands.

EGYPTIAN WRITING never reached the poetic heights that
Sumerian did. "The nearest approach to the epic," says Sir
Leonard Woolley (1963, p. 812), "is the long poem cele-
brating Ramses II's doubtful victory at Kadesh [ca. 1300–
1290 B.C.]; it comes late in time, and the narrative form, now
used for, apparently, the first time in Egyptian verse, may
have been modelled on some foreign original; but the style
is wholly Egyptian, with all the Egyptian faults of bombast
and cliché grievously exaggerated."

Far better is the tale of Sinuhe, an official who fled to
Palestine when Ammenenemes I was murdered. This is a
picaresque story about a presumably real person; even the
royal family is treated with a light touch that is rare in
Egyptian literature. "Sinuhe" is one of a collection of tales
about a shipwrecked sailor. The loose narrative structure
resembles *The Arabian Nights' Entertainments* (*ca.* A.D.
1450).

The ancient people of the Middle East could write literature, but they had only a vague idea of what history should
be. One reason for this was their conviction that not men
but gods were responsible for everything that happened and
that nothing could change an already destined course of
events. Fortunately, some of the better thinkers were interested in science. In Mesopotamia especially, they began to
lay down the foundations of mathematics and astronomy.
The Egyptians, who have been given more credit than is
due them as scientific innovators, nevertheless did make
some important contributions to our knowledge of the universe and the way it works. But many centuries were to pass
before man could rid himself of the heavy burden of super-
stition he had acquired.

Writing is what sets the historic period of man's existence apart from the prehistoric one. With the written word
man became modern. We have had a little more than 5,000
years to adapt ourselves to the complexities of a modern
world. A few people have done so very well, but most have

not. If the sword—and all the violence associated with it—rather than the pen still prevails in a good part of civilization, that is because man's dark heritage is yet with us. Whether we can learn to live with it and not die by it is the primary problem that faces us now.

HISTORY may have begun in the Middle East, but it did not get very far in those myth-ridden lands. One glimpses history in the accounts of battles, of conflict over political borders, and in the king lists, but true history did not come into being until Herodotus used the Greek word ἱστορίη for it in the fifth century B.C. He made it clear that he wanted to describe the deeds of men so they should not be forgotten by posterity. R. G. Collingwood (1946, p. 19) says that "Herodotus does not confine his attention to bare events; he considers these events in a thoroughly humanistic manner as actions of human beings who had reasons for acting as they did: and the historian is concerned with these reasons."

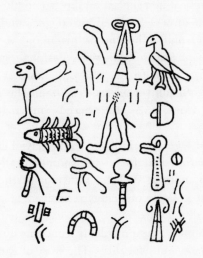

Hittite pictographs

30. How Civilization Came to Europe

SINCE CIVILIZATION REQUIRES cities with large populations and previously advanced cultures to build upon, it could not spread as easily as Neolithic ideas had. Suitable sites are needed for cities, and there is a limited number of such locations. When civilization came to Europe it could put down its roots only in a few places where it had a chance of flourishing.

It moved from the eastern shore of the Mediterranean to Crete and mainland Greece. Ancient people knew this, as is evidenced by the Europa myth. According to the story, this lovely young girl was the daughter of the King of Sidon, a city on the coast of Phoenicia. She was captured by Zeus disguised as a bull. When she sat on the seemingly gentle creature's back, he at once plunged into the sea and carried her to Crete. There one of the sons of this union, Minos, became an early ruler of Knossos. His wife, Pasiphae, gave birth to the Minotaur, the half-man, half-bull monster who dwelt in the Labyrinth until Theseus slew him. The word "labyrinth" comes from λάβρυs, the sacred—and magic—double axe.

Myths and legends originated in the days before writing when information had to be transmitted orally from one generation to another. Webster says that myth "deals with the actions of gods or of beings conceived of as divine or possessed of divine attributes," whereas "legend, though it may include supernatural incidents, concerns human beings, and often some definite locality." The story of Europa is both myth and legend, but there are evidently elements of history in the fanciful tale because it tells the truth about the route that civilization took on its way from Asia to Europe. And the name of its heroine is, of course, of high significance.

Just who the original people of the island of Crete were is a matter of dispute. R. W. Hutchinson, who spent many years studying the excavations there, said (1962, p. 91): "There is no evidence of an indigenous Neolithic culture

*Europa and the Bull.
Designed by Sidney Waugh
[Courtesy Steuben Glass]*

developing out of a Paleolithic one in Crete. . . . The first Neolithic settlers must have come by sea." But a few years later, Ares Poulianos, a Moscow-trained Greek anthropologist, made public the results of a study of 1,200 modern Cretans which showed that they are "basically descendants of aborigines who lived on the island as early as . . . 12,000 B.C." He disagreed with previously held ideas that "the Cretans might have come from North Africa, the Middle East, or the Greek mainland" (*New York Times*, April 17, 1966).

Whatever the origins of the earliest Cretans may have been, civilization seems to have arrived there some time after 2800 B.C. Settlements began on the eastern end of the long, narrow island, which is natural, for that is the part nearest to Asia and Egypt. It is possible that the new migrants might have come from more than one place. Connections with these two areas remained close as trade with them flourished. Since Crete soon became a naval power, its cities did not need strong fortifications; the sea was its best defense.

About 1900 B.C. impressive palaces were built in Knossos, Phaistos, and Mallia. It is with these buildings that what

337

GREECE

CORFU

TROY

ARGOS

THERMOPOLAE

ITHACA

MARATHON

ATHENS

MYCENAE

SALAMIS

SPARTA

MYKONOS

PYLOS

DELOS

KNOSSOS

CRETE

MALLIA

PHAISTOS

*Greece, Crete, and
the Aegean Islands*

we think of as Minoan civilization begins. The excavations
at Knossos made by Sir Arthur Evans at the turn of the century—and at his own expense—brought the great palace of
that city to light. Of all the civilizations that the world had
yet seen, Minoan seems to have been the most pleasant.
Mesopotamia was dark and bloody ground; Egypt, for all
its brilliant sun and color, was run for the benefit of the kings
and the priests. In both countries, war was a sport, a diver-
sion, and an accepted means of acquiring wealth.

Crete, however, was apparently a fairly happy place
during the centuries that followed, although earthquakes
and volcanic action on nearby islands sometimes leveled the
palaces. The one at Knossos had to be rebuilt at least three
times. Gordon Childe, who was often a harsh critic, praised
338 Minoan civilization as it was portrayed by its artists (1957,

p. 27): "In beholding the charming scenes of games and processions, animals, and fishes, flowers, and trees that adorned the Middle Minoan II and III palaces and houses we breathe already a European atmosphere."

Aside from their colorful decorations, Cretan buildings were the forerunners of the kind of architecture that was to rise in Europe. Mesopotamian and Egyptian palaces and temples were rather austere and were intended primarily—and sometimes exclusively—for gods, kings, priests, and

How the bull jumpers made their daring leaps [After Sir Arthur Evans]

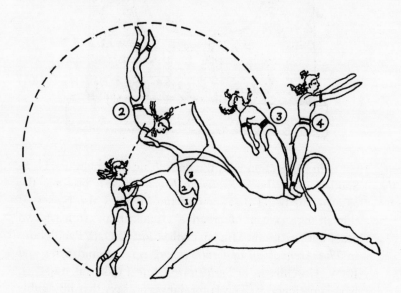

courtiers. But Minoan architecture was more domestic in plan and execution. Even its finest palaces seem to have been designed for living rather than for show. Stairways in some of the five-story buildings were made for use and not merely to impress visitors. The courtyards had spaces where the famous bull-leaping games were played by lithe young men and maidens who jumped through the charging animal's horns to land unharmed on his back.

Archeology can never tell us everything about the lives of vanished peoples, so there undoubtedly are gaps in the information we have about the ancient Cretans. As in Malta, life in the Minoan palaces could not have been completely idyllic. But when compared with the cruelty of Mesopotamian civilizations it seems attractive.

The peculiar eidetic ability to project a mental image of an object and then trace its outlines was described in Chap-

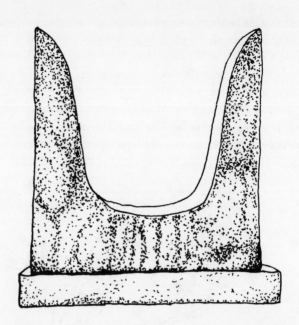

*"Horns of consecration"
from the
Palace of Knossos*

ter 13 in connection with the Paleolithic cave painters. G. A. Snijder, in his book *Kretische Kunst* (1936), presents the case for his belief that some of the Minoans also possessed this strange power of creative visualization. At least two other authorities on Minoan civilization, J. D. S. Pendlebury in *The Archeology of Crete* (1939, pp. 248 and 275) and R. W. Hutchinson in *Prehistoric Crete* (1962, pp. 129–33), have mentioned it. The latter, however, says that he doubts "whether this is a satisfactory explanation of Minoan art in general."

Whatever special gifts Minoan artists may have had, it is certain that they made great strides forward on an island that had had no previous record of creativity. Pendlebury says that "their representations of wild life, animals and birds, and in their sense of the surroundings in which the action takes place, the Minoan artists are not approached in ancient art until the days of Tell-el-Amarna" (in Egypt under Akhenaton *ca.* 1350 B.C.). He also believes that the Minoans may have had a great deal of influence upon the Egyptian art of that extraordinary period (1939, p. 276).

Certain motifs occur again and again in Minoan art to express things that were obviously of great importance in the lives of these island people. Pre-eminent among them is the bull, the symbol of masculine strength and fertility.

Figures of this powerful animal appear on engraved seals, statuary, and murals, sometimes represented only by a pair of spreading horns. The second omnipresent symbol is the double axe, or labrys, which was often mounted between the tips of the horns, perhaps to give the cult object added force. The third is the Mother Goddess, who often becomes the Snake Goddess. The double axe was her emblem, parti-

cularly when she was in household guise, for she ruled the home and presided over death as well as birth. She is also "the Mistress of Trees and Mountains and the Lady of the Wild Animals. . . . When pictured on the rings and seal stones, the goddess is always bareheaded, with her long tresses floating in the wind" (Pendlebury, 1939), p. 273). As the Snake Goddess she is dressed in the Cretan costume of the time with wide, flaring skirts and breasts exposed. Doves flutter around her, and lions walk by her side. Compared to earlier representations of the Mother Goddess, she seems very modern, very European, terrifying sometimes, but also enchanting. Of all ancient figures she appears to be the most sympathetic.

Above: a double axe. Left: bull heads and double axes from a Mycenaean vase

IF THE Minoans had a literature, it is lost except as possible echoes in later Greek myths. It is lost because their writing, so far as we know, never got beyond the business-record stage. But it is an important step in the history of communication. The lists and inventories make dull reading for the layman, but they have told specialists a great deal about those times.

The basic idea of having symbols stand for letters, syllables, or complete words almost surely came to Crete from the Middle East or Egypt. Pictographic characters were used first. Among them was the double axe; others, such as the eye, a leg, a ship, a jar, a bird, or an ox head, had already appeared in earlier forms of writing. In Crete they can be seen on engraved seals and baked clay tablets.

In 1908 a flat clay disk, slightly more than six inches in diameter, was found at Phaistos. Arranged around it in spiral form, 45 pictorial symbols were "separately impressed on the soft clay by means of a punch or type cut for the purpose. . . . Only one each of the set of punches was needed; nevertheless, this use of standard forms was a remarkable anticipation of the invention of engraving and printing" (John Chadwick, 1958, p. 20). The brilliant notion of using individual relief-cut character stamps, as was done about 1700 B.C. on the Phaistos disk, did not occur again until A.D. 1045, in China.

Some of the symbols on the Phaistos disk

In connection with such innovations it should be noted that Daedalus, the perhaps not entirely mythical innovator who built the Labyrinth and made wings for himself and his son Icarus to fly, was said to be an exiled Athenian who came to Crete to work for King Minos. Crete, in myth and reality, nurtured invention. It had some of the world's first interior plumbing, carefully planned rain-water drains and sewers, and in general was far in advance of the rest of Europe in the art of living.

Linear A

THE FAMOUS Linear A and Linear B scripts were found on Crete and in Greece by Sir Arthur Evans and others. Linear B was deciphered in 1952 by Michael Ventris, a young architect who applied cryptographic analytical techniques to the problem and solved it just before he was killed in an automobile accident at the age of 34. Linear A, as well as the Phaistos disk, have been worked on by Professor Cyrus Gordon, who believes that they represent Semitic languages. The Phaistos inscription, he says, is a ritual text associated with the worship of Baal.

The messages written on these early tablets are short, factual, and rather dull. But the methods devised to decipher them will always be helpful to archeologists who want to read long-dead languages inscribed in characters that have no apparent connection with other known scripts.

Linear B

STUART PIGGOTT (1965, p. 123) says that "the great age of Mycenaean Greece, the first civilisation of mainland Europe . . . probably began in the late seventeenth century B.C." He adds that it was "profoundly influenced by Minoan art and architecture" and also points out that the "horse-drawn chariots on the stelae (of the Shaft Graves) are the first monumental and representational stone carvings in Greece, and all mark the first appearance of this engine of war in Europe."

The Mycenaeans were a bellicose people, and the swift-moving chariot was a powerful weapon in their ruthless hands. The chariot long precedes the mounted horseman because stirrups, which enable a cavalryman to remain effectively seated in the shock of combat, did not come into use until shortly before the beginning of the Christian era. Men rode to the battlefield but ordinarily dismounted to fight on foot. The chariot, however, like the much-later tank, was a fear-inspiring mobile weapon.

When Henry Schliemann, fresh from his discoveries at Troy, excavated the Grave Circle at Mycenae he found that the city had been as rich in gold as Homer said it was. And one of the Shaft Graves contained 90 bronze swords. Some of Mycenae's great wealth had been obtained by looting and piracy, for such practices were then regarded as normal in the violent Aegean world. Yet much of Mycenae's treasure came from trade; her ships went to ports in Italy and Sicily, while her artifacts have been found in England and central Europe. The ever-pressing need for tin and copper to make bronze drove her on. That metal was as essential to her as steel is to us. Amber was also sought for. In exchange for raw materials, Mycenae sent out pottery, glass and faience beads, and arms and armor. Among her exported goods are the magical double axes.

A soldier from the Warrior Vase, Mycenae

343

Trade and war made Mycenae powerful. If her traders were as determined as her warriors, they must have driven hard bargains wherever they went.

Much as Mycenae owed to Crete, she did not hesitate to plunder Knossos when the opportunity arrived early in the fifteenth century B.C. But in the thirteenth century, when the Dorians came down from the north shortly after the fall of Troy, both Mycenae and Crete were overwhelmed, and civilization in the Aegean entered a long dark phase.

During the ninth century, when the Greek alphabet was coming into use, Homer told the story of the Trojan War in the *Iliad* and of the wanderings of Odysseus afterward in the *Odyssey*. European literature begins with Homer, and, by good fortune, it began on the highest level.

Homer has dominated the literature of the Western World ever since he wrote his immortal poems. He has naturally been the subject of much inquiry. Did he really exist? Are the poems actually his or were they written by several people? Were they written at all or were they composed orally? And how historically true are they?

For a long time it was thought that the *Iliad* and the *Odyssey* were probably produced by a number of authors whose joint work was given Homer's name. It was also believed that the poems had to be written because they seemed to be too long to be retained in the memory as oral compositions. Since no one expected a poet to follow truth literally, it was taken for granted that the author or authors took free advantage of poetic license and invented most of the material, paying scant attention to facts about a world that had existed centuries before the Homeric epics were composed.

But in recent times scholars have changed their minds about many of these questions, and it is now thought that a single author was responsible for both the *Iliad* and the *Odyssey*, although he, like Shakespeare, used material from earlier sources. It has been shown by comparison with other oral literatures that the poems are not too long to have been produced by one man. As for historical truth, the stories told in the poems may have large areas of fancy but basically they are founded on fact. This applies especially to the *Iliad*, which deals with events that can be traced. The *Odyssey* is a picaresque novel with mythical overtones.

344

The Homeric epics are more than literature, for they tell

us more about ancient Greece than its ruins, artifacts, and works of art can. Such relics are nearly always broken or incomplete, and at best they give us information about material things. From them one has to infer what life was like when they were new and in daily use. They, along with the human bones dug up with them, belong in a cemetery in which what is left of the past is interred. We are grateful to have them, particularly for the periods before written history, for they are all that remain of that preliterate stage.

Writing, even when it recorded nothing but business records, tells us much more than artifacts do. Inventories give us an idea of quantity, value, wealth, and the nature of perishable things that people then wanted to own. And so many of the cherished objects of the past no longer exist. Where, for instance, is the goddess Ino's veil that protected Odysseus? Or the purple blankets that covered Helen's bed?

When writing becomes literature it gives us a truly intimate view of the personal lives of long-ago people. With Gilgamesh we begin to see into the heart of man and are told something about his desires, ambitions, and fears. With Homer we get more than generalities. He takes us to the battle plain before the walls of Troy, to the beach where fair Nausicaä is playing with her maidens, to Odysseus' home when he settles accounts with his wife's suitors and cuts them down, one by one, with quick-flashing arrows. Gilgamesh talks about the past; Homer makes it come alive.

THE ACTUAL DATE of the ten-year-long Trojan War is still a matter of dispute. Tradition puts the fall of Troy at 1184 to 1180 B.C., although some ancient commentators said that it was as early as 1334 or as late as 1135. Modern archeology pins it down to about 1200 B.C. The "long" chronology used by Trojan expert Carl W. Blegen says 1260.

Homer's lifetime is equally vague; so is his birthplace. In fact, practically nothing is known about him. He is believed to have been blind and is said to have been poor. Modern scholars place him—with some uncertainty—in the eighth century B.C., say about 725. If he lived about that time, Troy would have been as far behind him as the discovery of America is from us. But things changed slowly then, so he was able to gather oral data, fragments of facts, and bits of legends for the background of his tales. The rest he did him-

Homer
[Courtesy of Museum of
Fine Arts, Boston]

self. "There is no evidence at all," says Cedric Whitman (1958, p. 14), "that the poet of the *Iliad* invented a single character or episode in his whole poem. He may not have invented a single phrase. His invention was the *Iliad*."

Ancient people may have had something that we have lost. To preserve large segments of the past without recourse to written records could be one of them. That may be the price we pay for the enormous advantage of having the written word at our disposal.

HOMER portrays the first civilization of the mainland of Europe. His people are still half savage, given to swaggering and boasting, to violence, and to a moral code that sometimes seems more than dubious to us. The barbarian strain was still strong in them, but they were brave, loyal, and dedicated men. Their costumes and accoutrements, chariots, houses, ships, and living customs foreshadow those of classical Greece, which was only a few centuries ahead.

Its center, Athens, had been settled long before classical times, as recent excavations show. And unlike Egypt, with its rigid caste system, a citizen, and later on even a slave, had certain rights. This greater freedom was evidenced in the form that writing took. The Greek alphabet "was no hieratic secret guarded by priests, or confined to archival accounts, records, or business operations. It was a fairly public accomplishment by the late eighth century, and people already wrote verse with it" (Whitman, 1958, p. 79).

After Homer's time, mainland Greece began to develop rapidly. The first Olympic games were held in 776 B.C. Colonies were established in Italy and southern France. Athens grew steadily. By 480 B.C. it became a target for conquest by the Persians under Xerxes. They took the city and burned it. Then they were turned back at Salamis, and Athens was free to become the first great city of the Western World. At that point civilization was firmly planted on the mainland of Europe.

But Athens was more than just a city. It had been purified in the Persian wars and now stood for something that was to dominate the West as gods and priests and kings had dominated the East. "It was *Demos*, men said, who had won the war, who safeguarded the peace. The men who had fought at Marathon were a legend, but the seafaring men of

*A model of the Acropolis
at Athens [Royal
Ontario Museum, Toronto]*

the fleet had won Salamis; it was they who still kept out the Persian and held the aliens in hand; they were the people; and one by one the old traditions were changed, and Athens became the standard democracy of the world, and of all time" (T. R. Glover, 1935, p. 112).

THE RUINS OF Athens were replaced by some of the finest buildings in the history of architecture. On the imposing heights of the Acropolis the Parthenon was erected as a temple to honor Pallas Athene. Near it were placed the Temple of Nike, the Erectheum, and the Propylaea Gateway. Sculpture flourished; so did all the fine arts. But the true glory of ancient Greece was not to be counted in material things. Its greatness came from its people, the long roll of distinguished men who lived after the Persian War. The period included Periclean Athens, and among the outstanding creators, philosophers, and leaders were Phidias, Aeschylus, Pindar, Sophocles, Plato, and the historians Herodotus, Thucydides, and Xenophon. Then came Aristotle and Archimedes. There are others, many others, for the next few centuries in Greece saw one of the greatest concentrations of the human spirit that has ever been witnessed.

Such genius could not last, but the essence of it was passed on to Etruria, to Rome, to the Roman colonies, and was carried by the legions to Britain and the barbarian north.

The apelike creatures who had come down from the trees reached their fullest development in classical Greece. There human beings had gone as far as they are ever likely to go.

347

The rest is history, more than 2,000 years of it. But that is another story, and we have already trespassed on its threshold.

Prehistory is a record of fairly steady progress, but in recent times the very idea of progress has been questioned. The men who shaped the first stone hand-axe, built the first fire, drew the first picture, planted seeds, and invented writing never stopped to raise questions about the ultimate values of what they were doing. They simply went on to do something else. Progress and improvement sparkled in their brains, emanated from their creative fingertips. Curiosity tirelessly drove them on. There were always new worlds to explore, new ideas to conceive, untried theories to devise and test.

We have inherited all that they created. We should cherish the gifts, carry on the resolute drive, and encourage the probing mind. We are still motivated by our ancient ancestors. Some of our worst traits come from them—and so do some of our best. Deep in our unconscious selves are the vague stirrings of stooped figures moving under the trees, of the warm glow of fires burning in dark caves while the cries of animals echo through the night. Murmuring voices rise and become speech. All the elemental things are there, basic and unchanged. Man is their essence. Prehistory and history added together are his story. It is a great narrative, filled with terror and tears, with conflict and creation, with defeat and accomplishment. Look at the pictures on the walls of time, and you will see, as our ancestors did, that they are always on the move.

BIBLIOGRAPHY

Bibliography

AGIUS, A. J.
1968. *The Hal-Saflieni Hypogeum,* Paola-Malta
AITKEN, M. J.
1961. *Physics and Archeology,* New York
ALBRIGHT, W. F.
1949 and 1960. *The Archeology of Palestine,* London
ALDRED, CYRIL
1961. *The Egyptians,* London
ALSOP, JOSEPH
1964. *From the Silent Earth: A Report on the Greek Bronze Age,* New York
ANATI, EMMANUEL
1961. *Camonica Valley,* New York
1962. *Palestine Before the Hebrews,* New York
ANGRESS, S., AND C. A. REED
1955. *An Annotated Bibliography on the Origin and Descent of Domestic Animals,* Chicago
ARDREY, ROBERT
1961. *African Genesis,* New York
1966. *The Territorial Imperative,* New York
ASHBEE, PAUL
1960. *The Bronze Age Round Barrow in Britain,* London
ATKINSON, R. J. C.
1956. *Stonehenge,* London
1967. "Silbury Hill," *Antiquity,* XLI
BACON, EDWARD
1961. *Digging for History: Archeological Discoveries Throughout the World, 1945 to 1959,* New York
BAILIT, HOWARD L., AND JONATHAN S. FRIEDLANDER
1966. "Tooth Size Reduction: A Hominid Trait," *American Anthropologist,* June
BANDI, HANS-GEORGE, ET AL.
1961. *The Art of the Stone Age; 40,000 Years of Rock Art,* London
BANDI, H., AND H. MARINGER
1953. *Art in the Ice Age,* London
BANNISTER, B.
1963. "Dendrochronology" in Brothwell and Higgs, 1963
BECKER, C. J.
1955. "The Introduction of Farming into Northern Europe," *Journal of World History,* II, 4, Paris
BIBBY, G.
1956. *The Testimony of the Spade,* London
1961. *Four Thousand Years Ago,* London

351

BIRDSELL, JOSEPH B.

1957. "Some Population Problems Involving Pleistocene Man," *Cold Spring Harbor Symposia on Quantitative Biology*, XXII

BLANC, ALBERTO C.

1958. "Torre in Pietra, Saccopastore, Monte Circeo . . . the Mousterian Culture in the Pleistocene Sequences of the Rome Area" in *Hundert Jahre Neandertaler, 1856–1956*, Utrecht

BLEGEN, CARL W.

1963. *Troy and the Trojans,* London

BONIFAY, EUGENE AND MARIE-FRANÇOISE

1963. "Un gisment a faune épivillafranchienne à Saint-Estève-Janson (Bouches-du-Rhone)," *Comptes Rendus,* Académie des Sciences, 256, Paris

BORDES, FRANCOIS

1961. "Mousterian Cultures in France," *Science,* September 22

BOUCHER DE PERTHES, JACQUES CRÈVECOEUR

1839. *De la Création: essai sur l'origine de la progression des êtres,* Paris

1847–64. *Antiquités celtiques et antédiluviennes,* Paris

BOULE, MARCELLIN, AND HENRI V. VALLOIS

1921 and 1957. *Fossil Men,* Paris and London

BRACE, C. LORING

1964. "The Fate of the 'Classic' Neanderthals; a Consideration of Hominid Catastrophism," *Current Anthropology,* February

BRACE, C. LORING, AND M. F. ASHLEY MONTAGU

1965. *Man's Evolution: An Introduction to Physical Anthropology,* New York

BRAIDWOOD, ROBERT J.

1952. "From Cave to Village," *Scientific American,* October

BRAIDWOOD, ROBERT J. AND LINDA

1953. "The Earliest Village Communities of Southwestern Asia," *Journal of World History,* I

BRAIDWOOD, ROBERT J., ET AL.

1953. "Did Man Once Live by Beer Alone?" *American Anthropologist,* LV

BRAIDWOOD, ROBERT J., AND CHARLES A. REED

1957. "The Achievement and Early Consequences of Food Production: A Consideration of the Archeological and Natural Historical Evidence," *Cold Spring Harbor Symposia on Quantitative Biology,* XXII

BRAIDWOOD, ROBERT J., B. HOWE, ET AL.

1960. "Prehistoric Investigations in Iraqi Kurdistan," *Oriental Institute Studies in Ancient Oriental Civilizations,* No. 31, Chicago

BRAUCOURT, JEAN DE HEINZELIN DE

1962. *Manuel de typologie des industries lithiques,* Brussels

BREA, L. BERABÒ

1957 and 1966. *Sicily,* London

BREASTED, JAMES HENRY

1905 and 1912. *A History of Egypt,* New York

BREUIL, ABBÉ HENRI

1952. *Quatre cents siècles d'art parietal,* Montignac

BREUIL, HENRI, AND M. C. BURKITT

1929. *Rock Paintings of Southern Andalusia,* Oxford

BREUIL, HENRI, AND RAYMOND LANTIER
1951 and 1959. *The Men of the Old Stone Age*, New York
BRIFFAULT, ROBERT
1927. *The Mothers*, 3 vols., New York
BRODRICK, A. H.
1949. *Lascaux, a Commentary*, London
1963. *Father of Prehistory: The Abbé Henri Breuil: His Life and Times*, New York
BROOKS, C. E. P.
1949. *Climate Through the Ages*, London
BROOM, R.
1950. *Finding the Missing Link*, London
BROTHWELL, DON, AND ERIC HIGGS (EDITORS)
1963. *Science in Archeology*, New York
BROWN, G. BALDWIN
1928. *The Art of the Cave Dweller*, London
BUCKLAND, DEAN WILLIAM
1823. *Reliquiae Diluvianae, or Observations on the Organic Remains contained in caves, fissures, and diluvial gravel attesting the action of a Universal Deluge*, London
BUETTNER-JANUSCH, JOHN
1966. *Origins of Man*, New York
BURKITT, MILES
1933. *The Old Stone Age*, Cambridge
BUTZER, KARL W.
1964. *Environment and Archeology: An Introduction to Pleistocene Archeology*, Chicago
CAMPBELL, BERNARD G.
1964. "Quantitative Taxonomy and Human Evolution" in *Classification and Human Evolution*, edited by S. L. Washburn, London
CARTAILHAC, E., AND HENRI BREUIL
1906. *La caverne d'Altamira à Santillane, près Santander*, Monaco
CHADWICK, JOHN
1958. *The Decipherment of Linear B*, Cambridge
CHAD, CHESTER S.
1963. "Implications of Early Human Migrations from Africa to Europe," *Man*, August, London
CHILDE, V. GORDON
1925 and 1957. *The Dawn of European Civilization*, London
1929. *The Most Ancient East*, London
1930. *The Bronze Age*, Cambridge
1931. *Skara Brae*, London
1936 and 1951. *Man Makes Himself*, London
1950. *Prehistoric Migrations in Europe*, Oslo
1950. "Cave Men's Buildings," *Antiquity*, XXIV
1958. *The Prehistory of European Society*, Harmondsworth
CLARKE, GRAHAME
1939 and 1957. *Archeology and Society*, Cambridge
1940. *Prehistoric England*, Cambridge
1948. "Fishing in Prehistoric Europe," *Antiquaries Journal*, XXVIII
1952. *Prehistoric Europe: The Economic Basis*, London
1954. *Excavations at Star Carr*, Cambridge
1961. *World Prehistory, an Outline*, Cambridge

CLARKE, GRAHAME, AND STUART PIGGOTT
    1933. "The Age of British Flint Mines," *Antiquity*, VII
    1965. *Prehistoric Societies*, New York
CLARK, J. DESMOND
    1958. "Early Man in Africa," *Scientific American*, July
CLARK, SIR WILFRED LE GROS
    1955 and 1964. *The Fossil Evidence for Human Evolution*, Chicago
    1960. *The Antecedents of Man*, Chicago
    1965. *History of the Primates*, Chicago
CLES-REDEN, SIBYLLE VON
    1961. *The Realm of the Great Goddess*, London
CLUTTON-BROCK, J.
    1963. "The Origins of the Dog" in Brothwell and Higgs, 1963
COHEN, M.
    1958. *La grande invention de l'écriture et son evolution*, Paris, 3 vols.
COLBERT, E. C.
    1953. "The Record of Climatic Changes as Revealed by Vertebrate Paleocology" in *Climatic Changes*, edited by Harlow Shapley, Cambridge
COLE, SONIA
    1961. *The Neolithic Revolution*, London
    1963. *The Prehistory of East Africa*, London
COLLINGWOOD, R. G.
    1946. *The Idea of History*, Oxford
CONRAD, J. R.
    1959. *The Horn and the Sword*, Oxford
COOK, R. M.
    1961. *The Greeks Until Alexander*, London
COON, CARLETON S.
    1954. *The Story of Man*, New York
    1962. *The Origin of Races*, New York
    1963. "The Rock Art of Africa," *Science*, December 27
    1965. *The Living Races of Man*, New York
CORNWALL, I. W.
    1956. *Bones for the Archeologist*, London
    1958. *Soils for the Archeologist*, London
    1964. *The World of Ancient Man*, New York
COUGHLAN, H. H.
    1951. *Notes on the Prehistoric Metallurgy of Copper and Bronze in the Old World*, Oxford
CRAWFORD, O. G. S.
    1957. *The Eye Goddess*, New York
CRENSHAW, JOHN W., JR.
    1964. "Human Evolution" in *Culture and the Direction of Human Evolution*, edited by Stanley M. Garn, Detroit
CRISLER, L.
    1959. *Arctic Wild*, London
DANIEL, GLYN
    1950a. *The Prehistoric Chamber Tombs of England and Wales*, Cambridge
    1950b. *One Hundred Years of Archeology*, London
    1960. *The Prehistoric Chamber Tombs of France*, London
    1962. *The Idea of Prehistory*, London

1963a. *The Megalith Builders of Western Europe,* London
1963b. *The Hungry Archeologist in France,* London
DARLINGTON, C. D.
  1963. *Chromosome Botany and the Origins of Cultivated Plants,* New York
DART, RAYMOND
  1959. *Adventures with the Missing Link,* New York
DARWIN, CHARLES
  1839. *Narrative of . . . H. M. S. Adventure and Beagle,* London
  1859. *On the Origin of Species by Means of Natural Selection,* London
  1868. *Animals and Plants Under Domestication,* London
  1871. *The Descent of Man,* London
DAWKINS, W. BOYD
  1880. *Early Man in Britain,* London
DAY, MICHAEL
  1965. *Guide to Fossil Men,* London
DE CAMP, L. SPRAGUE
  1960. "Before Stirrups," *Isis,* June, Brussels
DEEVEY, E. S., JR.
  1960. "The Human Population," *Scientific American,* September
DE GEER, BARON GERALD
  1912. "A Geochronology of the Last 12,000 Years," Proc. 11th Inst. Geol. Congress, Stockholm 1:241–58
DEGERBØL, M.
  1962. *Tierzüchtung U. Züchtungs-Biologie,* Copenhagen
DE LAET, S. J.
  1958. *The Low Countries,* London
DE QUINCEY, THOMAS
  1845. "Levana and Our Ladies of Sorrow," in *Selected Writings of Thomas De Quincey,* New York, 1937
DE VRIES, M., AND KENNETH P. OAKLEY
  1959. "Radiocarbon Dating of the Piltdown Skull and Jaw," *Nature,* 184, London
DIGBY, GEORGE BASSETT
  1926. *The Mammoth and Mammoth-Hunting in Siberia,* London
DIMBLEBY, G. W.
  1963. "Pollen Analysis" in Brothwell and Higgs, 1963
DIRINGER, DAVID
  1962. *Writing,* New York
DOBZHANSKY, THEODOSIUS
  1944. "On Species and Races of Living and Fossil Man," *American Journal of Physical Anthropology,* September
  1951. *Genetics and the Origin of Species,* New York
DUBOIS, EUGÈNE
  1894. *Pithecanthropus erectus,* Batavia
DYSON, ROBERT H., JR.
  1953. "Archeology and the Domestication of Animals in the Old World," *American Anthropologist,* December
EDMONSON, MUNRO S.
  1961. "Neolithic Diffusion Rates," *Current Anthropology,* April
EISELEY, LOREN C.
  1958. *Darwin's Century: Evolution and the Men Who Discovered It,* New York
  1954. "Man, the Fire-Maker," *Scientific American,* 191, No. 3

EMERSON, RALPH WALDO
1841. "History," in *Essays, First Series,* Boston
EMERY, W. B.
1961. *Archaic Egypt,* Harmondsworth
EMILIANI, CESARE
1968. "The Pleistocene Epoch and the Evolution of Man," *Current Anthropology,* February
ERDTMANN, D. B.
1954. *An Introduction to Pollen Analysis,* Waltham, Chronica Botanica
ERICH, ROBERT
1965. *Chronologies in Old World Archeology,* Chicago
ERICSON, DAVID B., AND GOESTA WOLLIN
1964. *The Deep and the Past,* New York
ERMAN, ADOLF
1927. *The Literature of the Ancient Egyptians,* London
EVANS, J. D.
1959. *Malta,* London
EVANS, JOHN
1872. *The Ancient Stone Implements, Weapons, and Ornaments of Great Britain,* London
EVANS, SIR ARTHUR J.
1921 to 1935. *The Palace of Minos: A Comparative Account of the Successive Stages of the Early Cretan Civilization as Illustrated by the Discoveries at Knossos,* 4 vols., London
EVERNDEN, J. F., AND G. H. CURTIS
1965. "The Potassium-Argon Dating of Late Cenozoic Rocks in East Africa and Italy," *Current Anthropology,* October
FERGUSSON, JAMES
1872. *Rude Stone Monuments in All Countries; Their Age and Uses,* London
FORBES, R. J.
1950. *Metallurgy in Antiquity: A Notebook for Archeologists and Technologists,* Leiden
FORSDYKE, JOHN
1964. *Greeks Before Homer,* New York
FOX, AILEEN
1964. *South West England,* London
FOX, SIR CYRIL
1932. *The Personality of Britain,* Cardiff
1959. *Life and Death in the Bronze Age,* London
FRANKFORT, HENRI
1951. *The Birth of Civilization in the Near East,* Bloomington, Indiana
1954. *The Art and Architecture of the Ancient Orient,* London
FREEMAN, KATHLEEN
1950 and 1963. *Greek City-States,* New York
FRERE, JOHN
1800. "Account of Flint Implements Discovered at Hoxne," *Archeologia,* XIII, pp. 204–5, London
GARDINER, SIR ALAN
1961. *Egypt of the Pharaohs,* Oxford
GEIKIE, JAMES
1874. *The Great Ice Age and Its Relation to the Antiquity of Man,* London

1881. *Prehistoric Europe*, London
1914. *The Antiquity of Man*, Edinburgh

GIEDION, S.
1962. *The Eternal Present: The Beginnings of Art*, New York

GIMBUTAS, MARIJA
1963. *The Balts*, London

GIOT, P. R.
1960. *Brittany*, London

GLOVER, T. R.
1935. *The Ancient World*, Harmondsworth

GORDON, CYRUS H.
1953 and 1965. *The Ancient Near East*, New York
1962. *The Common Background of Greek and Hebrew Civilization*, New York
1966. *Ugarit and Minoan Crete*, New York

GRAHAM, JAMES WALTER
1962. *The Palaces of Crete*, Princeton

GRAVES, ROBERT
1948. *The White Goddess*, New York

GRAZIOSI, P.
1960. *Paleolithic Art*, New York

GREENE, JOHN C.
1959. *The Death of Adam: Evolution and Its Impact on Western Thought*, Ames, Iowa

GRIGSON, GEOFFREY
1957. *The Painted Caves*, London

GROENEWEGEN-FRANKFORT, H. A., AND BERNARD ASHMOLE
1967. *The Ancient World*, New York

GROSJEAN, ROGER
1961. *Filitosa et son contexte archéologique*, Paris
1964. *Filitosa, haut lieu de la Corse préhistorique*, Strasbourg

GUIDO, MARGARET
1964. *Sardinia*, London

HAGEN, ANDERS
1965. *Rock Carvings in Norway*, Oslo

HALL, E. T.
1963. "Dating Pottery by Thermoluminescence" in Brothwell and Higgs, 1963

HALL, K. R. L.
1963. "Tool-Using Performances as Indications of Behavioral Adaptability," *Current Anthropology*, December

HAMILTON, EDITH
1942. *The Greek Way to Western Civilization*, New York

HAMMEL, H. T.
1960. "Response to Cold by the Alacaluf Indians," *Current Anthropology*, March

HARDEN, DONALD
1962. *The Phoenicians*, London

HARRIS, DAVID R.
1967. "New Light on Plant Domestication and the Origins of Agriculture: A Review," *The Geographical Review*, January

HAWKES, C. F. C.
1940. *The Prehistoric Foundations of Europe to the Mycenaean Age*, London

HAWKES, J. AND C. F. C.
1958. *Prehistoric Britain,* London
HAWKES, JACQUETTA
1963. *Prehistoric Europe,* Volume I of UNESCO's *History of Mankind,* London
1967. "God in the Machine," *Antiquity,* XLI
HAWKINS, GERALD S.
1963. "Stonehenge Decoded," *Nature,* October 26, London
1965. *Stonehenge Decoded,* New York
HAYES, WILLIAM
1953 and 1959. *The Sceptre of Egypt,* 2 vols., New York
HERRE, W.
1963. "The Science and History of Domestic Animals" in Brothwell and Higgs, 1963
HIBBEN, FRANK C.
1958. *Prehistoric Man in Europe,* Norman, Oklahoma
HOCKETT, CHARLES F., AND ROBERT ASCHER
1964. "The Human Revolution," *Current Anthropology,* June
HOLE, FRANK, AND ROBERT F. HEIZER
1965. *An Introduction to Prehistoric Archeology,* New York
HOWELLS, W. W.
1954–63. *Back of History,* New York
1959. *Mankind in the Making,* New York
1960. "The Distribution of Man," *Scientific American,* September
1966. "Homo Erectus," *Scientific American,* November
HOWELL, F. CLARK
1960. "European and Northwest African Middle Pleistocene Hominids," *Current Anthropology,* May
1966. "Observations on the Earlier Phases of the European Lower Paleolithic," *American Anthropologist,* April
HOYLE, FRED
1966. "Speculations on Stonehenge," *Antiquity,* December
HRDLICKA, A.
1930. *The Skeletal Remains of Early Man,* Washington, D.C.
HULZE, FREDERICK S.
1963. *The Human Species,* New York
HUTCHINSON, R. W.
1962. *Prehistoric Crete,* London
ILLUSTRATED LONDON NEWS
1949. "A Stone-Age Settlement in Yorkshire" (Star Carr), October 29, London
ISAAC, ERIC
1962. "On the Domestication of Cattle," *Science,* July 20
JAENSCH, ERICH, R.
1933 and 1955. *Eidetic Imagery and Typological Methods of Investigation,* London
JAMES, E. O.
1959. *The Cult of the Mother Goddess,* London
JAŻDŻEWSKI, KONRAD
1965. *Poland,* London
JOLY, N.
1883. *Man Before Metals,* London
KEILLER, ALEXANDER
1965. *Windmill Hill and Avebury,* edited by Isobel Smith, Oxford

KEITH, SIR ARTHUR
   1915 and 1925. *The Antiquity of Man,* London
KELLER, FERDINAND
   1866. *Lake Dwellings of Switzerland and Other Parts of Europe,* London
KENYON, KATHLEEN
   1957. *Digging Up Jericho,* London
KITCHING, JAMES W.
   1963. *Bone, Tooth, and Horn Tools of Paleolithic Man,* Manchester
KITTO, H. D. F.
   1951. *The Greeks,* Harmondsworth
KLINDT-JENSEN, OLE
   1957. *Denmark Before the Vikings,* London
KOENIGSWALD, G. H. R. VON
   1956. *Meeting Prehistoric Man,* London
   1962. *The Evolution of Man,* Ann Arbor, Michigan
   1964. "Early Man: Facts and Fancy," Royal Anthropological Institute *Journal,* July–December
KRAMER, S. N.
   1956 and 1959. *History Begins at Sumer,* New York
   1963. *The Sumerians,* Chicago
KROEBER, A. L. ET AL.
   1953. *Anthropology Today,* Chicago
KÜHN, HERBERT
   1955. *On the Track of Prehistoric Man,* London
   1956. *Rock Pictures of Europe,* London
LAMING-EMPÉRAIRE, ANNETTE
   1959. *Lascaux: Paintings and Engravings,* London
   1962. *La signification de l'art rupestral paléolithique,* Paris
   1964. *Origins de l'archéologie préhistorique en France,* Paris
LANCASTER, JANE B.
   1968. "On the Evolution of Tool-Using Behavior," *American Anthropologist,* February
LARTET, LOUIS, AND H. CHRISTY
   1875. *Reliquiae Aquitanicae,* London
LAURING, PALLE
   1957. *Land of the Tollund Man,* London
LEAKEY, L. S. B.
   1934 and 1960. *Adam's Ancestors,* New York
   1951. *Olduvai Gorge,* Cambridge
LEROI-GOURHAN, ANDRÉ
   1964. *Les religions de la préhistoire,* Paris
   1965. *Préhistoire de l'art occidental,* Paris; American edition: *Treasures of Prehistoric Art,* New York, 1967
LEROI-GOURHAN, ARLETTE
   1968. "A Neandertal Burial in Shanidar Cave," *New York Times,* June 13
LÉVI-STRAUSS, CLAUDE
   1966. *The Savage Mind,* Chicago
LHOTE, H.
   1958 and 1959. *The Search for the Tassili Frescoes,* New York
LIBBY, WILLARD F.
   1952. *Radiocarbon Dating,* Chicago

LILLIU, GIOVANNI
1956. *Scultura della Sardegna Nuragica*, Venice
1959. "The Proto-Castles of Sardinia," *Scientific American*, December
LOË, BARON DE
1928. *Belgique ancienne: Les ages de la pierre*, Brussels
LORENZ, KONRAD
1966. *On Aggression*, New York
LUBBOCK, SIR JOHN
1865. *Prehistoric Times*, London
LUKIS, WILLIAM C.
1885. *The Prehistoric Stone Monuments of the British Isles*, London
LUQUET, G. H.
1926. *L'art et la religion des Hommes Fossiles*, Paris
1930. *L'art primitif*, Paris
LYELL, SIR CHARLES
1863. *The Geological Evidences of the Antiquity of Man*, London
MACGOWAN, KENNETH, AND JOSEPH A. HESTER, JR.
1950 and 1962. *Early Man in the New World*, New York
MACKENDRICK, PAUL
1962. *The Greek Stones Speak*, New York
MACKENZIE, DONALD A.
1926. *The Migration of Symbols and Their Relations to Beliefs and Customs*, New York
MACNEISH, RICHARD S.
1964. "The Origins of New World Civilization," *Scientific American*, 211, No. 5
1965. "The Origins of American Agriculture," *Antiquity*, XXXIX
MARINGER, JOHANNES
1960. *The Gods of Prehistoric Man*, New York
MARSHACK, ALEXANDER
1964. "Lunar Notation on Upper Paleolithic Remains," *Science*, November 6
MASSOULARD, E.
1949. *Préhistoire et protohistoire d'Égypt*, Paris
MATSON, FREDERICK R.
1963. "Some Aspects of Ceramic Technology" in Brothwell and Higgs, 1963
MAYR, ERNST
1963. *Animal Species and Their Evolution*, London
MELLAART, JAMES
1965. *Earliest Civilizations of the Near East*, London
1967. *Çatal Hüyük: A Neolithic Town in Anatolia*, New York
MERTZ, BARBARA
1964. *Temples, Tombs, and Hieroglyphs*, New York
MILLER, GERRIT S.
1915. "The Jaw of Piltdown Man," *Smithsonian Misc. Coll.*, 65, pp. 1–31
1918. "The Piltdown Jaw," *American Journal of Physical Anthropology*, I, pp. 25–52
MINOT, RENÉ SERGE
N.D. *Les Monuments Megalithiques de l'Île aux Moines*, Vannes
MONGAIT, ALEXANDER
1959. *Archeology in the U.S.S.R.*, Moscow

MONTAGU, M. F. ASHLEY
    1945 and 1960. *An Introduction to Physical Anthropology,* Springfield, Illinois
    1957. *Man, His First Million Years,* New York
    1968. (EDITOR) *Man and Aggression,* New York
MONTELIUS, GUSTAV OSCAR
    1888. *The Civilisation of Sweden in Heathen Times,* London
    1889. *Bronze Age Chronology in Europe,* London
MOORE, RUTH
    1953. *Man, Time, and Fossils,* New York
MORRIS, DESMOND
    1967. *The Naked Ape,* New York
MOVIUS, H. L.
    1950. "A Wooden Spear of Third Interglacial Age from Lower Saxony," *Southwest Journal of Anthropology,* 6, 140
    1961. "Radiocarbon Dates and Upper Paleolithic Archeology in Central and Western Europe," *Current Anthropology,* September, November, and December
NEUMANN, ERICH
    1955. *The Great Mother,* New York
NEUSTUPNY, E. AND J.
    1961. *Czechoslovakia,* London
NILSSON, SVEN
    1868. *The Primitive Inhabitants of Scandinavia,* London
NOUGIER, LOUIS-RENÉ, AND ROMAIN ROBERT
    1958. *The Cave of Rouffignac,* London
OAKLEY, KENNETH P.
    1961a. *Man the Tool-Maker,* London
    1961b. "On Man's Use of Fire" in *The Social Life of Early Man,* edited by S. L. Washburn
    1962. "Dating the Emergence of Man," *Journal for the Advancement of Science,* January, London
    1964. *Frameworks for Dating Fossil Man,* London
    1966. "Discovery . . . at Vérteszöllös," *Proceedings of the Geological Society of London,* No. 1630
OBERMAIER, HUGO
    1910 and 1924. *Fossil Man in Spain,* New Haven
O'KELLY, CLAIRE
    1967. *Guide to Newgrange,* Wexford
ÓRíORDÁIN, SEAN P., AND GLYN DANIEL
    1964. *New Grange,* London
PALLOTTINO, M.
    1950. *La Sardegna Nuragica,* Rome
PALMER, LEONARD R.
    1961 and 1965. *Mycenaeans and Minoans,* London
PARROT, A.
    1961. *Sumer,* London
PATTERSON, BRYAN
    1967. *San Francisco Examiner and Chronicle,* January 22
PENDLEBURY, J. D. S.
    1939 and 1965. *The Archeology of Crete: An Introduction,* New York
PERICOT-GARCIA, L., AND E. RIPOLL-PERELLÓ
    1960. "Recent Research on the Prehistory of Spain," *Current Anthropology,* March

BIBLIOGRAPHY   PIGGOTT, STUART
          1950. *William Stukeley,* Oxford
          1954. *The Neolithic Cultures of the British Isles,* Cambridge
          1961. *The Dawn of Civilization,* New York
          1965. *Ancient Europe: From the Beginnings of Agriculture to Classical Antiquity,* Edinburgh
          1965. (WITH GRAHAME CLARK) *Prehistoric Societies,* New York
        POWELL, ANTHONY
          1948. *John Aubrey,* London
        PRADEL, L.
          1966. "Transition from Mousterian to Perigordian: Skeletal and Industrial," *Current Anthropology,* February
        PULL, J. H.
          1932. *The Flint Mines of Blackpatch,* London
        RAINEY, FROELICH G.
          1965. "New Techniques in Archeology," Philadelphia
        RAINEY, F., AND E. K. RALPH
          1966. "Archeology and Its New Technology," *Science,* September 23
        RAPHAEL, MAX
          1945. *Prehistoric Cave Paintings,* New York
        REED, CHARLES A.
          1957. See Braidwood and Reed, 1957
          1963. "Osteo-Archeology" in Brothwell and Higgs, 1963
        RICE, TAMARA TALBOT
          1957. *The Scythians,* London
        RODDEN, ROBERT J.
          1965. "An Early Neolithic Village in Greece," *Scientific American,* April
        ROUX, GEORGES
          1964. *Ancient Iraq,* London
        RYDER, M. L.
          1963. "Remains of Fishes and Other Aquatic Animals" in Brothwell and Higgs, 1963
        SACCASYN-DELLA SANTA, E.
          1947. *Les figures humaines du paléolithique supérieur eurasiatique,* Antwerp
        SAINT-MATURIN, SUZANNE DE, AND DOROTHY GARROD
          1951. "La frise sculptée de l'Abri du Roc aux Sorciers à Angles-sur-Anglin," *L'Anthropologie,* 55, Nos. 5–6, Paris
        SANDARS, N. K. (EDITOR)
          1960. *The Epic of Gilgamesh,* Harmondsworth
        SANDERSON, IVAN T.
          1967. *"Things,"* New York
        SAUER, CARL O.
          1952. *Agricultural Origins and Dispersals,* New York
        SAUTUOLA, MARCELINO
          1880. "Breves apuntes sobre algunos objetos prehistóricos de la provincia de Santander," Santander
        SCHALLER, GEORGE B.
          1964. *The Year of the Gorilla,* Chicago
        SCHLIEMANN, HEINRICH
          1875. *Troy and Its Remains,* London
          1878. *Mycenae, a Narrative of Researches and Discoveries,* New York
   362   1880. *Ilios: The City and the Country of the Trojans,* New York

SCHMID, ELISABETH
  1963. "Cave Sediments and Prehistory" in Brothwell and Higgs, 1963
SEMENOV, S. A.
  1964. *Prehistoric Technology,* London
SHAPLEY, HARLOW (EDITOR)
  1953. *Climatic Change,* Cambridge
SHAPIRO, HARRY L. (EDITOR)
  1956. *Man, Culture, and Society,* New York
SHOTTON, F. W.
  1963. "Petrological Examination" in Brothwell and Higgs, 1963
SIEVEKING, ANN AND GALE
  1962. *The Caves of France and Northern Spain,* London
SIMONS, ELWYN L.
  1964. "The Early Relatives of Man," *Scientific American,* July
SIMPSON, GEORGE GAYLORD
  1951. *The Meaning of Evolution,* New Haven
  1951 and 1961. *Horses,* New York
  1964. "The Meaning of Taxonomic Statements" in *Classification and Human Evolution,* edited by S. L. Washburn
SINGER, C., ET AL.
  1954. *A History of Technology,* Oxford
SMITH, PHILIP E. L.
  1964. "The Solutrean Culture," *Scientific American,* August
SNIJDER, G. A.
  1936. *Kretische Kunst,* Berlin
SNODGRASS, A. M.
  1967. *Arms and Armour of the Greeks,* London
SOLECKI, RALPH S.
  1957. "Shanidar Cave," *Scientific American,* November
  1963. "Prehistory in Shanidar Valley," *Science,* 139
SOLLAS, WILLIAM J.
  1911. *Ancient Hunters,* London
SPEKKE, ARNOLDS
  1957. *The Ancient Amber Routes,* Stockholm
STACUL, G.
  1963. *La Grande Madre,* Rome
STEKEL, WILHELM
  1929. *Sadism and Masochism,* 2 vols., New York
STENBERGER, M.
  1962. *Sweden,* London
STERN, PHILIP VAN DOREN AND LILLIAN
  1967. *Beyond Paris: A Touring Guide to the French Provinces,* New York
STONE, J. F. S.
  1958. *Wessex,* London
STRAUS, WILLIAM L. JR., AND A. J. E. CAVE
  1957. "Pathology and the Posture of Neanderthal Man," *Quarterly Review of Biology,* 32
TAYLOUR, LORD WILLIAM
  1964. *The Mycenaeans,* London
THOM, ALEXANDER
  1966. "Megaliths and Mathematics," *Antiquity,* June
THOMAS, HOMER L.
  1967. *Near Eastern, Mediterranean, and European Chronology,* Lund

BIBLIOGRAPHY   THOMAS, NICHOLAS
                      1960. *A Guide to Prehistoric England,* London
                   THOMAS, W. L. (EDITOR)
                      1965. *Man's Role in Changing the Face of the Earth,* Chicago
                   TYLECOTE, R. F.
                      1961. *Metallurgy in [British] Archeology,* London
                   TYLOR, SIR EDWARD BURNETT
                      1865. *Researches into the Early History of Mankind,* London
                      1871. *Primitive Culture: Researches into the Development of Mythol-
                      ogy, Philosophy, Religion, Language, Art, and Custom,* London
                   USSHER, JAMES
                      1650. *Annals of the Ancient and New Testaments,* London
                   VARAGNAC, ANDRE, ET AL.
                      1959. *L'homme avant l'écriture,* Paris
                   VARRO, MARCUS TERENTIUS
                      1912. *On Farming,* London
                   VÉRTES, LAZLO
                      1966. See Oakley, K. P., 1966
                   WARD, ANNE
                      1968. "The Cretan Bull Sports," *Antiquity,* June
                   WASHBURN, S. L.
                      1960. "Tools and Human Evolution," *Scientific American,* September
                      1961. (EDITOR) *Social Life of Early Man,* New York
                      1964. (EDITOR) *Classification and Human Evolution,* London
                   WECKLER, J. E.
                      1954. "The Relationship Between Neanderthal Man and *Homo
                      sapiens,"* American Anthropologist, 56
                   WEIDENREICH, FRANZ
                      1937. "The Dentition of Sinanthropus pekinensis," *Paleont. Sin.,*
                      N. S. D. No. 1, whole series, No. 101
                      1943. "The Skull of Sinanthropus pekinensis," *ibid,* whole series, No.
                      127
                      1946. *Apes, Giants, and Man,* Chicago
                   WEINER, J. S.
                      1955. *The Piltdown Forgery,* London
                      1958. "The Pattern of Evolutionary Development of the genus *Homo.
                      S. Afr.,"* South African Journal of Medical Science, 23
                   WELLS, CALVIN
                      1964. *Bones, Bodies, and Disease,* London
                   WHITMAN, CEDRIC H.
                      1958. *Homer and the Heroic Tradition,* Cambridge
                   WILLIS, E. H.
                      1963. "Radiocarbon Dating" in Brothwell and Higgs, 1963
                   WILSON, DANIEL
                      1851. *The Archeology and Prehistoric Annals of Scotland,* London
                      1862. *Prehistoric Man,* London
                   WINDELS, FERNAND
                      1949. *The Lascaux Cave Paintings,* London
                   WOOD, ERIC S.
                      1963. *Field Guide to Archeology,* London
                   WOOLLEY, SIR LEONARD
                      1929. *Ur of the Chaldees,* London
                      1963. *The Beginnings of Civilization,* Volume II of UNESCO's *History
         364   of Mankind,* London

WORSAAE, J. J. A.
    1849. *The Primeval Antiquities of Denmark,* London
WYCHERLEY, R. E.
    1949. *How the Greeks Built Cities,* London
ZEHREN, ERICH
    1962. *The Crescent and the Bull,* London
ZEUNER, FREDERICK E.
    1946 and 1958. *Dating the Past,* London
    1954. "Domestication of Animals" in Singer *et al.,* 1954
    1959. *The Pleistocene Period: Its Climate, Chronology, and Faunal Successions,* London
    1963. *A History of Domesticated Animals,* London

INDEX

Index

Skara Brae

Tollund Bog

New Grange

Folkton
Star Carr

Creswell
Crags and Pinhole Cave

Pesse

Grime's Graves
Hoxne
Swanscombe
Clacton-on-Sea

Windmill Hill
Avebury
Stonehenge
Maiden Castle

Kit's Coty
Piltdown

Trou de Châleux

Neandertal
Ehringsdorf

Abbeville
Omal
Spy
Saint-Acheul
Levallois
Chelles

Heidelber
Steinh

Grand-Pressigny
Carnac

Arcy-sur-Cure

Nidau-Steinberg
Kesserloch

Niederwy
Ober Meilen

Chaffaud
Le Placard
Teyjat
Fontéchevade
Chancelade
Rouffignac
Les Eyzies (see p. 104)
Combe-Chapelle

Angles-sur-Anglin
La Marche

La Tène

Solutré
Le Veyrier

Lascaux
La Chapelle-aux-Saints
Chabot

Camoni
Valley

Pindal
Candamo
Altamira
Pasiega
Castillo

Cougnac
Pech-Merle

Brassempouy

Isturitz
Montmaurin
Gargas
Marsoulas
Montespan
Les Trois Frères

Mas d'Azil

Saint-Estève-Janson
Roquebrune

Grimaldi

Le Portel
Tuc d'Audoubert
Niaux

CORSICA

Filitosa

Ambrona
Torralba

Li Muri
Ozieri

SARDINIA

Cogul
Los Casares

Senorbi

Los Millares

Gibraltar

A.M. JAUSS